A New Order

A collection of short articles and miscellanea from The Followers of The Apocalypse.

By David Ker

Introduction by Brian Lamb (@brlamb, http://ab

Front cover art by Rob Englebright (@rob_work, http://www.strange

For Viv, and for Ben. And for Brian, whose fault this whole thing is.

ISBN: 978-1-326-05888-3

CONTENTS

INTRODUCTION: A USER'S MANUAL

by Brian Lamb

Congratulations on your acquisition of A New Order. We hope you will find this a worthy volume. Sturdy, well-constructed, highly resistant to empty sentiment and received wisdom. If looked after with care and attention, this collection will serve you faithfully for a lifetime.

As you read these pieces, you will be welcomed deeper into the world inhabited by the Followers of the Apocalypse. The FOTA are a noble and hardy order, if too easily dismissed as scruffy and incorrigible malcontents, unfit for participation in serious enterprise.

Some readers are advised to proceed with special care. Be particularly cautious if you have a history of intoxication via certain common tropes, such as those that spread "disruptive innovation", or "There Is No Alternative". Sudden immersion into the FOTA mindset after simmering in consensus reality can be a jarring and dizzying sensation. Finding oneself unexpectedly absorbed in British higher education policy wonkery can be difficult to comprehend, at least at first.

Whatever their orientation or attributes, it is common for the Followers to experience sensations of disorientation, agitation, and occasional discomfort when reading. Do not be alarmed. Indeed, these symptoms suggest that the Follower of the Apocalypse is still capable of feeling outrage, sadness, and a refusal to accept the triumph of jive bullshit as inevitable. In many respects, reading FOTA is facing the horror we are building without the comforting escape of chipper buzzmemes that promise a happy ending. Without the consolation of not caring.

To relieve these pains, David Kernohan has provided numerous means of relief. Elegant phrasing. LOLs and love of LOLs abound. Keep your ears on for esoteric and cleverly placed musical notes. Sense the camaraderie and fellowship that warms so much of the writing. And understand that the stories and the struggles being shared in this collection are not ended.

Invocation

On Writing, 2014

- a Triolet.

For writing copy that must go to press,
Are we writing or just making content?
Like writing - but somehow sadly less,
And I am less; and I am less content

"Short and punchy", simple - but a mess,
Wrote to be! - but just with that intent
Unread and unloved on readers it will press
Not prose, not poetry, just content.

-

Make art, dammit.

Aside: a quick note on the apocalypse

Seems like everyone is predicting the end times these last few years, either as a rhetorical device or a cut-off point for existing practices. Years and dates have been mentioned - so much for "no man may know the day or the hour!"

I realise that I've never really written properly about the apocalypse on here, which is odd given the title of my blog. My interest in eschatology is not a ghoulish fetish (those of you who have met me will know that I'm actually pretty cheerful and upbeat most of the time), but a fascination with narrative structures.

Stories are brilliantly structured: they have a beginning, a middle and an end. And we (as a society) love stories- we love them so much that we expect events that we experience to have these attributes too. But actual human life is seldom as forthcoming, especially regarding endings. Things tend to peter out, tail away or flat-out stop being interesting. In an increasingly diverse and connected world, this becomes more readily apparent. The advent (so very 1990s!) of post-modernity has highlighted just how important these narrative structures have become.

Enter the apocalypse. This is the ultimate "end", a profound way of saying "this story is now finished". My little boy says "The End" after every story he tells, even if it is a story I clearly want to know more about! I think he does it because endings are linked inextricably with beginnings. He wants to start telling a new story.

In art we've seen an increase in the use of "apocalyptic" imagery as we entered this economic downturn. I'd argue that this is a wider cultural wish to end this story and switch to a new one. And idly watching speculative Hollywood fiction about some natural disasters is easier than actually doing something about the several man-made ones we are now in the middle of. At the end of the Hollywood apocalypse we see the triumph of humanity, justice, and the American way. In reality this is never quite so certain- and the final triumph is more of a few more snatched days, weeks or months before the next onslaught.

To conclude, apocalypses beguile and dazzle because:

- they are dramatic. Saying "X is dead" is much more exciting than saying, "I don't think X is really working".

- Linked to this, they are irrevocably final, they appeal to the idea of completion-

- and thus to the idea of a new, fresh beginning.

- they offer the possibility of individual and group heroism. Apocalyptica is littered with heroes: the prophet crying in the wilderness, the action man with the crow-bar caked with zombie, the well organised vault dwellers, Bruce Willis-

- Wish fulfilment: from St John of Patmos to the Swedenborgians to the DIYU crowd - it's incredibly seductive to imagine all the things that you don't like being swept away so you can be proven right all along-

- especially politically. The far right dream of bunkers and guns, the far left of riots and revolution. If my involvement in OER has taught me one thing politically, it's that the bridge from right libertarianism to left anarchism is surprisingly solid.

As a follower of the apocalypse, I'm interested in what happens after all this heroism. Because amid the collapse and the destruction, war never changes. And the slow decline of ideas, the trickle of enthusiasm, is neither dramatic nor inspiring. But it is more true than all the stories we can tell.

The Past

What about those clangers, eh?

Note to readers that don't live inside my head - The Clangers was a 1970s UK TV kids programme which could have been entitled "LOLs with Swanee Whistles". It was (and most likely remains) impossible to survive your first month at university without having a conversation during a dull evening in a rubbish Student Union bar about retro children's TV, how strange it was, and how everyone involved was clearly on drugs.

So. It's official. The cool kids of EdTech snarking are now, nauseous with the dizzying headlong rush to whatever TechCrunch reckons is the future, looking in the recently discovered other (non-future) direction: alias "The Past".

It is, as LP Hartley noted during what must have been a particularly dull evening in the Student Union Bar, a foreign country. Things were done differently. Depending on your point, this may have been with a charming naiveté or a jejune gaucheness, but it generally boils down to the idea that at the time we knew less than we do now - with the inevitable implied corollary that here in 2014 we somehow know more.

And the more we know, the less work we need to do. Or so we would think.

Brian Lamb and Jim Groom recently wrote about "innovation fatigue":

> *"The practice of outsourcing itself seems to have become the pinnacle of innovation for information technology in higher education."*

If this is the case, it is little wonder we hark back to the time we would change the world for ourselves.

The word and condition of "nostalgia", interestingly enough, were originally invented in the 17th Century by a 17th century doctor named Johannes Hofer, and was pretty much synonymous with homesickness. He hypothesised that Swiss mercenaries were particularly troubled with this "neurological disease of essentially demonic cause" because of the constant ringing of cowbells in the Alps. Over the years the meaning of "nostalgia" has mutated to describe a longing for the type of homecoming that one could only achieve with a heavily modified DeLorean.

In his book "Retromania" Simon Reynolds cites the story above in the introduction of a becomingly scholarly look at why popular culture is obsessed with its own past. He divides nostalgia from "retro", with the latter being a specifically twisted form of the new nostalgia:

> *"[...] that you can feel for the glory days of 'living in the now' that you didn't- actually - live through" (page xxix)*

One of his central theses is that the ageing and gentrifying of the original *prime movers* of popular music has led to the growth of retrospectives that are aimed at this time- and money-rich market. Because of this, it is argued, those attempting to establish a culture of their own are hamstrung by these cultural behemoths - which become a pattern for the idea of cultural revolution against which newer attempts are measured and found wanting. Leaving us with a range of attempts to recreate the novelty and freshness of experiments of the past by explicitly following the recipe.

But we cannot. We know too much. In edtech, as in music.

Much of the talk at the CETIS14 conference focused on the past, even the opening keynote (Jisc's Phil Richards) began by citing his own heritage within the lineage of Jisc- and TLTP- supported projects. His former sparring-partner Phil Barker's session on metadata was similarly reflective, and although Lorna Campbell's session on Open Policy didn't have quite the same lengthy pedigree, we still got back as far as the filo-rice-pudding-wastes of 2008.

These are hardly "hidden histories" - they are documented and described in project plans, reports and blog posts - but they are "unpopular histories". Their unpopularity stems solely from the fact that they failed to change the word and remind those who would still try of the near-hopelessness of their task.

One imagines an inscription at the back of the Yellow Book (the colour books themselves were standardised with the support of a forerunner of Jisc) or within the old Janet NRS-

> *"Look on my works, ye Mighty, and despair!'*
> *Nothing beside remains. Round the decay*
> *Of that colossal wreck, boundless and bare*
> *The lone and level sands stretch far away"*

(or should that be "away far stretch sands level and lone The-."#bigendianLOLs)

We, as the institutionally and systemically based agitators of yore, are now a backwater, professional Cassandras that either maintain the reviled legacy platforms or feed the new disruptive ones with content, effort and time - for little esteem and less money in both cases.

It seems almost redundant to point out that it is these academic and support staff that make the greatest impact on the actual experience of actual students - not that it stops me doing it, mind - and likewise that the institution now exists as a means to sustain itself as a corporate body rather than to sustain and develop a collegiate community.

But I think we're at, in the argot of the times, "peak student". The current policy obsession with shaping the system around "student needs" is increasingly seen as representing a concerted attack on the professionalism of academic and support staff, especially when coupled with a parallel investment focus on estates and the seemingly expected infrastructure.

"Peak student" offers us a fetishisation of the tangible facets of student experience coupled with a desire for an impression of novelty, both of which are seen as a means to enhance the experience of the largely imaginary student that is at the heart of the system. (The needs of the real student - advice, challenge, inculcation into a community of scholarship, the skills to learn and adapt to a very uncertain world, and suchlike - don't really figure here).

All of which is a round-about way of saying that the fact that we do have 50+ years' experience of the ins and outs of sharing learning materials electronically is a beautiful irrelevance to those holding the purse-strings. The fact that we can neatly and deftly critique the strengths and weaknesses of something like Coursera or FutureLearn pales into insignificance against a well-designed infographic and the fact everyone else (of note) is involved.

You could describe overwhelming sarcasm at the ahistoricism amongst the "next generation" of innovators as sheer sour grapes. But it is not as if they are succeeding where others have failed.

Rather, it is that technology parted company from the shock of the new some time ago. And this painful separation will take years to become apparent - whilst the chance to refocus on culture, community, collegiality and cohesion is lost.

The bubble of openness?

Is openness (in the form of open access to knowledge, and the open sharing of distilled knowledge) a contemporary bubble, destined to collapse as universities and industries seek to tighten their budgets? Or is it a wider phenomenon, intrinsically bound to its antithesis - the modern industry of publishing?

The industrial revolution in the UK coincided with the growth of a new industry, that of the publisher - which applied the lessons of manufacturing to the production of art. And a sample of legislation across that time demonstrates the increasing emphasis of the rights of the publisher over that of both the reader and author.

The Copyright Act of 1709 (The Statute of Queen Anne, subtitled *"An Act For The Encouragement of Learning-"*, afforded the 18th century reader the right to complain about an unfairly high book price to the Archbishop of Canterbury, who could fine booksellers up to £5 for every overly expensive book sold.

Around a hundred years later, an 1814 Act of Parliament permitted the author (as a protection against unscrupulous publishers!) full control of the exploitation of their work for *"the remainder of his or her life"*.

However, at the very beginning of the 20th Century the emergence of the model of "net prices" marked the institutionalisation of the right of the publisher to maximum profit - and highlighted the increasing separation between the bookselling, bookbinding and publishing industries. As the 1911 Britannica puts it:

"After much discussion between authors, publishers and booksellers, a new scheme was launched on the 1st of January 1900. Books began to be issued at

net prices, from which no bookseller was permitted to make any deduction whatever. This decree was enforced by the refusal of all the publishers included in the [Publisher's] Association to supply books to any bookseller who should dare to infringe it in the case of a book published by any one of them. In other words, a bookseller offending against one publisher was boycotted by all. Thus, what is known as the "net system" depended absolutely upon the close trade union into which the publishers had organized themselves"

And in 2009, 300 years after the promulgation of the Statute of Queen Anne, the Digital Britain Report recommended the statutory codification of the rights of publishers to police the "piracy" of their digital assets, via the disconnection of the reader from the network of computers that had become a primary means of obtaining knowledge.

In these 300 years the publisher has gone from a possible impediment to the advancement of learning, under the strictures of no less than an Archbishop, via the establishment of a cartel dedicated to the preservation of an artificially-raised "market value", to a state-sponsored business model enforcement unit. Whilst this has happened publishers have divested themselves of every vestige of the "work" of publishing - hiving off printing, bookselling and latterly quality review, to ancillary units with expensive overheads - whilst still maintaining a position as arbiters of "quality" and "trustworthiness" to the reader. A "published" work is seen as a greater achievement than any other indicator of intellectual labour, and is used as the primary measure of research effectiveness in academia.

Despite this, those 300 years have seen a growth in literacy and the free exchange of ideas via mass literacy and the extension of school provision (starting with the Factory Act of 1802, the gradual increase in the availability of knowledge via the establishment of public libraries (particularly after the 1850 Public Libraries Act), and now the explosion of freely-available information online. Each of these advances, though largely brought about by the judicious use public funding (lest we forget, the first multi-platform web browser was developed by a student from Leicester Polytechnic on placement at an institute co-funded by European governments), was greatly enhanced by the support of philanthropy and private investment.

So, on the one hand we have a trend supporting the growing access to, and demand for, free knowledge, on the other we have an industry devoted to reducing access to knowledge via the levy of fees. Viewed like this, the current cultural interest in "openness" is not a bubble, rather a continuation of a trend almost as old as the publishing industry that has grown to support the demand for knowledge.

A further interesting factor is the idea of a body of cultural reference. Giulia Forsythe paraphrases Lessig (via Jim Groom) to say:

> *"I believe this is OUR culture. We have a right to review, remix, and make meaning of the media we grew up with through the tools new media provides."*

Just because the majority of the media of our formative years (music, television, film, literature-) belongs to one or other of the big publishing conglomerates does not mean that it does not also belong to us. Part of the reason such intellectual property is so valuable to publishers is because of the value we (as readers in the widest sense of everything being a text) invest in it.

Which is very 17th century really - the land we are fighting over is in our minds rather than on managed farms, we want to own the means to grow ideas, not crops - but culture, like the earth, is a common treasury for all.

OER Hero? OLGA and Open Education (pt. 1)

Sometimes the clearest precursor of an academic development comes from outside academia. I'd argue if you want to understand open learning, you've got to look beyond distance learning and the learning object. You've got to look at guitar tablature.

As long as there has been written music, there has been tablature (or tab) - it represents a far older, and less formal, system for notating music than "traditional" western notation. When writing tab, one records the actual movement of the fingers, rather than the notes produced, and timing information is explicitly approximate. For this reason, tab is very popular with students of the guitar and other stringed instruments - it provides exactly the information needed to play, it is easy to read, and - like playing by ear - it requires the development of listening (especially rhythmic listening skills).

I'd argue that it is a better fit for most music outside of the classical tradition, as it notates what is possible to perform on the instrument, rather than limiting performance to what it is possible to notate. It also presents a close analogue to "learning by listening and watching", the traditional way that tunes and arrangements were spread throughout pre-literate society.

So, to look at an arbitrarily chosen piece of guitar tablature, you'll see that each string of the guitar is represented by a line, and each line has numbers on it - which indicate which fret you should have your finger on when you play that string. The position of the numbers along the lines give an indication of timing and relationship, and a fluid and adaptable language of additional markings has developed to represents the huge arsenal of non-classical techniques and effects the modern guitarist has access to.

You'll also have noted that tab is very easy to share electronically. All you need is a fixed-width font and a text editor. Such as your email client. So it should come as little surprise that tab was shared via newsgroups such as rec.music.makers.guitar and alt.guitar.tablature (both now pretty much dead, sadly), and eventually archived on the On Line Guitar Archive (OLGA). It was a participative, networked process - tabs requested, presented, tested, argued, refined and finally published in a way that feels more like a modern MOOC (Massively Open Online Course) than the later parallel of mp3 sharing on Napster.

Like movements around sharing more conventional learning material (because isn't a tab simply a learning object?), the online guitar tab movement had to deal with issues of licensing. It chose the "dealing" route, providing one of the first serious digital-age tests of this defence.

But - and, I need hardly add, the resulting IPR story is both tragic and uplifting - the real interest to OER folks comes within a short 2004 paper by Thomas Chesney in the Journal of Computer Mediated Communications, detailing participants motivations. At OER11, I summarised these as follows:

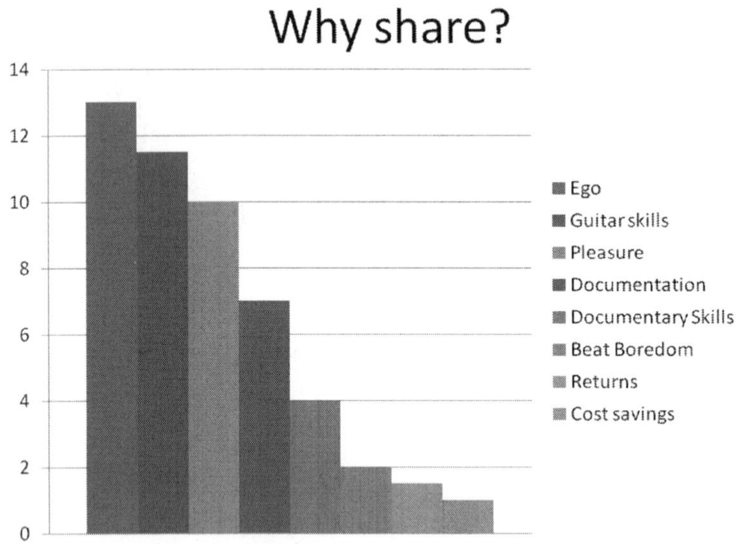

From Chesney 2004 – sample size was 259, 34% [72] usable response rate

Chesney also provides a number of quotations from survey responses concerning the benefits that participants felt they got from participating:

> *get my name out there*
>
> *[o]nce I've transcribed them for myself, it's not hard to send them to OLGA or another site.*
>
> *I have worked them out and someone else might want to learn that song*

23 of the 72 respondents claimed they received no benefit from publishing tabs. Referring to benefits, one respondent claimed he got "*none. others benefit. i benefit from their work.*" Chesney concludes:

> *The act of preparing (collecting, collating etc.) the material to be shared should have meaning in itself for the person who is preparing it. This was seen in the fact that most self-motivations were motivations to transcribe a song and store that transcription in electronic form, and not motivations to publish the tabs. The publishing came later and all that publishing involved was emailing a file to OLGA. This result could be used by organizations with a little imagination.*

To me, this sounds a long way from the received wisdom that academics are unlikely to share materials without some system of codified reward and recognition. Of course, your young guitar player - fixated on mass adulation and random sexual encounters in anonymous global hotels rather than becoming a professional transcriber - could not be further from our traditional view of an academic, but we do see in their reported comments the idea that the work is involved in creating the materials, and after they have been created sharing is little or no effort. In Martin Weller's terms this is very much an argument for little OER.

I hinted darkly at the IPR-mageddon that essentially ensued from this proto-academic behaviour - and it was as far back as the late 90s that music publishers started to claim rights over transcriptions. Just to bring home how odd that is, imagine Damien Hirst claiming rights over a book about biology preservation techniques. The stream of takedowns and legal challenges ending in 2006 served to remove the fundamental folk idea of "playing by ear" from the commons. As Rob Balch from "Guitar Tab Universe" put it in The Register:

At what point does describing how one plays a song on guitar become an issue of copyright infringement? This website, among other things, helps users teach each other how they play guitar parts for many different songs. This is the way music teachers have behaved since the first music was ever created. The difference here is that the information is shared by way of a new technology: the internet.

When you are jamming with a friend and you show him/her the chords for a song you heard on the radio, is that copyright infringement? What about if you helped him/her remember the chord progression or riff by writing it down on, say, a napkin-infringement? If he/she calls you later that night on the phone or emails you and you respond via one of those methods, are you infringing? I don't know. It was an audacious attempt by music publishers not just to defend their rights but to own our interpretation and critical response to "their" products, which has as many implications for academics as it has for guitar students.

Needless to say, it failed.

How it failed is very interesting, has further parallels to the world of OER, and will be the topic of post two in this little series.

OER Hero? OLGA and Open Education (pt. 2)

We left our intrepid song-learning heroes in something of a quandary. The simple act of recording and sharing your learning had been deemed detrimental to the financial interests of the music industry. In 2006 the Online Guitar Archive (OLGA) had been hit by "take down" letters.

Links to a scan of the 7 page letter soon became the only material available from OLGA. The music business had won, and it seemed like an amazing learning resource was gone forever. Other claims began to appear based on the same understanding, for example:

The versions of these publishers' musical works that you post on your website are not exempt under copyright law. In fact, U.S. copyright law specifically provides that the right to make and distribute arrangements, adaptations, abridgements, or transcriptions of copyrighted musical works, including lyrics, belongs exclusively to the copyright owner of that work. (reprinted in "Red Hat" Magazine,

2006)

However, things didn't quite work out that way. Whereas OLGA complied with the law and removed access to the archive, other sites were able to capture and redistribute the archive. And as the industry went after OLGA rather than source of the tabs (rec.music.makers.guitar and alt.guitar.tablature), the informal transcription and sharing of tabs continued.

Numerous sites came and went, using the OLGA archive and supplementing it with other sources - new tabs from the newsgroups, transcriptions from fan-sites, direct submissions. As access to the web widened, the potential sources increased exponentially - with new destinations springing up faster than they were taken down

In 2007, we saw a change of tack from the industry. Formerly illegal site MXtabs became the first "legal" free tab repository, having signed an agreement with the Harry Fox Agency. Income from advertising displayed alongside shared tabs, with site and publisher sharing the profits. But this proved unsustainable, the site closing after 2011- three years after a delayed launch.

Keeping abreast of the multiple tab sources available had become a full-time job, and players were looking for a means of simplifying their search. TabCrawler had launched at the turn of the century, eight years after OLGA but a long time before the legal difficulties became apparent. But the fact that it primarily searched (crawled) other sites for tabs rather became a huge advantage during the volatility of the mid-late 00s.

Though many sites claimed "fair use" and similar defences, and no case was ever brought to court, it was clear that the harassment from music publishers would continue. This, after all, was a battle on their historical turf - sheet music piracy was the first battle they fought, and with fists and boots rather than legal redress.

Sites like 911tabs entered into licensing arrangements with publishers in order to crawl and display content from multiple sites. Again advertising revenues were shared, but rather than hosting - and clearing rights for - individual tablatures, the site obtained a license to the rights of any tab that may or may not exist. When a tab was added to one of the host sites, 911tabs would automatically had the right to display ads alongside it.

This may strike you as a peculiar business model:

- Publishers and the aggregator share income from advertising displayed alongside the free tab.
- The transcriber is not paid for their work
- Those who review and improve the transcription are not paid for their work
- Sharing of this unpaid work outside of the aggregator may be illegal, but this is generally not pursued as it actually aids the aggregator.

Or, it would strike you as a peculiar model if you had not been exposed to the exciting modern world of academic publishing.

The guitar tab newsgroups are long dead, just spam and the occasional doomed request. One note from a stalwart was particularly poignant:

> so far this year no tabs have been posted on alt.guitar.tab -- last year there was only one tab posted on rec.music.makers.guitar.tablature (and that was by me)

> i've been posting to Usenet since 1993, and posting tabs for almost as long (rock, blues, folk,&classical) -- for over 10 years i've looked after one of the major guitar tab sites, and i used to encourage people who sent me tabs to also post them here -- but no longer...
>
> Oniscoid, rec.music.makers.guitar.tablature, Feb 26 2010, 2:00 am

But the sheer volume of players using and sharing tabs has grown so large that it would no longer be possible for a single mailing list to work. To submit a tab you can use any of the major sites, to request a tab likewise (Ultimate Guitar is another aggregator with a license). The process, however, is now owned and monetised by the music industry.

You'd think that the involvement of the industry would result in better quality tabs - but you would be wrong. It is very common to find materials from the original OLGA archive in any search- unedited, uncorrected and still as patchily awful but brilliantly human as they were in the 90s. The eagerness to share and to learn shines through.

I'm no open fundamentalist - I've no problem with publishers publishing and letting the artists get on with making art. But I expect publishers to actually publish stuff, and add value by doing so. Imagine if you could find tab for any song you wanted, musically accurate , laid-out beautifully, supported with lessons and techniques: I'd *subscribe* to that, never mind stand up for the rights of the publishers to sell rights around it.

All it would require would be a little investment, a little work. Maybe a community micro-payment of bounties for requested tabs. The tiniest bit of innovation, a little thought. But as things stand, the music publishers profit from the work of thousands of keen amateurs and contribute nothing in return.

Is this the future of education resources more generally? We share our resources freely, but see publishers damage sharing and reuse by demanding payment and restrictions?

The price of everything

So, that Andrew McGettigan tweeted about the ThinkBelt today - Cedric Price's mid-60s designs and concepts for a distributed, community-based, industrial university in the Potteries district (basically Greater Stoke-On-Trent).

Price was keen to design a campus that was adaptable and flexible to changing needs, but an institution that could offer a scale and intensity that could have an impact on the economy of the region and nation. He felt that:

> *"Because education beyond 18 is not accepted as a prime national industry, universities and colleges risk seeming to lack (a) recognisable social relevance, and (b) the capacity to initiate progress rather than attempt to catch up"*

His designs relied heavily on temporary and mobile structures using industrial methods of production, and an internal transport network based on an existing, disused, railway line. He postulates that both age and length of study would be far more flexible than in traditional universities, and that computer-aided instruction and administration would have a central place to play. But it is clear that he sees the institution as an experiment in community and infrastructure regeneration rather than as a new form of learning and practice [although those with an interest in networked learning make find some of Price's diagrams of interest]

Which makes the geographical site of the proposed 100km^2 campus very interesting for any student of the way that UK Higher Education has grown over the past 70 years. Established as a university college in 1949, The University of Keele received a royal charter in 1962, conferring degree awarding powers as the second (after Sussex) of the 60s wave of new ("plate glass") universities.

Initially a project of Alexander Dunlop Lindsay, an advocate of adult education and a fellow of Balliol College, Oxford, the University College of North Staffordshire (as it was then known, was founded to provide a wider and deeper education for the working man. As Lindsay himself said:

> *"If we are going to try and keep a democratic country and maintain understanding of one another, we have to send out people from our universities who can do the technical stuff and who at the same time have an understanding of political and social problems and of the values that lie behind them"*

He worked closely with the local Workers Education Association, and eventually became the first Principal of the new organisation.

Keele, though predating the Robbins Report, could be said to have been the first to fully take on board the influence of paragraph 262 of the report, which states:

> *"A higher proportion should be receiving a broader education for their first degrees. This in itself calls for change. But if greatly increased numbers of undergraduates are to come into the universities in the future, change becomes essential. Indeed we regard such a change as a necessary condition for any large expansion of universities. Greatly increased numbers will create the opportunity to develop broader courses on a new and exciting scale, and we recommend that universities should make such development one of their primary*

> *aims."*

It claims to be the first UK institution to offer a modern Joint Honours Degree, and (until 1990) required that all undergraduates spent a foundation year studying the development of western civilisation before commencing their studies.

On the Keele experiment Cedric Price merely notes:

> *"Keele, the first (sic) post-war New University, has shown the slowest growth of all British universities (present student population approximately 1,000). It has little contact with the area and few faculties linked to local industries."*

What we are seeing in these two parallel dreams of using university education to revitalise a stagnating industrial area is the difference between the industrial and academic perspective.

Both represent a change from current practice, but one is short term and focused on industry and short-term gain, the other on the wider concerns of civilisation. One arrives on an unknown landscape as a disruption, the other is based around existing structures and communities in the area. One takes little or no account of the small-scale but successful existence and work of the other.

It's an age old story of the needs of commerce and the concerns of academia, which makes me think of Neal Stephenson's Anathem world of Concents and Extramurous as perhaps the last great campus novel.

Fifty Shades of Black: conservative education policy, GCSEs and London Met

There is a possibly apocryphal story, told in lowered tones wherever two or three HE policy wonks are gathered, about a certain former Minister who approached their staff with a wizard HE wheeze. "I want to close a University", they said. On being asked why, few credible answers were forthcoming. Clearly they'd discovered that they could, and felt that the wielding of this power would encourage the others into mute compliance.

However, then, as now, there was a candidate University in place. This was an institution which had distinguished itself by doing many of the non-university-like things that ministers had asked for. It had aped the conventions and shibboleths of private business, sought efficiencies and expanded in to new markets. But crucially, it was not fashionable, and did not have the ivy-strewn patina of a "proper university".

Appearances matter. For all the reports and white-papers that envisage a thrusting, dynamic business going around leveraging things and increasing valorisation in suits and bright ties, there is a ministerial daydream that involves drifting down the Cherwell on Mayday in a punt with two jugs of Pimms and a pretty girl who's Daddy owns Hampshire.

Meanwhile in the compulsory sector, anger rages over a return to norm-referenced grading at GCSE level. Is this an attempt to drive up academic quality, or to return top grades to the preserve of the elite?

Be they red, blue, or yellow Tories - the right is fundamentally split on education. A rift deeper than any European quarrels, or the evidence-based/Daily Mail editorial argument on law'n'order'n'hanging'n'flogging. And to understand why, we need to look at the publication of a very peculiar set of books from way back in the 70s - in a story that includes Brian Cox, Francis Maude's dad, Mrs Thatcher, Kingsley Amis and many others luminaries-

Brian Cox (no relation to the other Brian Cox) was a Professor of English Literature, an early advocate of University teaching in creative writing and (at the time) a lifelong labour voter. Having been on sabbatical in Berkeley in 1968, he returned to Britain in time to catch the student unrest at LSE. Being in proximity to two such outbursts, he made the unlikely decision to blame the rise of "expression" in schools following the "10/65"government edict to move further along the road to a fully comprehensive system.

Incensed, he spoke to his friend AE Dyson- who had recently been one of those who drove through the reform of laws around homosexuality, and who now edited the Creative Review Quarterly (which he had co-founded with Cox). Together they decided to co-edit a collection of essays around the general theme of the excesses of progressive education, which (perhaps mischievously) they entitled The Black Papers.

Whilst by no means - in 2012 - a page turner, the first Black Paper is a fascinating historical document concerning a turning point in UK educational thought. What stood out for me is how measured the criticism is, in places. This (the first volume at least) is not the radical preservationist clarion it has subsequently been characterised as. It does not explicitly criticise the comprehensive system as an idea, just the worst - unthinking - excesses of it.

The collection of essays has three main targets: the rise of student radicalism, the excesses of progressive education and the value of private education. The three are connected by an overarching theme of the need for elitism, not just to favour the naturally gifted but to provide the best possible education for all children. The collection saw progressive education as one approach amongst many to be used by skilled teachers with consideration and support - the excesses it decried concerned "progressive" ideas becoming the unthinking status quo. As the opening words of the opening essay made clear:

> *"Taking a long view, one must conclude that the most serious danger facing Britain is the threat to the quality of education at all levels. The motive force behind this threat is the ideology of egalitarianism"*

Contributors included Kingsley Amis, John Sparrow (warden of All Souls College, Oxford), and Angus Maude (at the time a rebel Conservative MP, and the source of the quote above). It was perhaps Maude and Amis's contributions that led to the whole pamphlet being perceived as a Rightist initiative. Certainly it was seen as such by the Labour Education Minister of the time, Edward Short, who said "In my view the publication of the Black Paper was one of the blackest days for education in the past century". Cox's later career gave lie to the initial label, and he was delighted to be labelled a "woolly liberal" following the publication of the (very progressive) 1989 Cox report on the teaching of English.

The traditional education mooted in response is cultural rather than utilitarian in perspective. As Dyson puts it:

> *"It seems indisputable, though alarming, that education, which ought to be particularly concerned with transmitting the heritage of reason*

> *on which civilisation is founded, has turned its back on this reason to a disturbing extent"*

Or Robert Conquest:

> *"A wide diversity of ideas, many merely voguish and picked up from television, replace a proper training in the thought and history of the western world. I would urge a very simple reform - no admittance to University without passing a broadly based general paper"*

Such a publishing coup (more than 15,000 copies sold in less than a year - very much the "Fifty Shades of Grey" of the early 70s education policy world) required a sequel, so Cox and Dyson edited a second volume, along with another Conservative MP in waiting, Rhodes Boyson. The editorial board meeting between gay-rights pioneer Dyson and noted homophobe ("It is wrong biblically, is homosexuality. It is unnatural.") Boyson must have been very interesting indeed. At the time Boyson was the headmaster of a school (Highbury Grove) that marketed itself based on a renewed emphasis on corporal punishment.

SchoolboyLOLs aside, the Black Paper series was causing a range of people from across the political spectrum to coalesce around the very broad idea of a return to "traditional education", however they personally conceived it. Not least amongst these was Margaret Thatcher, whose stance on education was initially at odds with a more business-focused Conservative party.

Prior to this, the education policies of the right had been much more proto-Cameronite, suggesting a desire to *"prioritise economic stability over costly egalitarian social spending, selectivity over universality and minimal rather than optimal levels of state provision"*. But Thatcher -

though for completeness it should be noted that she created more comprehensive schools than any other Education secretary - was at least diverted by the dream of traditionalism.

Her version, however, required an active centralised intervention in nearly every aspect of educational activity: there was little room for accidental learning in the centrally planned GCSE curriculum, and in (Thatcher and Major's) expansion of university provision to meet the needs of employers for graduates. This was a top-down conservatism with much more in common with the "progressives" Cox and Dyson railed against than with Gove.

There is a romantic and utilitarian strand within the "traditional" education policies of governments of all stripes, and some of the most confusing errors occur when this tension is highlighted. Be this the romantic notion of a university against the economic reality of mass provision, or the romantic ideas of egalitarianism against the utilitarian need to stratify society, the background to the current debate draws heavily on this little read and little understood collection of essays.

Further reading:

A History of Education In England, Derek Gillard.

The Black Papers and the debate about standards, Conservative History Journal

The Black Papers, CB Cox and AE Dyson (WorldCat link, no online version)

The Onrushing Avalanche of Pedagogical Technology (1936)

[This is a sketch of a 5-7 minute presentation in that style (which I freely admit I stole the idea of from Brett Victor's mind-blowing "Future of Programming" presentation at DBX2013) and it owes something of a methodological debt to Jim Groom's ongoing paleoconnectivism.]

> *"A college education for anyone who wants it. A complete course in practically any of the subjects now named in the college curriculum - for five dollars; an elementary course in these subjects for one dollar, and a single far-reaching lecture on one of them by a worldwide authority for ten cents"*

Professor Michael Pupin, Professor of Physics at Columbia University, sets out a compelling vision for the future of higher level instruction in a "Popular Science" interview. In this vision of the future there is no need for a campus, or for textbooks.

Both university and private money is being invested in this and similar schemes - after recent upheaval in the financial markets it appears that technology-led speculation has moved to the world of education, bypassing existing industries entirely. A glance through the content of the rest of "Popular Science" for the month in question sees a number of advertisements for various forms of remote learning, for business or for pleasure.

Remote instruction has since become far more widespread, and we are on course to see more than 200 city school systems, alongside numerous colleges and universities, broadcasting materials by 1938. Both Columbia and Harvard, along with many other famed institutions, are a part of this movement. Often, credit is offered linked to self-administered examinations.

But, despite the obvious boon to those thirsty for knowledge without the capability to attend a physical campus, not everyone is a fan. Bruce Bliven of The New Republic asks: *"Is radio to become a chief arm of education? Will the classroom be abolished and the child of the future be stuffed with facts as he sits at home or even as he walks about the streets with his portable receiving-set in his pocket?"*

Bliven is highlighting the need for a social aspect to learning. Advances combining learning theory and psychology at Yale (notably the work of Clark Hull) suggest that the act of learning is one constituent of the wider formation of character, and that the act of imitation is key to this. The person of the teacher, and of the more mature peer, is key here - and as yet we cannot transmit character via radio waves.

Or via the printed press. None of these concerns about technology in education are new. In Plato's account of the dialogue between Socrates and Phaedrus the idea of learning from books is discussed:

> *"[T]his invention will produce forgetfulness in the minds of those who learn to use it, because they will not practice their memory. Their trust in writing, produced by external characters which are no part of themselves, will discourage the use of their own memory within them. You have invented an elixir not of memory, but of reminding; and you offer your pupils the appearance of wisdom, not true wisdom, for they will read many things without instruction and will therefore seem to know many things, when they are for the most part ignorant and hard to get along with, since they are not wise, but only appear wise." [274c-275b]*

Our UK coalition government is presiding over a number of far reaching changes to the education sector, not least the raising of the compulsory school leaving age and the development of new types of schools to meet the needs of new forms of employment. But, in this context, the 1928 Hadow report recommendation that *"the books used in schools should be excellent in quality as well as adequate in numbers"* suggests that as a reference and as a model, high-quality published material should be around for a long time yet. As the report notes (p112) *"[C]hildren should learn from them to admire what is admirable in literature, and to acquire a habit of clear thought and lucid expression."*

Whatever the advances in pedagogy that the future may see, it is difficult to imagine a time where the expertise of the tutor, the lucidity of published materials and the discipline of classroom dictation are not central to the learning process.

The Rome Act of the Berne Convention, nearly 10 years ago, added a whole range of additional publication types to those protected globally by copyright. It is to be hoped, that as technology develops, these global treaties protecting the rights of publishers will develop with them, but that this would not be to the detriment of access to published works by learners and scholars.

But how are the publishers using new technologies to support education? Already we have seen the Milwaukee Journal experiment with Facsimile transmission of newspaper pages via the airwaves to a range of receivers in department stores and other public places. Although, at present this is a proof-of-concept led by the struggling newspaper industry as a way to cope with the threat of radio news, it is possible to imagine academic materials transmitted in a similar way.

We know that certain enterprises, for instance the innovative start-up "Penguin", are experimenting with newer, more portable formats for books. The team are also looking to revolutionise distribution via a number of platforms in railway stations. Admittedly, these have been cheap mass productions, and I for one would not be surprised if a newspaper business like Pearson doesn't become involved. But what today is only a way of selling gaudy crime novels for the price of a packet of cigarettes may tomorrow cut into the core business of many academic publishers - imagine if a consortia of university presses owned an operation like Penguin - or the proposed Pelican factual imprint?

Increasingly, readers are expecting "more" from books, and are paying less for them. Competition from broadcast channels has so far been focused on the newspaper industry, but who is to say that the in-depth engagement with an educational institution or a textbook would not be next to fall to the immediacy of new sources of information? In 80 years or so, would we be discussing a global marketplace in scholarly publication that doesn't involve printing at all? A few years ago I would have said no, but these days - in the words of the popular song by Mr Cole Porter - "Anything Goes"!

Former Yale President becomes Coursera CEO

Anything Goes (EdTech 2014 Version)

Time once was
In New Haven Connecticut
Richard Levin did instruct
All the scholars Yale could induct
If today
That scholar sought a dollars gain,
He'd brush up on his netiquette
To join the MOOCing game…

In olden days a glimpse of data
Was news to a course creator.
But now, God knows, Anything Goes.
Professors who were once pedagogues,
Pour over charts of server logs',
Fire Hose! -Anything Goes.

The world's mistook today
And just look today,
There's eBooks today,
And there's MOOCs today,
And the hook today
Is they're took today
By everyone one knows

And as I'm not a proud Courserian
I feel so antiquarian
A-pro-pos anything goes

When Andrew Ng and Daphne Koller
Raise $40million dollars with videos,
Anything Goes.
When Thrun would pivot in Fast Company
Disrupting entire industries full of pros.
Anything Goes.
If some TED you'd like,
Not higher ed you like
Venture Cap. you like,
And free crap you like,
M.C.Q.s you like,
Money too you'd like,
Well, see how it flows!

When investors are always hoping
Your course will pretend to be open when it's closed,
Anything Goes.

And though I am no educator
I know that you'll comment later
If I propose,
Anything goes-

Anything goes!
(with apologies to Cole Porter)

Dickens on big data

It has become one of those common place go-to riffs in education reform. Not quite up there with "education is broken" or that bloody Ferris Beuller video. But if you're listening to someone with pretensions of a literary background you may well catch an earful of that classic indictment of useless educators:

> *"Now, what I want is Facts. Teach these boys and girls nothing but Facts. Facts alone are wanted in life. Plant nothing else, and root out everything else. You can only form the minds of reasoning animals upon Facts; nothing else will ever be of any service to them"*

If you are lucky, you may be introduced to the fact that the character speaking is named Gradgrind and the book is Charles Dickens' "Hard Times". Gradgrind, of course, wasn't a teacher - this was the charmingly named Mr M'Choakumchild - nor had he any real reason to be in the school at that point.

For what is (to my mind) one of Dickens' more incisive and political books it is not often read. Certainly it has its share of unexpected familial coincidences and grotesque characters, and naturally poverty is compared with the moneyed classes with a situationally unlikely set of instances of social mobility - but at heart it is a dystopian novel based on the excesses of a certain persuasion of utilitarianism.

"The greatest happiness of the greatest number" is the Benthamite cry, and this led indirectly to Jeremy sitting in on UCL committee meetings more than 150 years after his death. But a great deal of the ongoing utilitarian work was finding reliable methods of identifying when people were happy, and the conditions that were preventing this.

There is a charming passage in Hard Times where Dickens reflects on the earnestly pursued data-driven diagnoses:

> *"[-] there was a native organisation in Coketown itself, whose members were to be heard of in the House of Commons every session, indignantly petitioning for acts of parliament that should make these people religious by main force. Then came the Teetotal Society, who complained that these same people would get drunk, and showed in tabular statements that they did get drunk, and proved at tea parties that no inducement, human or Divine (except a medal), would induce them to forego their custom of getting drunk. Then came the chemist and druggist, with other tabular statements, showing that when they didn't get drunk, they took opium. Then came the experienced chaplain of the jail, with more tabular statements, outdoing all the previous tabular statements, and showing that the same people would resort to low haunts, hidden from the public eye, where they heard low singing and saw low dancing, and mayhap joined in it; and where A. B., aged twenty-four next birthday, and committed for eighteen months' solitary, had himself said (not that he had ever shown himself particularly worthy of belief) his ruin began, as he was perfectly sure and confident that otherwise he would have been a tip-top moral specimen."*

The strikingly modern aspect of this, to me, is not just the reliance on "tabular statements" to define social and moral ills, but also the reliance on coercion and behavioural engineering based on these tabular statements.

Quite what conclusion I draw from this quote I'm not yet sure. But there is some link between the aggregation of quantified selves as data trails within a larger quantitatively driven policy process and the excesses of utilitarianism that Dickens was satirising.

And you should (re)read "Hard Times". Because it strikes home regarding the almost unnameable something that austerity-battered populations cling to that is almost the precise opposite of data-driven policy making.

"You can't always get what you want. But if you try sometimes well you just might find you get what you need"

"The VLE is dead" is not dead. The past month has seen posts from Peter Reed, Sheila MacNeill, and D'Arcy Norman offering the "real world" flip-side to the joyous utopian escapism of edtech Pollyanna Audrey Watters. Audrey's position - that the LMS (learning management system [US, rest of world])/VLE (Virtual Learning Environment, formerly Managed Learning Environment - MLE [UK]) constrains and shapes our conception of technology-supported learning (and that we could and should leave it behind) - is countered by the suggestion that the LMS/VLE allows for a consistency and ease of management in dealing with a large institution.

To me there are merits in both positions, but to see it as a binary is unhelpful - I don't think we can say that the LMS/VLE is shaping institutional practice, or that institutional practice is shaping or has shaped the LMS/VLE. To explain myself I need to travel through time in a very UK-centric way, but hopefully with a shout-out to friends overseas too.

We start at the end - an almost-random infrastructure of tools and services brought into being by a range of academics and developers, used to meet local needs and supported haphazardly by a loose network of enthusiasts. Its 1998, you're hacking with (the then new) Perl 5, and your screensaver is SETI@home.

But how do we get the results of the HTML quizzes that you are doing for your students on an ~-space website (after having begged your sysadmin to let you use CGI) across to the spreadsheet where you keep your other marks, and/or to your whizzy new student records system that someone has knocked up in Lotus Notes? Copy and Paste? Keep two windows open? Maybe copy from a printout?

What if there was some automagical way to make the output of one programme input into the other? Then you could spend less time doing admin and more time teaching (isn't that always the promise, but never the reality?)

Remember, this was before Kin Lane. We were not quite smart enough to invent the API at this time, this was a couple of years down the line. But the early work of the Instructional Management System project could easily have proceeded along similar lines.

IMS interoperability standards specified common ways in which stuff had to behave if it had any interest whatsoever in working with other stuff. The founding of the project, by EDUCAUSE in 1997, sent ripples around the world. In the UK, the Joint Information Systems Committee (JISC) commissioned a small project to participate in this emerging solution to a lack of interoperability amongst tools designed to support learning.

That engagement with IMS led to the Centre for Educational Technology Interoperability Standards- CETIS.

As I've hinted above, IMS could very easily have invented APIs two years early. But the more alert readers amongst you may have noticed that it is 1998, not 1997. So all this is ancient history. So why 1998?

In a story that Audrey hinted at the CETIS 2014 conference- it's like she knew! - some of those involved in IMS were imagining an alternative solution. Rather than bothering with all these crazy, confusing standards wouldn't it be much easier if we could get a whole educational ecosystem in a box. Like an AOL for the university.

Everything would talk to everything else (via those same IMS standards), and you would have unlimited control and oversight over the instructional process. Hell, maybe you could even use aggregated student data to predict possible retention issues!

Two of those working for IMS via a consultancy arrangement at the time were Michael Chasen and Matthew Pittinsky. Sensing a wider market for their understanding of the area, they formed (in 1997) a consultancy company named Blackboard. In 1998 they bought CourseInfo from Cornell University, and started to build products based on their idea of a management system for learning.

The big selling point? It would allow courses to be delivered on the World Wide Web. Let's put a date on it. 29th April 1998.

In the UK, this development looked like the answer to many problems, and JISC began to lead a concerted drive to manage take-up of "instructional management systems", or (as "instructional" is soo colonial) "managed learning environments".

JISC issued a call for institutional projects in 1999. The aim of these projects was not simply to buy in to emerging "in a box" solutions, but to join up existing systems to create their own managed environment. Looking back, this was a typically responsive JISC move, there was no rush to condemn academics for adopting their own pet tools, merely to encourage institutions to invent ways of making this feasible on an increasingly connected campus.

JISC was, as it happened, undergoing one of their periodic transitions at the time, because:

> *"[...] PCs and workstations are linked by networks as part of the world wide Internet. The full impact of the potential of the Internet is only*

> *just being understood."*

One of the recommendations stated:

> *"The JISC [...] finds itself trying to balance the desire to drive forward the exploitation of IT through leading edge development and pilot projects with the need to retain production services. [...] At present about 20% of the JISC budget is used for development work of which less than a quarter is to promote leading edge development work. This is lower than in previous years. This run down of development work has been to meet a concern of the funding councils that the predecessors of the JISC were too research oriented. [...]Given that the future utility of the JISC depends on maintaining UK higher education at the leading edge there should be more focus on development work."*

(Sorry for quoting such a large section, but it is a beautifully far-sighted recommendation. For more detail on JISC's more recent transition, please see the Wilson Review.)

So, there was an emphasis on home-grown development at the leading edge, and a clear driver to invest in and accelerate this - and there was funding available to support it. In this rich and fertile environment, you would imagine that the UK would have a suite of responsive and nuanced ecosystems to support academia in delivering technology-supported tuition. What happened?

Some may try to blame a lack of pedagogic understanding around the tools and systems that are being deployed. JISC commissioned a report from Sandy Britain and Oleg Lieber of the University of Bangor in 1999: " A Framework for Pedagogical Evaluation of Virtual Learning Environments". By now (one year on), the UK language had shifted from MLE to VLE.

The report notes that as of 1999 there was a very low take up of such tools and systems. A survey produced only 11 responses (!), a sign of a concept and terminology that was as yet unfamiliar. And of course, institutions were being responsive to existing practice:

> *"Informal evidence from a number of institutions suggests that few are currently attempting to implement a co-ordinated solution for the whole institution, rather many different solutions have been put into operation by enterprising departments and enthusiastic individual lecturers. [...] It may not be an appropriate model for institutions to purchase a single heavyweight system to attempt to cater for the needs of all departments as different departments and lecturers have different requirements."*

Like many at the time, Britain and Lieber cite Robin Mason's (1998) "Models of Online Courses" as a roadmap for the possible development of practice. Mason proposed: The "Content Plus Support Model", which separated content from facilitated learning and focused on the content. The "Wrap Around Model", which more thoughtfully designed activities, support and supplementary materials as an ongoing practice around a pre-existing resource. The "Integrated Model", which was primarily based around student-led interaction with academic support, content being entirely created within the course.

This is an astonishingly prescient paper, which I must insist that you (re-)read. Now.

It concludes:

> *"Just as the Web turns everyone into a publisher, so online courses*

> *give everyone the opportunity to be the teacher. Computer conferencing is the ideal medium to realize the teaching potential of the student, to the advantage of all participants. This is hardly a new discovery, merely an adaptation of the seminar to the online environment. It is not a cheap ticket to reducing the cost of the traditional teacher, however. Designing successful learning structures online does take skill and experience, and online courses do not run themselves. It is in my third, "integrated model" where this distinction is most blurred, as it provides the greatest opportunities for multiple teaching and learning roles."*

This is a lesson that even the UK Open University (to whom Mason was addressing her comments) have struggled to learn. I leave the reader to add their own observation about the various strands of MOOCs with respect to this.

Britain and Lieber, meanwhile end with a warning.

> *"This [...] brings us back to the issue of whether choosing a VLE is an institutional-level decision or a responsibility that should be left in the hands of individual teachers. It raises the question of whether it is possible (or indeed desirable) to define teaching strategy at an institutional rather than individual level"*

A footnote mollifies this somewhat, noting that issues of interoperability and data protection do need to be considered by institutions.

In 2003, JISC undertook their first review of MLE/VLE activity. The report (prepared by Glenaffric Consulting) suggested that the initial enthusiasm for the concept had been tempered both by a general disenchantment with the potential of the web after the first dot-com bubble had burst, and by an understanding of the pressures of running what was becoming a mission-critical system. One key passage (for me) states:

> *"[A] tension is apparent between the recognised need for generally applicable standards for the sector, and the institutions' need for systems that provide the functionality that they require for their specific business processes. In this context, witnesses were critical of the drive to impose a standards-based approach when the specifications themselves were not complete, or adequately tested for widespread application."*

The pressure to "get it right first time" outweighed the ideas of building for the future, and it was into this gap that commercial VLEs (as a single product) offered a seemingly more practical alternative to making myriad systems communicate using rapidly evolving standards.

By 2003, only 13% of institutions did not use at least one VLE. By 2005, this had dropped to 5%, and by 2008 the question no longer needed to be asked, and the dominance of Blackboard within this market (through acquisitions, notably of WebCT) was well established.

But remember that the VLE emerged from a (perceived or actual) need to allow for interoperability between instructional and learning systems. A need amplified by funding and advice designed to future-proof innovative practice. We may as well ask why Microsoft became a dominant desktop tool. It just worked. It was there. And it became the benchmarks by which other solutions were measured.

To return to my opening tension - I wonder if both institution and system have been driven to current norms by a pressure for speedy and reliable ease of use. To manage the growing administrative burden in a newly massified and customer focused higher education.

Reliability. Standardisation, not standards-informed development. And the ever-flowing pressure for rapid and transformative change. Where did *that* come from?

And that is why we talk about politics and culture at education technology conferences. *I saw her today, at the reception…*

"Don't make a fuss, just get on the bus"

Increasingly, MOOCs seem like buses to me. Not because I wait for ages and then three million all turn up at once (though you can see why I might think it), but because they seem to be drawing us in to the first stages of the Higher Education Bus Wars.

Before the 26th October 1986, (when I was 8 and lived quite near Darlington) each local council in the UK ran its own bus service. Which you might think would be sensible, as it meant they could design services around local needs rather than profitability.

Alas the logic of the market prevails, with the 1985 Transport Act allowing pretty much anyone with a bus to start whatever-the-hell kind of commercial service they liked providing they gave 56 days' notice.

This ushered in a glorious new era for the UK bus user.

What actually happened was that local councils had to spin off and sell their own bus services, which were largely bid for by the same five large companies. It was in their interest to reduce the value of these existing services, so they could buy the local company more cheaply or demolish it entirely to bring in their own services.

So to start with, residents saw loads more buses about the place. These new buses ran the same routes as the existing buses people were used to, but charged a fraction of the price (or were in some cases entirely free).

And who could be against cheap (or free) bus travel?

But eventually, the loss-making buses made the others on the route unviable. And then, with a monopoly in place, those prices rose sharply to the absolute maximum the market would bear. Local and smaller companies went to the wall.

The big five (Arriva, First, GoAhead, National Express, Stagecoach) then effectively carved up the country between them, with sporadic and limited local competition easily quashed. Prices rose sharply, passenger numbers fell and services outside of the profitable routes largely disappeared.

The problem was that local transport is basically a guaranteed income. People aren't just going to stop needing to get around, and governments (even the right-wing fantasy ones) pretty much know that if you can't move people between minimum wage jobs, expensive rented accommodation and shopping centres then the economy is stuffed. So there is money to be made, and a system has been designed that favours money making ability over actual ability to provide a service.

In the same way, no government is likely to stop supporting education. Even people who are solely concerned with making money admit that people need education. And that they can profit from both the results (educated people) and the process.

Now read the above again, but imagine that these new bus companies had somehow convinced existing and experienced bus drivers to drive their new, enormous and unwieldy vehicles (from which 90% of passengers fell and injured themselves on each journey) without wages.

And that these new buses were plastered in the logos of the old, trusted bus companies (who even paid for the privilege), and accompanied by acres of uncritical news coverage and dubious quality testimonials about how a single free low-quality bus journey had changed people's lives.

And that people tried to make existing companies feel old-fashioned for not having these new buses that were free to all passengers, even though the more experienced companies knew that it was a far worse service and completely unsustainable.

And that these new services were backed by limitless money, from huge publishers and venture capital, whilst existing services were squeezed again and again by their own funders.

Imagine.

Bonus video about bus wars in the south of England from 1986 local TV.

Graduate Employability and the New Economic Order

> *"A new publication issued today by the Higher Education Statistics Agency (HESA) sets out, for the first time, figures describing the First Destinations of students leaving universities and colleges of higher education throughout the UK."*

No, not today. The 9th of August 1996, when a still-damp-behind-the-ears HESA published the results of a ground-breaking survey concerning where students end up after they complete their degree. More than the rise (and rise) of fees, more than the expansion of the system, more (even) than the growth of the world wide web; the publication of these numbers has defined the shape and nature of modern higher education.

Before this time (and records are hazy here, without disturbing my local library for bizarre out of print 90s educational pamphlets from the National Archive) universities and colleges careers advisory services did their own surveys of graduate destinations, which were annually grouped by the DfEE. Though this produced interesting data, national ownership across a relatively newly unified HE sector was clearly the way to integrity.

And also league tables.

Here at last was a metric that promised to convert investment in Higher Education into "real world" economic benefit. Beyond the vague professorial arm waving, and the lovely glowy feeling, some hard return on investment data.

We're pre-Dearing here, so obviously Lord Ron and team had a thing or two to say in their 1997 report. Though being careful not to provide a "purely instrumental approach to higher education" (4.2), the report makes a number of gestures towards the need to encompass employer requirements in the design and delivery of HE courses. Some of these (4.14) recommendations are as stark and uncompromising as anything in Browne (or Avalanche)

> *above all, this new economic order will place a premium on knowledge. Institutions are well-placed to capitalise on higher education's long-standing purpose of developing knowledge and understanding. But to do so, they need to recognise more consistently that individuals need to be equipped in their initial higher education with the knowledge, skills and understanding which they can use as a basis to secure further knowledge and skills;*

"New Economic Order", eh? Of course, I've gone over some of this history before, in particular the 20 year English habit of building new universities at the drop of a capitalist's stovepipe hat. What was new in Dearing was the idea of embedding these values into a wider definition of what it means to be a university.

The Blunkett-led DfEE commissioned a report entitled "Employability: Developing a Framework for Policy Analysis" from the Institute for Employment Studies, which was delivered by Jim Hillage and Emma Pollard in 1998. (If the idea of a framework for policy analysis is ringing faint alarm bells in the ears of alert FOTA readers, then yes - the late 90s saw a certain Dr Barber influencing the development of education policy in England.)

What Hillage and Pollard do is provide three key elements of scaffolding to the burgeoning employability agenda in education (note: not solely HE) A literature review, and definition of the term. A "framework" for policy delivery, to (yes) "operationalise" employability. Some initial analysis of the strengths and weaknesses of the various available measures of employability.

I'm very close to just quoting huge chunks of this report as it is such a perfect encapsulation of the time

> **In simple terms, employability is:**
>
> *being capable of getting and keeping satisfactory work.*
>
> **A perhaps more accurate, but more wordy, definition identifies employability as:**
>
> *'The capability to move self-sufficiently within the labour market to realise potential through sustainable employment.'*
>
> **This definition not only centres on transitions in the labour market but also the importance of moving independently of external intervention. It also includes a subjective element of 'realising potential' (which implies a qualitative side to work and also a labour market efficiency element of people using their skills to the maximum) and 'sustainable employment' (which does not just mean a job, but work in general (eg self-employment or project work) and not necessarily with the same or a single employer).**

Their definition (p11)

You have to love "labour market efficiency", don't you?

Hillage and Pollard make an attempt to split the employability of an individual into a set of attributes (e.g. p21); "Assets" (knowledge, skills and attitudes), which are "deployed" (career planning and goals), then "presented" (interview and application). "Context" dangles off the end as a late admission that other things going on in the world, or in the life of an individual can have a powerful effect.

Again, very much of the time, the report is cautious but optimistic about the methods of measuring employability - noting that although "output measures" (such as our first destination survey) can be useful, the wider context of the state of the labour market needs to be taken into account.

"Intermediate indicators" (the possession of appropriate skills and knowledge) are easier to measure. You could read across to competency-led course design and the whole world of "learning outcomes" here.

The final indicator type analysed is "perceptual" - broadly, what do employers think of the "employability" of their intake? Again context is key here, and there is an immediacy bias - in that the skills required to do a particular task (I'll call them "role skills") are separate from the wider concerns of the individual in being "employable" in a wider way.

But if this document has a theme, it is that the individual needs to take responsibility for their own employability. The learner is complicit in their own subservience to an economic and value-generation system, with the educator merely a resource to be drawn on in this process.

It is this model of education - now measured without qualification - that has come to dominate HE. It is a conceptualisation tied in with institutional (and often academic) support of a neo-liberal system without question. (A neoliberal system, I may add, that is looking none-too-healthy at the moment). This is a model that is being problematised by Professor Richard Hall and others. And this is why (Lawrie) that HE in England is markedly less political than in countries without a fully integrated and developed employability agenda.

Here's the 2011 White Paper:

> *"To be successful, institutions will have to appeal to*

> *prospective students and be respected by employers"* (14)

And

> *"We also set out how we will create the conditions to encourage greater collaboration between higher education institutions and employers to ensure that students gain the knowledge and skills they need to embark on rewarding careers"* (3.2)

Good luck.

Entrepreneurs and Enigmas

Bletchley Park- rightly - has a semi-mythical status amongst UK geeks as the birthplace of modern hacking. As the wartime employer of Alan Turing and his peers, many of the underpinnings of the information age - from super-computers to advanced cryptography - were developed here. Certainly in my imagination it was a small, close-knit, community of the finest minds in the UK - a place where sustained concentration and flashes of genius changed the course of the war.

Except of course, it wasn't. It was a huge organisation - employing over 9,000 people by 1945, something you would never know from the official history. I was genuinely taken aback to hear this on an edition of BBC Radio 4's "Thinking Allowed" (from about 15mins) which was discussing a recent book on Bletchley Park by Professor Christopher Grey of Warwick University. The book, "Decoding Organisation", takes an organisational analysis approach to the work of the station, and draws some surprising conclusions.

The fundamental shock being that - in any modern sense of the term - it was in no way organised. There were no clear lines of reporting, often different parts of the organisation had no idea of the existence of other parts, much less what they were doing and why. A very small initial elite group, drawn primarily from interpersonal contacts, barely held together what Grey describes an "anarchistic" system. It had no (or nearly no) job delineation, no strategic or policy function, and (surprising for a quasi-military wartime function) very little hierarchy. The small, close-knit social circle at the top was nominally "in charge" of the establishment - but they didn't have a remit or regular committee meetings, or -really- any idea what was going on.

And this isn't a story of "despite this, Alan Turing won the war and invented modern computers". As Grey makes clear in the interview, it was *because* of this chaos that such things were possible.

This is by no means a single example. To me the Bletchley management parallels the classic British University structure of a similar vintage. In both cases you see a commitment to a single overarching cultural goal - the "defence of Civilisation", with surprisingly little codification of such a goal. And universities - loosely organised, loosely managed - have produced many of the advances that have advanced and defended Civilisation: from DNA at Cambridge to the Web at CERN.

When we hear stories of these efforts, we hear about individual genius, we hear about sudden flashes of brilliance, things falling in to place. We hear - in essence - a revisionist history informed by the myth of the entrepreneur. We seldom here anything of the conditions that make such breakthroughs possible, and we never hear anyone arguing for the establishment of quasi-anarchistic organisations that provide support and resources without obsessing over outputs and accountability.

Which is a very dangerous state of affairs when coupled with our current cultural enthralment with the quantification and demonstration of value. There are few infographics with question marks. Little performance data with error bars. And the irony comes with the realisation of the sheer expense of doing all of this measurement - both in terms of human and financial cost - is the most effective way of ensuring that no innovation ever happens.

Unfit for purpose? - Organisational resilience and Bletchley Park

Again, fate and fascination draws me back to Bletchley Park. My initial stumble upon the Christopher Grey's book " Decoding Organisation" has now been compounded by me actually reading the thing (thanks again to the good folks at Thompson Rivers University), and just this week I was lucky enough to engage with Dr Sue Black(her of Saving Bletchley Park fame) at her amazing JISCEL12 keynote.

There are many books and articles that will tell you some of the history of Bletchley, more about some of the amazing people working there, and the astonishing intellectual and technological triumph that was the repeated breaking of ciphers and encryptions previously considered unbreakable. As previously, and not to in anyway denigrate the amazing work that was done there, my interest is in Bletchley Park as a knowledge organisation and an innovative organisation - and the parallels between Bletchley and those other great repositories of genius and intellectual labour, universities

By referring to "Bletchley Park" as an organisation, I am already making a very obvious error. The work referred to above was conducted by the Government Code and Cipher School which happened to be based in and around the Bletchley Park estate during the Second World War, itself born in 1919 of various intelligence functions within the Armed Forces and Foreign Office, and a forerunner of GCHQ. The school was technically placed under the purview, though not controlled or directed by, SIS (a forerunner of MI6) and the various subcultures within what we know as "Bletchley Park" rubbed together uneasily for much of the war.

Some of you may have spotted the unlikely use of the word "school" in the organisational title. The school was founded to support and train staff in the emerging field of "signals intelligence (SIGINT) during peacetime - primarily in the effective use of encryption and ciphers rather than decoding the signals of others.

At the time the centre undertook it's most famous work, the following roles were implicit within the activity of the school:

- Interception of signals, at distributed centres across Europe
- The delivery (via transport or transmission) of the content of these signals, to Bletchley.
- Decryption of signals
- Translation into English, and the de-corruption of this intelligence
- Traffic analysis (who sent signals, where, how often?)
- Intelligence assessment (what did it say? what can we learn from it?)
- Distribution to customers/ end users. Use of information (or not)

(list adapted from Grey (2012) p37)

Each of these processes had their own champions, just as each of the services and cultural tendencies within Bletchley had their advocates. There were frequently heated disagreements concerning the value and needs of each interest group, so much so that an external review (the Van Cutsem report, conducted by Brigadier W.E. Van Cutsem) was conducted in 1941.

Nineteen Forty-One was, of course, a year of great peril for the UK and Europe - so the conduction of a major enquiry into the organisational structure of GC&CS in December 1941, followed by a transition to a new structure by February 1942 may strike some as faintly absurd.

Certainly the kinds of arguments that were being made have an other-worldly feel to them. Nigel De Grey, himself a superb code-breaker, wrote up a review of the work of the GC&CS after the war (which Grey quotes widely from [pp58-59]):

> *there was never - any clear understanding about the staffing of the service stations or any uniformity of procedure between them [...]*
>
> *GC&CS created a most complicated structure internally violating the official ladder of command and at the same time causing an intricate and illogical series of channels of reporting*

There is an amazing amount of primary evidence in Grey's book, which I would strongly urge the interested to take a look at, especially the first section "The Making of Bletchley Park". Much of this is taken from National Archive documents which are sadly not (yet) available online. I particularly want to read what Grey describes as a "satirical sketch of the various organisations involved that was written in 1940" entitled "The Kitchen Front"!

As I don't just want to re-write the entire book, I just want to give one further example from 1941. In October a group of leading cryptanalysts wrote to Winston Churchill asking for more funding, bypassing the entire management structure at Bletchley. The interesting thing is not the obvious "a few great men" narrative, but the fact that they chose to implicitly criticise one key administrator by defending the work of another - thus leading to the demotion of the man who brought the initial structure and staff of Bletchley together, Alastair Denniston. It was office politics, writ large.

Do bear in mind also that I am not telling the story of the organisational reshuffle that broke the enigma code - many forms of Enigma has been broken even by 1940. Rather, this is the story of an organisation in transition - a research centre that needed to add production lines to meet insatiable customer demand. (because who *doesn't* want more intelligence?)

-

I awoke on Monday to learn from our Prime Minister that we are at war. However, we appear to be at war with ourselves, with bureaucracy and our human rights. As always, universities are a microcosm of wider society, wherein we can plainly see that bureaucracy is an easy target but also an essential support mechanism. The lean, mean, fit-for-purpose, more-with-less language of business and innovation does not provide us with the safeguards and loopholes that make organisations work.

Remember, Enigma was broken whilst Bletchley was apparently in chaos. The reorganisation was primarily a way to scale up what were basically research findings into a product. Even within the new structure (post Van Cutsen), there was a research team working amongst and within the process-driven large scale decryption functions. And even in the process driven areas - you see the tales of Hut 3 (translation, evaluation and decryption of Army and Airforce intelligence) descending into near mutiny in 1942.

If you are lucky enough to work in an innovative organisation, you will see these tensions simmer and erupt again and again. Precisely because people care so much about the value of what they are doing, different conceptions can lead to heated argument. And then (hopefully) new understandings and new links forged. Often the complexities of these organisations are founded on the fractures and reformations of the positions and people involved.

-

I was lucky enough to revisit the Hawthorn Building at DMU recently - it was my "first" university building, wherein I studied (and failed) pharmacy for a year in the mid-90s. If you were going to build a set of rooms to teach Pharmacy, you wouldn't design the Hawthorn Building. Huge windows (a former arts college), a medieval archway preserved in the basement, a main lecture hall where Hendrix once played, rooms in turrets accessible only by hidden external staircases.

You wouldn't design it like that, but you wouldn't undesign it from that either. It is beautiful, ungainly, inspirational and the faculty doesn't so much inhabit the building as colonise it. But in doing so it has adapted the building to suit needs passing and long term, in a way it could never do with a purpose-built facility. Organisational structures can be self-adapting and self-nurturing in the same way.

MOOCs and the War on Terror

I'm still thinking about (and digesting) the "Organisation" book that the good folks of TRU decided to buy me. But this quote from another source made me sit up in recognition:

> *In the early 1970s [sociologists] carried out a large survey of superintendents, principals, and teachers in San Francisco school districts. The initial reports indicated that something was amiss in these organizations. Reforms were announced with enthusiasm and then evaporated. Rules and requirements filled the file cabinets, but teachers taught as they pleased and neither principals nor superintendents took much notice. State and federal money flowed in and elaborate reports went forth suggesting compliance, but little seemed to change in the classrooms. Studies of child-teacher interactions in the classroom suggested that they were unaffected by the next classroom, the principal, the district, the outside funds, and the teacher training institution.*

Or so quotes Robin Hanson, from a paper he can't be bothered to cite properly (!). He sees this as a "dictator-like teacher autonomy": "Schools are designed to, and do, stifle student imaginations. So why would we care much if teacher imaginations get stifled in the process? Do we care if prison guard imaginations gets stifled?"

So far, you may think, so standard edtech 'disrupt all of the things!' talk - though the main pull-quote has lovely implications for the analysis of the university as a chaotic organisation, which is what I'm currently warming up to do. But Robin Hanson is an interesting chap and worthy of further consideration. He takes most of the credit (pdf) for one of strangest ideas in US foreign policy in the last 10 years.

First coming to light in 2003, the Policy Analysis Market (PAM) was an audacious attempt to harness the power of the free market in order to identify likely terrorist threats. Participants (who needed to show no evidence of expertise in foreign policy, or indeed identity) could bet (and win) actual money on a range of likely acts. This approach seems to sit neatly between crowd-sourcing and rewarding "informants" in a traditional intelligence industry manner.

It is easy, and indeed was easy, to write this idea off as a right-wing fantasy - the invisible hand of the market solves everything. And that, coupled with a hefty dollop of 'nothing is more serious than the safety of our nation' rightist hand-wringing is pretty much what happened- sparking a scandal so great that it even caused John Poindexter (of Iran-Contra fame) to resign. So with all of this media frenzy, the actual research project (and it was only a research project) never got started.

I'd started thinking about PAM again after reading Mike Smithson's analysis of political punditry versus the (UK!) betting markets during the US election:

> *Throughout the long night of the White House race the most striking feature for the punters was how the betting markets were much faster responding to events and the information available than any of the so-called pundits.*

Again, lots of anonymous predictions come closer to the mark than a smaller number of "expert" ones, and the offer of reward to predictors leads to the possibility of non-open information being used ("cheating", as academics would call it).

And as the press began to call it, in relation to activity on Coursera massive online courses. A large number of participants, with varying levels of expertise, competed to answer non-trivial questions. And clearly some used "forbidden" information to do so.

Now Coursera is not so much a new model of education as a tool to produce test data in order to draw quantitative conclusions on every aspect of educational performance. [just realised as writing, I'm also describing a traditional university in maybe 3-5 years' time]. This approach (at least, on this huge scale) was pioneered by Candace Thille's team within Carnegie Mellon's OLI project.

Where PAM and political predications via betting markets actively hope for "cheats" in order to gain better quality data, Coursera and OLI are looking for an honest failure to predict correctly in order to improve what I can only, in this context, describe as market intelligence products (or as I might used to have called them, lectures). As Andrew Ng (co-founder of Coursera) described:

> *[...] While reviewing answers to a machine learning assignment, [I] noticed that 2,000 users submitted identical wrong answers to a programming assignment. A k-means clustering analysis revealed that the student errors originated with switching two lines of code in a particular algorithm. This information was used to improve the underlying lecture associated with the assignment.*

[a useful academic counter-example here would be Galaxy Zoo]

Now the casual reader (hello both!) will probably be wondering what I am getting at here! It's clear that both PAM and Coursera/OLI, whilst ostensibly set up for widely differing reasons, both are really looking for what you might call the "interesting outlier" in order to improve and expand upon the intelligence resources provided by in-house experts. It was Pauli who famously remarked of an uninteresting paper "It is not even wrong" - my suspicion is for both examples that a "right" answer is "not even wrong" and thus uninteresting.

And the top quotation on teacher autonomy - is the subtext not that it is impossible to get good quality comparable data on teaching methods whilst classroom practices are so varied?

But - finally, and chillingly - a university substitute that is actually hoping for wrong answers from students? That raises far deeper ethical questions than PAM ever did.

[edtech diaspora postscript: Hanson is clearly sensible enough to read - and cite - Martin Weller]

[further reading postscript: And Hanson maintains a great archive of PAM related materials on a dedicated corner of his web presence]

The 2003 White Paper on teaching, revisited.

For a fair number of years the 2003 DfES White Paper ("The Future of Higher Education") was my life, to the extent that I could quote paragraph numbers. I've just had reason to dive back in to check a reference, and I got to looking at the key recommendations on teaching (chapter 4). Can the impact of the recommendations still be seen eleven years on?

– We are rebalancing funding so that new resources come into the sector not only through research and student numbers, but through strength in teaching.

This was a general aspiration (that underpinned the rest of the chapter to a greater or lesser extent) rather than a specific policy.

– Student choice will increasingly work to drive up quality, supported by much better information. A comprehensive survey of student views, as well as published external examiners reports and other information about teaching standards, will be pulled together in an easy-to-use Guide to Universities, overseen by the National Union of Students.

The National Student Survey, of course! This has just been reviewed by HEFCE - and the review notes a number of practical and methodological issues, including significant changes to questions.

"[Both] stakeholders and students thought the NSS had conceptual weaknesses concerning what it measured, and methodological weaknesses related to what it covered. In particular, they were concerned that the NSS's scope was too narrow in terms of students' experiences and their engagement in learning and teaching which undermined the NSS's efficacy in informing

student choice and enhancing students' academic experience."

The wider collection of materials has been supplanted by Unistats, having previously been TQI - neither of which was ever run by the National Union of Students. Opinion appears to be mixed on the value of the data displayed by the service, some of which may be down to underlying issues with JACS coding.

The Key Information Set (KIS) also sits within this space. As does much of the thrust of the Browne Review and the 2010 White Paper ("Students at the Heart of the System").

But as a recent HEFCE review concluded, student choice is a bit more complicated than that.

– To underpin reform, we will support improvements in teaching quality in all institutions. Additional money for pay will be conditional on higher education institutions having human resource strategies that explicitly value teaching and reward and promote good teachers.

The DfES (as was) asked HEFCE to ensure that institutions had a policy to reward high-quality teaching, and then gave them some extra non-ringfenced money. Some institutions did (and continue to) have good processes for teaching-related promotion. For others it was more around lip-service. The new model of funding higher education pretty much undoes this reform, as all funding now follows student choice.

– New national professional standards for teaching in higher education will be established as the basis of accredited training for all staff, and all new teaching staff will receive accredited training by 2006.

There was an awesome multi-agency consultation, and then the then-new Higher Education Academy, took ownership of a set of professional standards on behalf of the sector (which initially looked the same as the old ILTHE standards. The UKPSF has been updated and continues to exist, the Academy accredits institutional courses based on it- and the indications are that it will continue to do so throughout the forthcoming reorganisations. However, the Academy is emphatically not a professional body, and has no wish to maintain lists of qualified HE teachers.

The standards never became compulsory ("a license to practice"), but most institutions now offer a PGCertHE to new staff, which leads to said staff member becoming a "Fellow" of the Academy. The University of Huddersfield is currently the only English university where all staff with substantive teaching roles are fellows, though data overall is not good enough to share with students.

– The external examining system will be strengthened by improved training and induction, including a national programme for external examiners by 2004-05.

Both the QAA and the Academy have published advice and guidance on external examining, but I'm not aware of a national programme either currently or in the past. (There is an active JiscMail list, however)

– We will also celebrate and reward teaching excellence. We are consulting on the establishment of a single national body - a teaching quality academy - which could be established by 2004 to develop and promote best practice in teaching.

And so it came to pass. The Academy was launched on Monday 18th

October 2004 (from the LTSN, ILTHE and TQEF NCT - HESDA headed for the Leadership Foundation instead) and has worked hard to win the support and trust of the sector as an independent champion of teaching in higher education. It has faced a number of cuts in recent years, losing the much loved subject centre network and faces further cuts in the next few years.

– Centres of Excellence in teaching will be established to reward good teaching at departmental level and to promote best practice, with each Centre getting £500,000 a year for five years, and the chance to bid for capital funding.

– The National Teaching Fellowships Scheme will be increased in size to offer substantial rewards to twice as many outstanding teachers as at present.

The other components of the support for teaching quality were systems of national rewards. The National Teaching Fellows continue with another clutch of excellent teachers made Fellows this year, but the £315m Centres for Excellence in Learning and Teaching have, with a small number of exceptions, largely disappeared.

The CETLs, on reflection, represented a particularly profound missed opportunity. They attempted both to be reward and beacon, a way of incentivising local excellence and sharing practice nationally. Years of hopes and dreams were poured into something that still had to maintain the constraints of the text in the paper. (Weeks were spent doing basic things like changing the name - from Centres OF Excellence to Centres for Excellence - and abandoning the "commended for excellence" consolation designation).

DfES originally hoped to expand this initiative as a counterweight to research funding, but even by the time of launch changing priorities made this look unlikely. Capital, in particular proved hard for HEFCE to allocate and there was a second allocation to existing centres.

– To recognise excellent teaching as a university mission in its own right, University title will be made dependent on teaching degree awarding powers - from 2004-05 it will no longer be necessary to have research degree awarding powers to become a university.

At the time this seemed revolutionary, but given what David Willetts ended up doing this looks tame on reflection. A small number of former Colleges of HE became Universities as a result of this change, and one new institution - The University of Cumbria- was founded.

-

All of these interventions have had some positive influence on the sector, but none have profoundly changed the sector. Looking back, this was evolution rather than revolution in teaching at least. The main thrust of the contemporary debates around the paper concerned the imposition of "top-up fees", themselves unwittingly laying the foundations of the Browne model of funding.

Whose university, and why? pt1.

If you asked an average, informed, observer (say an informed and observant Vice Chancellor, for instance) "What is a university" I imagine you'd get something like the following:

Universities (and colleges) are supported by public funds to do research. They teach students, at undergraduate and post-graduate level, with a combination of state funding and student contributions. They work (at least partially) to meet the needs of local and national employers, and of professional bodies. And they administrate themselves, via academic managers with professional managerial support. *(this isn't a real quote, but it sounds about right)*

This has all only really been the case since 1919, with the establishment of two bodies - the Department of Scientific and Industrial Research, which provided state research funding for what we now call STEM subjects, and the University Grants Committee, propping up an ailing higher education infrastructure after the First World War. Keen ironists will be delighted to note that both of these bodies and their underlying state-interventionist principles were established by a Conservative/Liberal coalition government. One Sir William McCormick was the first chair of both the DSIR and the UGC.

Prior to this, university funding by the state was piecemeal and arbitrary, with the primary policy actors being local authorities (in the establishment of Civic universities such as Liverpool, Birmingham and Manchester) and central government in establishing the Willetsian degree-awarding colossus that is the University of London (essentially a self-supporting 1836 fudge by the Privy Council so they didn't have to grant powers to multiple provincial universities that they didn't feel would be sustainable). Despite this, institutions continued much as they had in the middle ages, with the idea of the university famously described by the newly-Blessed John Henry Newman in 1850:

> *"The general principles of any study you may learn by books at home; but the detail, the colour, the tone, the air, the life which makes it live in us, you must catch all these from those in whom it lives already. You must imitate the student in French or German, who is not content with his grammar, but goes to Paris or Dresden: you must take example from the young artist, who aspires to visit the great Masters in Florence and in Rome. Till we have discovered some intellectual daguerreotype, which takes off the course of thought, and the form, lineaments, and features of truth, as completely and minutely as the optical instrument reproduces the sensible object, we must come to the teachers of wisdom to learn wisdom, we must repair to the fountain, and drink there. Portions of it may go from thence to the ends of the earth by means of books; but the fullness is in one place alone. It is in such assemblages and congregations of intellect that books themselves, the masterpieces of human genius, are written, or at least originated."*

Of course, there was no need for University research funding in those early days. Newman again:

> *"The nature of the case and the history of philosophy combine to recommend to us this division of intellectual labour between Academies and Universities. To discover and to teach are distinct functions; they are also distinct gifts, and are not commonly found united in the same person. He, too, who spends his day in dispensing his existing knowledge to all comers is unlikely to have either leisure*

or energy to acquire new."

Public funding for research (apart from a few special cases where specific non-university research institutes such as the Royal Society and the Royal Observatory were supported by the Crown and commissioned largely private individuals) is largely a 20th century invention - indeed you can pin the date down a rough date shortly after the first world war, and the above mentioned Department of Scientific and Industrial Research. But even here, the Department was more likely to commission and fund independent research bodies such as the National Physical Laboratory and the Building Research Establishment, occasionally bringing in University staff to work with them.

Two notable non-recipients of UGC (and DSIR) cash were the Universities of Oxford and Cambridge, both of whom felt that their autonomy would be compromised by accepting state funding. But even these two, enviously and nervously eyeing the investment in laboratory equipment facilitated by grants to other institutions, petitioned the UGC to support them in 1922.

UGC grants mainly covered the administrative and structural costs of a University, with teaching supported by learners and their sponsors. The availability of (near) universal public funding for teaching in Higher Education is a post second-world war invention, with a growth in local education authority funding for university fees from the mid '40s onwards. A national scheme of student grants in the early '60s after the recommendation of the Anderson Committee and the legislation of the 1962 Education Act built on the narrow availability of private and Board of Education scholarships. The 1962 act enshrined the right of all school leaves to local education maintenance grants in respect of their higher-level studies, with the exception of trainee teachers and mature students, both of which who were supported by the Board of Education. These interventions led to a rapid rise in the number of students who were able to take advantage of university provision.

Only with the passage of the Higher Education Act in 2004did the onus for the payment of (at least some) of the cost of their university education (in the form of what at the time was called "top-up fees") return to the learner in question.

But enough of these modern ideas of funding teaching and research! The position of the employer needs has become more prominent since the Dearing report in 1997 but it's been there since medieval times, with pretty much a 10-20 year cycle of interest through the 20th century. Indeed, giving life to the old Einstein maxim that the definition of madness is continuing to do the same thing and expecting different outcome, successive movements and eventually governments have created new kinds of UK universities, to better meet the needs of employers:

- The "redbrick" and "civic" universities, largely established by groups of industrialist benefactors, placed particular emphasis on meeting the technological demands of the fast-changing Victorian era.
- The "Robbins Report", or "plate-glass", universities, where all Colleges of Advanced Technology (originally organised to meet the industrial and commercial needs in a given locality) gained degree awarding powers

- The "New", or "post 92" universities, where polytechnics and HE Colleges already embedded in local employment markets gained degree awarding powers.
- The Open University specifically allowed students to study whilst in full time employment.
- And those readers sitting in "ancient" universities may want to consider the links between their seat of learning and the Church, the principal employer of university graduates for many centuries.

And as for the academic leadership of Universities, just to give one example the University of Cambridge Congregation appointed "proctors" to deal with the finance, infrastructure and PR activity of the medieval university.

With this in mind, we can surmise that the current state of the university system in the UK is a function of many interventions, by government and employers, over nearly 1000 years. But is what we have ended up with worth defending?

Selected background and further reading:

Anderson, Robert, "The Idea of a University Today", (History and Policy, March 2010)

"A Brief History of the University of Cambridge", (cam.ac.uk, accessed October 2010)

Dyhouse, Carol, "Going to University: Funding, Costs, Benefits"(History and Policy, August 2007)

Hutchinson, Eric, "The History of the University Grants

Committee"(Minerva vol 13 number 4, December 1975)

"A history of congregation and convocation", (ox.ac.uk, accessed October 2010)

Salmon, Mike et al, "Look back at Anglia"(http://www.iankitching.me.uk, accessed October 2010)

Also, the legend that is Joss Winn pointed me to this amazing paper, which covers the changes of the 80s in much more depth.

Finlayson, Gordon, and Hayward, Danny, "Education towards Heteronomy: A Critical Analysis of the Reform of UK Universities since 1978. " (http://www.jamesgordonfinlayson.net, accessed October 2010)

Whose University? Why? pt2: the cuts and the fees

So where are we today? (2010)

The total income of the UK Higher Education Sector is £23,440m. Direct funding council funding for UK institutions (taking into account teaching [64%], research [20%] and special funding allocations [16%]) currently constitutes 36% (£8,508m) of this income. 19% of UK Higher Education Funding comes from other government sources (mainly the research councils), 8% from standardised student "top-up" fees. The remaining 37% comes primarily from other income associated with students (including international student fees, profits on university halls of residence). Non-government funded research (on behalf of charities and the private sector), comes to only 7%, only a little over the 6% gained from residential and catering profits (source, HEFCE 2010, from 2008-9 HESA figures).

Two things are notable about these figures.

The first is that research is not especially profitable if you take a short term view of it. The vast majority of research is paid for by the government using funding that would probably otherwise make its way into the core allocation, and factoring in that some universities do an awful lot of non-government research, the average institution is probably more profitable as a hotel than a commercial research centre. Given the rumoured oncoming research funding cuts, even more so.

The second is that charging a student £3,000-odd pounds a year per student is not yielding much in the way of additional income. Fees are payable starting at the point of completion of each year with the Student Loan Company paying the fees and then reclaiming from graduates over their working lives. All this does is move (a small amount) of the long-term cost of higher education from public taxation to private debt. And in the short-term, the fees are paid by the SLC and guaranteed by the Government, so for at least the first three years it makes pretty much no difference at all to the taxpayer whether fees are £0, £3000, £7000 or whatever else. Incidentally, why are we trusting an ex-BP person to apply a cap correctly?

This is an important point and is worth bearing whenever you hear a politician talking about cutting costs and universal education being unaffordable. The government will start getting a tiny trickle of these fat fees back in round about 2014-15, by which time that nice Mr Osborne will have cleared the deficit and the sun will always be shining. Fee increases have NOTHING to do with clearing government deficit and anyone who tells you otherwise is a liar.

But - oh yeah - the cuts. One rumour I've heard is of all funding for bands C and D cut, with bands A and B cut by an equivalent amount. This (apparently) will be a 40%-ish cut. For many readers, the previous sentence will be nonsense, so allow me to explain.

HEFCE allocates funds on a weighed model, based on a complicated set of observations called TRAC-T which tells them pretty much what it costs to do any kind of teaching in a UK university. They then simplify this into four bands and apply a weighting to each band, something like this:

- Band A (Clinical Sciences) = standard unit of resource x4
- Band B (Other lab-based sciences, engineering and technology) = standard unit of resource x1.7
- Band C (Other lab, studio or fieldwork subjects) = standard unit of resource x1.3

- Band D (everything else) = standard unit of resource x1

Then they add on some further weightings for being in or near London and some non-traditional modes of study, and note that some subjects are in multiple bands (eg Psychology) which causes no end of trouble. But the question you are probably wondering is what is the "standard unit of resource"? Well, to figure that out you take the number of students in the system (weighted as above) and then divide the total available teaching funding by that. This year, the standard unit of resource happens to be is £3947. (and the £3225 of fees "tops up" this figure to something approaching a nominal total cost of tuition per year, which must be about £7172- hmmm-)

Let me start by apologising for not doing this next bit in as cool a way as Tony Hirst would.

So, if we take the cuts rumours as fact, and lose HEFCE funding for band C and D entirely, and cut bands A and B by the standard unit of resource, we look like this.

- Band A (Clinical Sciences) = standard unit of resource x3
- Band B (Other lab-based sciences, engineering and technology) = standard unit of resource = x0.7
- Band C (Other lab, studio or fieldwork subjects) = standard unit of resource x0
- Band D (everything else) = standard unit of resource x0

Assuming that the nominal standard unit of resource is kept the same (£3947), we get:

A: current system = £15896, would be £11841

B: current system = £6710, would be £2763

C: current system = £5131, would be £0

D: current system = £3947, would be £0.

Looking at the system as a whole in 2008-9 combined (which are figures that have handily and rather arbitrarily have been published by HEFCE) we can get a rough understanding of the effects this would have on the system as a whole. (note that this is really dodgy and I'm ignoring all the complicated stuff that is in more than one band, London weighting, other weighing- so this is indicative rather than exact).

So a 40% teaching funding cut by cutting Band C and D and reducing A and B by a similar amount would actually come to at least a 78% cut to core teaching funding! Clearly someone else out there has data standards as low as mine, I just hope that it isn't someone advising David Willetts and Lord Browne.

Now from above, we know that any higher fees coming in will make no difference to state spending on HE for at least 4 years, we can make one of two assumptions depending on our current state of optimism given the assumed truth of the rumours.

1. These cuts will be one great big short sharp shock, and we'll lose any number of institutions, with the government hoping that any extraneous costs in legal fees, redundancy etc. will be more than offset by the increased savings. Carnage, basically.

2. These cuts will be tapered, to mesh with the rising fee take. Given that we've calculated the total unit of resource is about £7000 anyway, we wouldn't see any overall loss in resource assuming that we see the same number of students overall. As that last clause is clearly not going to happen we will still see a certain amount of carnage, but not

as much as in option 1.

And if we had the kind of government who hadn't recently rushed in to quango cuts and child benefit cuts without weighing up all the implications, I'd be confidently if painfully predicting option 2.

But I'm going to end on an upbeat note. Option 3. These rumours are clearly fag-packet policy from within the Browne Review. The figures don't add up, the fee cap raise doesn't have the effect that is expected, and above all, the country gains £3 from every £1 it invests in Higher Education. Browne releases the report and plays the big bad capitalist, the Tories harrumph and nod, then make a big show of being beaten down to a lower cut and a lower rise in fees by the Lib Dems, those plucky defenders of student finance.

Academia breathes a sigh of relief, but really the bus is already leaving.

Whose university? why? pt. 3

As I write, we are mere hours away from the launch of the Browne Review of Higher Education Funding and Student Finance and the first whir of the fearful machine that will change the face of higher learning.

This is the same machine that has turned our private sector into the behemoth that we placate with government bailouts and job cuts, and protect or mollify with new laws and new crimes. The machine that turned friendship and trust- ideas and beauty - into one man getting richer as other toil.

And this is it. We've reached the end of the profit margin. We can patch up the business models, flutter life into the stock certificates, pump the corpse of commerce with tainted coins and bills clawed from the hands of the exploited masses. We've no oil, no energy, no growth. The crops are dying, the seas are dying. The stories that we tell ourselves - the American dream, the myth of the self-made man, the benevolence of the market, the meritocracy, the idea of perpetual growth - they never were true, and we always knew it. But now even the leaders can only parody the mechanisms of belief.

Or to put it another way - we are trapped in the belly of this horrible machine and the machine is bleeding to death. (& part 2)

If we have a last hope - is it too late to talk about hope? - it is our own ability to understand, to create, to synthesise and to draw together. The first academic was a man drawing patterns in the sand. And we all did it, we drew patterns, connections, network diagrams- we were nodes in the lattice of learning, explaining as we created, weaving the strands together.

And we are the only ones that truly understand this machine that is coming for us. In many ways we built it.

There are contradictions, flaws, logical errors. Who better than we to point these out? Even in the past week we've seen the hot ice and wondrous strange snow of cuts that cost money, price rises that bring in nothing, market fundamentalism that leads to Sir Green's call for the Government to exploit and twist the so-called natural and immutable market forces to benefit itself.

In a world where jobs and income are in danger we are urged to take on more debt.

In two major reports, days apart, we are called upon to collaborate and compete, monopolise and diversify, act local and buy global. There's no rationale here- they're as scared as we are.

More so, because they are cowering not because of what they are about to destroy or what is already falling around their ears, but because they know that we can and will hold their ideas to account and that those ideas will be found lacking. Lacking in a logical sense, incoherent, self-contradictory, divorced from the very cause and effect that they claim we need to "get real" and understand.

And lacking in a spiritual sense, without a dream, a vision, an inspiration, a sense of any purpose beyond one number rising as another falls. They show us a balance sheet, we show them the stars- and the gods, and the artists, and the dreamers dreaming.

We hold the very secrets of the universe in the University, a treasure beyond value, and we don't sell them, we share them.

Our Arcadian islands have gotten tarnished over the years. Our own "big society" of scholars and seekers of truth has taken in those who can advise us how to play their game (as if we couldn't if we wanted to). We have our own balance sheets now too, our own income/outgoings, shortfalls and profits. We even mutilate ourselves to fit their image - a department lost here, a lab there, a few thousand books and journals tipped into the great stack. Good people held back because they care more about truth than money and the corporate way.

The last thing we want is to claim that we can play that squalid game better. Our argument is that the game is wrong, the whole game, and if anyone can find another one it's us. Think of all the things we do that isn't make money- we invent, we reappraise, we reuse; we expose young people to worlds and ideas they never knew existed. We're a community, and we are part of other communities. And we dream, the last dreamers in a world that has forgotten how. But they'll be needing us, if not now then soon.

Departments that close, institutions that fold. They won't come back. They say that we shouldn't hand our children debt, but let's at least have something to hand on that we are proud of. Or the stories we'll be telling them of learning for all and the life of the mind will be of a land as far away from their daily experiences as fairy tales. And I want some new stories, some better stories, to tell my son.

This post owes a debt to some of the amazing writing around the Dark Mountain project, and to Joss Winn, Richard Hall, Dave White, Adam Cooper, Rob Pearce, Lou McGill, Brian Lamb, Amber Thomas and everyone else I've agreed and disagreed with over the past few months.

David Kernohan

Guidance for aspiring keynotes

How to be an eLearning Expert - How to be Controversial

*Any resemblance to celebrity e-learning experts - living, dead, or horrible flesh-eating zombie - is not intentional and is probably self-perceived due to over-active paranoia. If you *are* a controversial e-learning expert and think any of these steps are specifically aimed at you, please let me assure you that they not. Please leave a blog comment detailing which section you mistakenly think is an attack on you and why, and I will gladly change the text.*

So, you've followed Lou McGill's excellent guide to becoming an elearning expert. And you've made it!

Or have you?

Sure, you're seen at all the cool sessions at all the best conferences, but you're there at the bar listening to Helen Beetham talking to Diana Laurillard, Sheila MacNeill, Grainne Conole and Sarah Knight about evaluating the use of runnable learning designs in educational practice and pretending that you are intellectually capable of following the conversation by occasionally nodding and saying "mmm-mmmm-" - whilst THAT GUY* is being whisked away from his keynote address to speak to puckered-lipped senior mandarins at the Ministry before returning - you imagine - to a hotel suite filled with exotic alcohol, sherbet dips and semi-naked booth babes employed by major e-learning vendors. And gosh, you want to be THAT GUY so hard that it hurts.

What's THAT GUY got that you haven't?

CONTROVERSY.

But now, with this simple free 10 point plan, you too can experiment with controversy: the coolest bad-boy substance known to man. Feel the raw power coursing through your fingers. Feel the adrenaline rush of being up against popular opinion with only your wits and a collection of pictures from Google Images used in breach of their license to help you. Because "starting a debate" is exactly the same thing as having 600 people call you a prat on twitter.

1. IDENTIFY A HIGHER POWER AND SUBMIT TO IT. Choose market capitalism, everyone else does. Of course you wouldn't talk directly about this to an audience of lefty academic soap-dodgers, but you can carefully structure your argument so you leave them desiring service or technology X, which is available at a very reasonable price from certain commercial suppliers. They *could* set it up and do it themselves, but if you drop in words like "cuts", "time pressures", "professional quality" and "advertising" it will soon put them off. If you are canny, you already own or have shares in certain commercial suppliers that provide service or technology X.

2. BUILD A STRAW MAN. There are some practices in academia that don't work, some of the time. Hell, there are loads - here's a few to get you started: exams, libraries, application, feedback, lectures, seminars, contact time, online learning- Pick one and argue that because it is bad sometimes, it must be bad all the time. You could cite your own personal experiences, or if you don't have any experience (and don't be ashamed), use a scene from a cheesy 80s film to perfectly reflect reality. In fact, if you are really confident, suggest academia is bad all the time and we should replace it with something where private companies can more easily sell services and thus support student choice.

3. SEE VISIONS, DREAM DREAMS. There needs to be a simple ideal solution to the problem you have posed under point two. The fact that there actually isn't shouldn't stop you getting in to some serious technologo-determinism. All students should have iPhones! All teaching should be filmed in stroboscopic surround-sound 3D! Academics should pay for the development of commercial quality games for teaching! Academics should be available 24/7/365 via a bespoke chat client and brain implant! Don't worry about implementation, who is going to pay for it all, or whether anyone actually wants it, or even whether it would actually work the way you claim it would. You'll never have to make it happen.

4. TILT AT A SACRED COW. Conversely, there are some things in academia that quietly work really well: try autonomy, diversity, micro-specialist subjects, local community and employer links, academic rather than business management, supporting small scale embedded innovation. But as these don't fit in with your vision and dreams (see point 3) then they obviously don't work. Just because they have stupid compelling independent evidence to support them does not mean that your theory is wrong. Your theory is obviously right, because you are on the stage expounding it, whilst they are sitting in rows listening. Never forget that.

5. KICK A DOG WHEN IT IS DOWN. There are some things that people love to hate. If you feel like you are losing the crowd, have a cheap shot at a complaint common among those who don't really understand the issue in question, like PowerPoint slides, university administrators, lazy apathetic students, moaning academics or useless quangos. There - didn't that feel good? Now everyone is back on your side again. A good time to do this is immediately before you start selling something, be that an event, a workshop or a new shiny product. Then you sound populist enough to make people think you talk enough sense that they will trust your sales pitch.

6. POTTY MOUTH. The best way to "keep it real" is to swear like a lady's front bottom. Because your poo is from the streets and you sexually tell it like it is, incestuous person, you can really fornicate excrement up. You might initially think you sound like a cranially-mounted phallus, but really you are the canine's gonads. And don't you coitally forget it, female dog. (of course, if challenged, you always speak like this. Especially to ministers of state and at dinner parties with major elearning vendors.)

7. TWO PLUS TWO EQUALS FIVE. You know that deeply unpopular and stupid thing that isn't going to work that the government have announced? Well, they're right and the consensus of opinion amongst those who actually understand the issue is wrong. It is going to work and it's just what we need. It may be painful and result in massive job losses/institutional closures/international terrorism/students dropping out/greater expense but really it's for the greater good of the sector. Only you, the controversial elearning expert, understand this, by refusing to cloud your razor sharp brain with the dull grind of facts and evidence. Why, you could almost be in government yourselves.

8. GET WITH THE EDUPUNKS. No, I don't mean proper EduPunk, which is where the likes of Jim Groom use a whole grab-bag of tools for themselves to engage with students on a personal, meaningful level and produce great art like DS106. You don't even need to go to the bother of selling out, because to you edupunk only means that the technology that institutions use is rubbish, and you should buy and use better stuff. Punk is simply market capitalism in funny clothes. (and note the best stuff has a logo that looks like a bit of fruit). On a similar tip, always use "disruptive" when you mean "new and probably unwise" - it makes you sound edgy and cool, and makes everyone who disagrees with you sound staid and old-fashioned.

9. THINK BIG. It's a waste of time doing stuff on a small scale. Lots of people will never see it, and that's bad for the ego. The only good things are those that are massive, monolithic and visible from low earth orbit. Forget doing something linked to the identified needs of a small group, forget trials and experiments, ignore building sustainable innovation: let's mandate, baby, mandate. If everyone *has* to do it then it will definitely be good and it will definitely work. After all, we've had so many pilots, why not invest in some nice technical drawing instruments made by Rotring.

10. NEVER APOLOGISE, NEVER EXPLAIN. Contrition is a sign of weakness. If you turn out to be wrong about something (and you've about a 50% chance, statistically, just like any other monkey) the important thing is to keep being wrong, but louder. People will start to suspect that you've seen something they haven't and have a deeper understanding. After this wears off, the career of a professional contrarian is open to you - a life of being THAT GUY on a plenary panel. Any you did want to be THAT GUY, didn't you?

ONE FINAL NOTE: PLAYERS BE HATERS. Following this approach, you may find that some people begin to dislike you. If they do it is important that you appear to deal with them civilly and politely. Firstly characterise them as "out of touch". You spend all day talking to delegates at conferences, you obviously know more about what is really happening than them, stuck in their sub-specialism. Secondly, they clearly haven't understood your argument- best repeat it to them several times in slightly different words. Thirdly, they are probably a fan of one of the things you slagged of in point three, so you can dismiss them as being self-interested. Fourthly, if all else fails, appeal to your authority. You've been being an elearning expert for, ooh, ages now, you even started an elearning company and got some contracts. How dare they know more than you about higher education? How very dare they?

(* and THAT GUY is (almost) always a guy.)

Clay Shirky is our MP3

Dear Clay,

Please stop being wrong about the future of Higher Education. It's embarrassing, and it is damaging to those of us who actually work in the field and care about it.

But first up, could you stop being wrong about the record industry. The pattern of a newer, low quality format supplanting an old one is not an unusual experience for them. Cassette tapes were a lower quality than vinyl. CDs are a lower quality than vinyl (and to be honest, it is also arguable regarding cassettes). And record companies love this stuff because it means that they can sell us content we already own all over again. Why do we let them do it? Because the new formats are more convenient for some uses.

The recording industry has singularly failed to die as a result of the mp3. True, they didn't develop ways of selling mp3s online but - guess what? - they didn't develop record shops either. Record shops did that, and iTunes (etc.) are just online record shops. Very successful record shops. More music was sold last year in the UK than at any other point in history.

One of the reasons for this *was* a by-product of Napster. Record companies realised that mp3 meant it was now viable to sell more of their back-catalogue, and that the interest was there. Previously as long as the Beatles and a few others were always available, most music was allowed to fall out of print. Which led to people searching second-hand record shops for that elusive single.

What Napster meant was I could search for the rare music I wanted to hear and have a real expectation of being able to hear it. That was new, that was great. There was no other way I could hear the music I was now hearing. If I could have paid for it, I would. Eventually, I did buy recordings by artists I wouldn't have known about if it hadn't been for Napster. And it wasn't just me.

Mp3s cost much less to produce than CDs or records, so it was much easier to keep all the old music around. No need to store it in a warehouse, no need to distribute it to shops. And record companies didn't make any money out of second-hand record shops, but they do make money out of iTunes.

And of course, there is a load of things you *can't* do with new formats. If you are a serious DJ, you're probably into vinyl. Sales of which have soared. You can do things with vinyl that you cannot do with CDs or mp3s. Maybe you are an audiophile - maybe you have a great sound system and miss all of that harmonic stuff going on up there above 41 kHz. (of course, you can't *hear* stuff above about kHz but you can hear the way that it interacts with the stuff you can hear.) Vinyl is good for you, as are raw audio files, SA-CD and DVD-audio. More formats to sell.

And then there is stuff like Spotify and YouTube. New ways for record companies to get paid, by subscription or via advertising.

So the impact of the "disruptive" Napster was that the recording industry was able to sell more music to us, and a greater variety of music, at a lower cost to them.

Maybe cancel the flowers?

Another alarming component in your argument is that you managed to attend Harvard, hear great lectures, but didn't see the development of a scholarly community. Guess what Clay? - you messed up. You were kind of "lossy". Your education was riven with compression artefacts.

Scholarly communities of interest don't just form - you have to work at them. You have to make them happen by talking to people. Maybe you weren't bothered - maybe you had other interests, but don't hold the system responsible for your choice not to participate fully in it. If you do just want a pile of lectures and some essay questions maybe a MOOC would work for you, but many of the rest of us *did* get a lot more out of our university experience.

That would be a superb way of "screwing it up", to use your scholarly term. To think that all a university experience can be is a bunch of lectures and some essay questions. To think that the availability of a new format that suits some people's needs a bit better means that nothing else is viable. To think that a degree is something that you purchase and experience, not something you work for with a great degree of pain and personal change.

The needs that MOOCs satisfy are the needs of a bunch of middle-aged men (and it is - nearly - always men) who are comfortably tenured but seek the thrill of being on the cutting edge of technology and "innovation" (whatever that is - looks to me like inventiveness with all the fun sucked out of it). They make for great TED talks. Wonderful blog posts. But they are nothing more than a surface solution to the surface problems a non-specialist observer could see in higher education.

The problems Higher Education does face is that it is a marketplace when it doesn't need to be. We spend billions of dollars forcing universities to compete without any evidence whatsoever that this leads to a better or cheaper product. We spend more on HE than at any point in our history whilst departments are closing, services are withering and talented young academics are leaving in droves because they have reached their mid-30s without finding anything other than temporary hourly-paid work.

The last great hurrah of the baby boom. Grey-haired millionaires trashing our cultural heritage, denying to others the opportunities that they have benefited from, and using a free product to undermine the maturation of education systems in the developing world. Maybe that works for you -it doesn't work for the rest of us. There are other formats we would prefer.

Thanks for that.

David

[p.s: See also Aaron Brady]

Life with geeks

This is what I have learnt about geeks in the last 10 years - I've worked with them and hung out with them, and although I feel like I understand them I wouldn't claim to be one. On twitter [a few years ago] I was in full-scale Adam Curtis mode (or maybe just trying to get a slide all to myself in a Dave White talk) and came up with the following soundbites:

"The geeks are 2%. They've always been 2%. They always will be 2%. They'll always own the cutting edge."

"Geeks are The Culture. They share everything, they don't need profit, they trust each other, they have super-advanced tech, they are naive."

"Geeks have their own currency - reputation. In that respect they've a lot in common with what academics used to be."

So, to unpack that a bit I'm fundamentally seeing geeks as being defined as those who are living now the life we will all be living in 3-5 years' time. But they are doing so with a very different set of assumptions, values and interest.

Geeks are not technodeterminist.

It's a cliché to paint a geek as having an interest in technology - Technology for geeks is like bricks to a builder. It's a staple. You can do all kinds of cool stuff with it, but in itself it's barely worth thinking about. Show a geek and a non-geek technodeterminist a new gadget. The technodeterminist gibbers about UI and gigabits and pixels per square inch. The geek asks "what can I do with it?" - a question that is more concerned with openness and interoperability than specification.

Geeks are interested (almost unhealthily in some cases) in human interactions and ways in which they can be improved and better understood. Most of what is interesting in geek culture is based on their understanding of (or, attempts to better understand) human interaction, and is expressed in the medium of technology. Most geeks do not have a formal background in humanities, so insights are drawn from technical analogies and amplified/reinforced by popular philosophy/literature and *especially* the more interesting class of games.

Amongst themselves, they have perfected interactions to a terrifying level. Respect and reputation are key, but the unlocking capability is the ability to ask intelligent questions. If you can do this - even if you can't understand the answers - you are accepted into the community. However, a poorly expressed question can often be treated with derision and rudeness.

Geeks design systems of interaction based on mutual respect and trust, precise and concise communication of key ideas, and the assumption that everything will be shared. When these systems migrate into wiser usage, these underlying assumptions can cause major problems. Facebook, for instance, assumes that you want to share pretty much everything with pretty much everyone - a default that becomes more and more problematic as the service becomes more mainstream.

Commerce, or even profit, is frowned upon. Those who manage to profit whilst maintaining geek credibility are tolerated, those who do not retain standing in the community are reviled. Geeks are more likely to work on something they think is cool (often with superhuman levels of effort and time commitment) than on something that simply pays their wages.

They are using technologies on a daily basis that you will be using, as I say, in 3-5 years' time. But by the time you get there they will be gone, to a technology that is more efficient and/or (usually both) more open. Ideas and tools that excite them now are almost certainly not accessible for the rest of us, indeed we'll have very little chance of understanding them in their current state. UI comes later, the possibilities and efficiencies are what is initially important.

As I said above, I'm not a geek - just someone who knows some geeks and is dumb enough to think he understands them. I think there are some historical and cultural parallels, as Carl Vincent pointed out:

"[T]hey are equivalent to academics from 300yrs ago and engineers from 150yrs ago."

but I'll leave them for others to draw out.

The Present

The followersoftheapocalyp.se review of the year - 2011

2011, for many of us, has been predominately characterised by having everything we once cared about and held dear torn away from us - and not merely torn away but snatched, mocked and destroyed by gibbering fools who care for nothing but their own momentary pleasure. Things that we loved for their purity, truth and beauty have been turned into sewage by the very people who promised to protect and cherish them. We've seen ever spark of humanity, every twitch of the rotting corpse of the beautiful civilisation that once gave us Swift, Cervantes and Rabelais immediately extinguished by a world that confuses what it means to be authentic with what it means to be selfish.

Every piece of music that made our souls leap, every connection with a fellow-traveller, every idea that ever spoke to us has become tarnished and poisoned by the cult of immediacy and sensation. Creative acts are now simply opportunities for monetisation, every altruistic impulse is a way of serving advertisements. The idea of "choice" has been cited by politicians and businessmen as a reason to choose not to care.

It's no longer enough to shudder against the onslaught of uninformed speculation - we've developed entire industries dedicated to maximising our exposure to the dribblings of idiots, and another to provide those very dribblings freshly minted and cropped to the requisite number of characters. All of it slewn with the suffocating irony and dog-whistling crowd management lowest-common-denominator dreck that has left us flinching from joyless, spiritless puns and artless references to other nuggets of popular culture that have had any semblance of humanity sucked from them generations ago.

Looking back across 2011, we have been lied to by everyone who has ever pretended to have our interests at heart. We've moved from governments pretending to do the right thing to seeing them pretend to do the wrong thing as a cover for doing something even more wrong. Anyone attempting to speak up for anything approaching meaning has been marginalised, smeared with shit before being effectively subsumed into the same stinking machine they once wanted to smash. We have failed to stand in support, we've bickered, jeered or ignored anyone we've been told to.

It has been the year of the false binary, the cynical requests that we provided detailed and costed alternatives to acts of audacious evil before we earn some "right" to question it. We've seen selfishness and mendacity enclose our memories and pleasures, limit our search for meaning to those which can be sold at an eye-watering profit margin.

2011 was the year we gave up and bought in to the narrative where we settle for losing what we are most proud of unless we lose more. We've redefined education as a state-funded hothouse for junior executive recruitment programmes, we've sold the minds of our children to entrepreneurs and thought leaders. We've turned the pursuit of truth, via art and science, into a disgusting and demeaning plea for money and security.

This was also the year when we learnt the languages of business and finance - quoting thoughtless anti-profundities in the way we used to quote poetry and philosophy. We've watched people live and die by the whims of discredited economic theories, we've let people starve and wither as we've argued for ideas that have been wrong for more than 100 years. We've seen ancient prejudices and jealousies, thought long-managed, re-explode into ugly life. And we've watched on YouTube, pointed and sniggered, as if our own ill-considered opinions are being ratified.

Top amongst the great sales pitches of the year has been the industrialisation of the artisan. Supermarkets pile-high "hand baked" and "authentic" goods, but these are available at an even greater price from airbrushed and idealised "farmers markets". The ecological movement has become a smokescreen for the industries that celebrate inefficiency as if it were some kind of worthwhile goal.

2011 was the year we finally managed to sell love and friendship. Brands start conversations and launch memes, and the potentially beautiful platforms where we spread these to those we care about are able to carefully place the appropriate advertisements alongside them.

And this year marks the end of outmoded ideas like retirement, curiosity, dignity and mutual support. Solidarity is little more than a hashtag. Even the language of the old left has been plasticised into vague exhortations about the "big society" and "we're all in this together."

And all this is what we used to call the "first world", the supposed exemplar of all that is noble and intelligent about humankind. In less advantaged parts of the world things are also exactly as I have described above, the only difference is that 99% of the population of the world have never known it any other way.

It is traditional to end yearly reviews with an optimistic message for this happiest of all seasons. And it is true that 2012 would have to monumentally suck to have any chance of out-sucking 2011. So we can all be happy that it already shows every sign of doing so. Merry Christmas!

[This post originally featured a section dealing with the German Brothel Myth, at the time I didn't realise it was a myth but I'm very glad to hear that it is. However I guess it says something about the state of the rest of the year that I didn't notice this until the wonderful @amcunningham pointed it out to me]

The house always wins: big data and legal loan sharks

I've read and retweeted this amazing article from Charisma about the way Wonga (the payday loan company) uses big data to make loan decisions. You might think that your social media use may have little bearing on whether or not you are eligible for credit, but social networks like Facebook are one of a range of sources that the company uses to confirm identification and assess lending risk.

> This slate.com article on the same topic includes a wonderful quote from ex-Googler Douglas Merrill, now at ZestFinance (a company who sells aggregations of data to aid credit decisions):

"We feel like all data is credit data, we just don't know how to use it yet. This is the math we all learned at Google. A page was important for what was on it, but also for how good the grammar was, what the type font was, when it was created or edited. Everything."

Everything.

You'd think with all this big data goodness that Wonga and the like would have no trouble with getting their repayments on time, wouldn't you? But Wonga wrote off £77m of debt the year before last (when it made £46m of profit). UK Member of Parliament and campaigner against payday loan companies Stella Creasy notes that 57% of customers miss at least one payment and half are unable to repay entirely.

It would appear that many customers choose to "over" the loan - borrowing again to pay off the existing loan + interest. And companies like Wonga charge fees for missed payments, and have a very aggressive approach to debt collection.

Is it too much of a leap to suggest that maybe all this "big data" is being used to identify the most profitable customers, rather than the most suitable? Social media data can supposedly be used to make inferences about a person's lifestyle and IQ, after all.

Data may have presumptions of neutrality, but any commercial enterprise looking at using data to enhance decision making would most likely have an eye on profit. And what is good for business may not be good for people.

Why management is more than watching the numbers go up and down.

BEFORE YOU READ THIS POST, WHY NOT PLAY THE GAME? Take a look at the graph below - it represents the changing staff morale over time of a (fictitious) organisation, as measured by a regularly administered survey instrument. You'll see you have two buttons, one of which administers a rebuke to staff for poor performance, the other offers praise for excellent performance. Your task, as manager, is to ensure that morale remains within the orange-bounded band - too low, and staff are too demotivated to perform, too high and staff are insufficiently engaged with corporate brand values. There are 19 (equal) time periods, with a value given at the end of each. It moves quite quickly so you really need to focus on your strategy. The newest data point is always on the left, older points move towards the right. Click the arrow button to begin and see how you get on.

[and Ha! It was an animated gif, and the buttons had no effect. Oh the LOLs…]

So how did you get on? Did you find the right balance of rebuke and praise to maintain morale? Did you learn how to react when morale suddenly dipped or soared? How did your staff morale end up? What would you do if you played again? Did you realise you've been pressing buttons linked to absolutely nothing whilst watching an animated gif?

Chances are you developed a narrative around the data displayed and your "interactions" with it. It is only a 20 frame gif so you probably couldn't develop a truly compelling story based on the data (over which you had no control whatsoever). But if I'd expanded it (or if I was Martin Hawksey and was able to figure out how to do a live random number plot with Google Charts) you'd have eventually become as unshakably certain in your internalised policy rules as David Cameron.

Here he is, running the country. "Rebuke! Praise! Praise!- no! Rebuke!- "

His iPad visualisation displays a variety of socio-economic indicators in real time, including sentiment analysis (*and was developed by none other than Rohan " year of code" " silicon roundabout" " exploding cheese" Silva*). His iPad, of course, has an email function allowing him to request action on the hoof, as it were. As much as I'd love to tell you that his email actually goes to "null" I fear this is not the case.

Anyway, let's get back to how much you sucked at playing the "corporate morale management simulator". Here are some questions you didn't ask: What was the survey instrument used? Why was it chosen? What did it measure? Why were the only options to "praise" and "rebuke"? Why couldn't you do something else? How large was the company? What did it do? What did the staff do? Why did morale have to stay in the orange zone? Where did those values come from?

Why didn't you ask these questions? No, not because you suck, but because I presented the situation as a game. If you're playing Flappy Bird, you don't ask why the bird has to flap or why he can't just land on the green Super Mario Bros pipe-thing. It's more fun not to ask, and to go along with the premise.

Suspension of disbelief: great for games, bad for policy.

In Joseph Heller's " Closing Time ", the president (referred to only as "The Little Prick") plays a fictional computer game named "Triage", one of a suite of war-themed games he keeps in an annex to the Oval Office. Triage simulates the planning of preparations for ongoing life post nuclear strike, in particular allowing the player to decide who to allow access to underground bunkers.

Of course, policy becomes based around the constraints of the game, and when he (inevitably, after Chekov) triggers the "real" nuclear football, his subsequent choices are based on game logic - and are characterised by his unwillingness to question the logic of the "game".

In times of uncertainty and rapid change, an ability to question the rules of the game are an essential prerequisite in adding value to decision making. And though access to data is helpful, this must be coupled with a deep understanding of the limits and constraints of the data, something that requires that you are able to comprehend it as a messy and contradictory corpus, away from the clean lines of your dashboard app.

So - our great generation of leaders - look with concern at dashboard apps and anything else that restricts your decision-making by design. And imagine how the morale in our imaginary company must have dipped if you had been randomly praising and rebuking them in the mistaken belief that it was effective.

"And these children that you spit on as they try to change their worlds are immune to your consultations..."

Consultations are strange beasts. In most cases, they are used where government wants to enact a policy but doesn't have the body of evidence to just go ahead and do it. The myth is that you run a consultation to gauge the response of interested parties to a change in policy, the reality is that you use a consultation to gather evidence that supports what you were going to do anyway.

And White Papers are a curious form of consultation. In policy implementation circles, they very quickly assume the status of sacred texts, even though (technically) the policy within is still subject to consultation. "How white is this paper?" is a frequent question in such circles - meaning "is anyone actually going to pay any attention to consultation responses here?" But this government generally likes to go one better. In HE, they've gone ahead and implemented most of the policy, then run a consultation.

They could do this based on the evidence of an "expert" report, the Browne Review. So interested parties had no chance to comment directly on plans to shift to a model where government funding for tuition follows student choices, just to pluck one example out of the air. And even stuff announced in the White Paper has already been enacted (MarginCore, AAB- indeed from next year ABB based on the massive success - ahem - of AAB this year).

Consultation responses are funny things too - organisational responses (and the vast majority do tend to be organisational) are written by a tame in-house wonk whose job it is to draft consultation responses. These responses are seldom the genuine, unfiltered, opinions of experts - the pattern tends to be "how can this proposed policy be tweaked in such a way as it benefits my organisation". They tend to be qualified approval, even if the policy itself is shockingly awful, because the possibility of the organisation maybe getting some more money outweighs the overall effect on the entire sector.

So the summary or responses is, at best, a summary of what we'd mostly guessed would happen anyway. The questions were largely concerned with the tinkering-around-the-edges aspects of HE policy - the responses (especially to the technical consultation) were largely along the lines of "stop playing with it, you'll go blind".

The big news items for me are as follows:

Explicit confirmation that there would be **no primary legislation** on HE, despite the need to give HEFCE new statutory powers and to protect the loan conditions of students within the new funding system.

Confirmation of the eventual r**eduction of HEFCE grant to strand A and B subjects**. This makes it explicit that BIS wants to move away from direct institutional funding entirely (para 2.1.20)

Moves towards the idea of **releasing data on institutional use of fee income**. This is actually one of the more insidious themes as many organisations depend on institutional subscriptions, and many institutional projects are multi-year long term benefit investments, both of which will be difficult to justify for students conditioned to expect £9k of direct value-added to their experience for £9k of fees.

The HEFCE **exemptions from the margin policy** (largely for arts/music institutions that admit by portfolio/audition) now look a lot less temporary than we initially expected.

Expansion of OFFA. This is actually a rather lovely example of the confused nature of HE policy, as a small-state focused government attempts to further regulate a market via an expansion of civil service numbers!

Confirmation that **PQA won't happen**, as predicted on Wonkhe.com. It never happens, but always turns up in White Papers. Like compulsory teaching qualifications for academics.

A whole range of **further consultations**. Great news for wonks everywhere.

We're under fifteen feet of pure white snow

An avalanche is coming. An avalanche of nonsense.

This is not our language, which is fair - which is correct - because this is not written for us. This is written for the kind of people who are impressed by such language.

This is written for people who would not bat an eyelid that the formerly respectable IPPR are now publishing paid advertorials from Pearson.

One of the facets of this new discourse of "disruption" is the use of vaguely connected anecdotes to illustrate a point. Pearson run a college in the UK, who are imaginatively called Pearson College - leveraging their reputation for value for money textbooks into the mass higher education market. Except they don't really do the mass bit, accepting a cohort of around 40 students, twenty of which had their fees paid for them at the last possible minute.

Norman Davies, the esteemed and often controversial historian, was interviewed recently in the FT, and explained historical change this way:

> *'historical change is like an avalanche. The starting point is a snow-covered mountainside that looks solid. All changes take place under the surface and are rather invisible. But something is coming. What is impossible is to say when.'*

You may wonder why I cite a Financial Times restaurant review at this point of the article, without any obvious context. The IPPR/Pearson advertorial does similar, and omits the following paragraph which offers context.

> *It seems impossible that Giorgio is going to arrive with more food, but he does. There's a green salad, followed by fish - handsome slices of sea bass and bream, and more of those chunky jumbo prawns. "The older you get, the more large meals become something of an ordeal," Davies observes.*

The education 'revolution' that Barber, Donnelly and Rizvi are such keen advocates of is a comfortably fed one. This is not a cry from the barricades - not a populist movement of grass roots activists. The hand-wringing citation of unemployment statistics and rising student fees comes not from the unemployed and poor, but from the new education industry that wants to find a way into the marketplace.

And this is the underlying impression one takes from this report. The citations are shoddy, the proofreading abysmal - it reads like a bad blog post. Or a good Ted talk. It's a serving of handsome slices of invective which would leave anyone sick to the stomach. Falling graduate wages. The lack of good "quality measures" for universities. A neatly formatted table of annual academic publication rates - in 50 year slices from 1726 onwards - labelled "The Growth of Information over 300 years". (but "citizens of the world now cry out for synthesis"!!)

Again and again we, as citizens of the world, are encouraged to rail and protest about the broken system that somehow seems to have educated world leaders, scientists, lawyers, engineers and senior staff at academic publishers with pretensions at "thought leadership". A system which anyone would admit has problems; problems caused by the imposition of a wearying and inapplicable market.

Here's another aside for you. The "thought leader" (trendy term of the moment, up there with "disruptive innovator") in question is Sir Michael Barber - the section of his wikipedia page that describes him as such was added from an IP address registered to Pearson.

Section 6 of the report, "The Competition is heating up", re-treads familiar grounds concerning the all-conquering world of the MOOC - that well known reheating of early 00s internet education hype flavoured with a rich source of venture capital. But this is situated within a wider spectrum of globalised private for-profit providers - the lot of whom (poor reputation! high drop-out rates! difficulty in gaining degree awarding powers!) is bewailed at some length.

As far as this report has any meat in it (horsemeat, maybe?) this section is it.

> *The reputations of some of the new for-profit providers have been tarnished by high dropout rates (a US government report alleges an average rate of 64 per cent in associate degree programmes) and high spending on non-education related expenses such as marketing and profit-sharing. Perhaps the government, through lax regulation and student loan subsidies, has also contributed to the problem, but either way it would be a mistake to think that the innovation itself will be diminished by these abuses.*

I'm particularly impressed with the way they decided to blame the government. If only the government had told them to stop lying to prospective students, spend less on flashy marketing and pay themselves less then everything would have been OK. Pearson here are calling for more red tape to constrain and direct the activity of HE institutions.

UK readers will be delighted to note:

> *In addition to US-founded MOOCs, the UK has responded with FutureLearn, an online university, which builds on the foundations of the Open University but has content from institutions around the UK.*

Remember this. FutureLearn is an **online university**. An e-university, if you will. An e-university based in the UK. And incidentally, did we mention that Pearson run a MOOC platform?

League tables are next in line. Pearson/IPPR complain that league tables are unfairly weighted against new entrants because they include things like research performance. Many would agree that perhaps too much weight is placed on research performance. But university reputations are complex things, and league tables are themselves a radical simplification of the complex criteria that we use when we decided which of two almost indistinguishable middle-ranking universities are the "best" for a particular purpose.

We can skip over the box-ticking enumeration of the neo-liberal university dream that is section two of the report, and move on to where the serious money is. Unbundling.

Research is at risk from- think tanks and government funded centres.

Degrees are at risk from- private colleges. Alternative credentials (yes! they reference my favourite "education is broken" start-up DeGreed. Still no venture capital for them, sadly) And also the start-up culture wherein Peter Thiel gives smart teenagers $100,000 to do very little of any consequence. And sites like the (Open University supported) Not Going to Uni.

The effects of *universities on their surrounding areas* are at risk from- government investment in local services. (another deviation from the small government playbook there)

Faculty are at risk from- celebrities. The connected internet age apparently means that people want to learn only from celebrities, without actually being able to communicate with them.

Students are at risk from- actually it breaks down here, it's just some more stuff about the connected world. Bob Dylan is cited as a college drop-out, though few current undergraduates would cite a need to meet Woody Guthrie as a reason to drop out.

Administrators are at risk from- their own inefficiency. (Despite being described earlier in the advertorial as "top professionals in specialist fields [who] make up the engine that keeps the vast, complex organisation running smoothly.)

Curricula are at risk from- MOOCS! - which are themselves based on university curricula. (from prestigious universities, no less-)

Teaching and learning are at risk from- online teaching and learning. This section also contains a curious digression about the need for "practical" rather than "theoretical" learning - perhaps harking back to a desire to see the government pay for employee training.

Assessment is at risk from-computer games. No, really. There's one of those asides about some 22 year old who became manager of the Azerbaijan football team FK Baku after 10 years of experience playing Football Manager. Which must be disquieting news for the team's actual manager, Ibrahim Uzunca. The student in question, Vugar Huseynzade, actually appears to be more of a business manager - though I invite any Baku fans who may read this to correct me. Oh, and Pearson already own a chain of assessment centres.

The *experience* of attending university is at risk from- clubs and forums.

Vice-chancellors who have read this far will likely be convulsing with laughter at this point. But never fear, as Sir Michael has a prescription for your future success.

You can be an elite, mass, niche, local or lifelong learning institution. All are at risk from the oncoming juggernaut of private sector instruction, so each must respond in different ways.

Elite institutions must share their prestige with (private) partner institutions. Mass institutions must move online, maybe with the capable support of private sector experts. Niche institutions will all be private institutions (College of Law, New College of the Humanities should it ever become an actual institution with degree awarding powers-) so don't worry about them. Local institutions must add the vocational, employer-supporting finesse to elite content from around the world. And lifelong learning? Well that isn't institutions at all, that's young entrepreneurs "hacking" their education with the support of the private sector.

I'm not sure what the key thread is with these recommendations, but there does seem to be a common theme running through them.

So - having sold you the disease, Pearson now attempt to sell the cure. We must all work hard to support the brave and noble entrepreneurs as they seek to disrupt education, moving existing providers out of the way, adding or removing regulation to order.

It is essential to do this because it is essential that we prepare our young people for their lives as cogs in a machine that is already broken, as avatars of a discredited and poisonous ideology. Young people are not seekers after truth, they are consumers and their money must be allowed to flow as directly as possible to Pearson Education.

Unless there is a bigger avalanche coming.

Eighteen Percent?

> *"A recent poll in the UK suggests that just 18 per cent of people think that a university education is a good preparation for today's labour market. In response, Wendy Piatt, speaking for the top universities, rejected this perception and said that in fact the education was 'ideal'. If she is right, at the very least she has a major communications challenge on her hands."*
>
> *(p47 "An Avalanche Is Coming", Pearson/IPPR, 2013)*

For anyone reading at Pearson, that thing in the brackets above is called a "citation". It means that anyone reading this blog post can quickly refer to the sources of information I am referring to. I'd recommend them to you as good academic and journalistic practice.

The "eighteen percent figure" is regularly repeated in presentations linked to the Avalanche report. I remember commenting at the time that the report was badly referenced - alas this poor referencing seems to extend to the slides. It is a good soundbite, but we should always be suspicious of statistical soundbites without sources.

So I turned to google - thinking that Wendy Piatt at the Russell Group probably doesn't refer to things as "ideal" very often, especially not in reference to the figure 18.

There are in fact three results for searching "Wendy Piatt ideal 18" on google. The first is a BBC News story about vocational education, published on 28th November 2012. The opening paragraph?

> *"UK universities should offer more practical and vocational learning, a survey for a think tank suggests. A poll for Policy Exchange found 55% of adults believed too many people studied narrowly academic*

> *subjects. Only 18% said universities had the right balance between academic and technical subjects. Dr Wendy Piatt of the Russell Group of universities rejected this saying they were "the ideal learning environment which produces 'work-ready' graduates".*

The timescale and Piatt quote fit, but this report suggests that 18% of the surveyed adults felt that Universities had the right balance between academic and technical subjects. Which is a fair opinion, I suppose. But is emphatically **NOT** the same thing as saying 18 per cent of people think that a university education is a good preparation for today's labour market

But let's be fair, maybe the underlying work supports the inference that Sir Michael Barber draws. The survey was carried out by the fairly reputable YouGov for the less reputable right-wing Policy Exchange thinktank (seriously, it was founded by Michael Gove for godsake-) in support of a report called " Technical Matters", published by Policy Exchange on 21 January 2013. Page 16 deals with the poll:

> *"Polling carried out for this report indicated that -55% of people agreed that "Too many young people in Britain study academic subjects at university, we need more people to study for practical and technical qualifications", with 8% indicating that too many people study practical qualifications, and 18% indicating that the balance was about right"*

So the same issue remains. Even if you wanted to cite a figure suggesting that not many people felt that universities are good preparation for the labour market - and were prepared to overlook the issue that studying practical qualifications (whatever they might be) might not be a good preparation for the labour market - you would use either 26% (the % of the sample that felt that there were enough or too many practical qualifications) or 45% (the % of people who did not say that there were too many young people studying academic courses).

I know the second one is a bit dodgy, but it is such a bad question - containing two separate propositions, the second not leading directly from the first - that to be honest you might as well.

But YouGov did the poll, and they are fairly solid statistically. Even though they were co-founded by Michael "Belize" Ashcroft. Let's look at the source data. The note in the "Technical Matters" report (note 45, note fans) says:

> *"YouGov polling for Policy Exchange. All figures, unless otherwise stated, are from YouGov Plc. Total sample size was 1,624 adults. Fieldwork was undertaken between 25th - 26th November 2012. The survey was carried out online. The figures have been weighted and are representative of all GB adults (aged 18+)."*

And YouGov publish the majority of their results in an online archive. Searchable by month and year.

But alas, amongst the important polls about time travel and Nadine Dorries, results of this survey are nowhere to be seen. Neither have Policy Exchange published them - I checked.

So, this headline assertion by Pearson/IPPR is uncited, seemingly based on a BBC News Story about a Policy Exchange commissioned YouGov poll, for which full results are not available is not backed up by what we do know about the poll.

More Pearson stats LOLs

Pearson College and Ashridge Business School have chosen the launch of the Annual CBI employers' survey to announce their partnership. For the first time, the CBI survey included responses from new starters - employees less than two years out of full-time education just beginning their career at a business.

Despite the dangling the promise of the possibility of an iPad mini, only 106 (no, really) new employees completed their survey. And it did not make promising reading for our friends in the Pearson press team, who were hoping to make an argument that new employees were crying out for workplace skills. More than two thirds (69%) of employees felt **they already had the skills they needed for the role they had just started**. Just under two thirds (60%) felt that **workplace skills were already well covered by colleges and universities.**71% of new employees cited a "**lack of work experience**" as their main issue when starting a new job, 44% felt that their **understanding of the world of work** was an issue (p35, CBI report)

This is all, of course, assuming that you think a response of 106, from employers that employ only 4.9% of people in the UK, is in any way representative. You look in vain for any kind of control or compensation for any skew in these results.

The "new starters" had to be less than two years outside of full-time education, a fact not mentioned in the report or the press release. So maybe a lack of work experience, and of understanding concerning the world of work, is understandable in such cases?

But none of this inconvenient fact-based stuff was going to stop the Pearson College press team:

> *"The new research, conducted alongside the annual Pearson/CBI Skills survey, found that many new starters felt unprepared for the world of work:*
>
> *Over 70% of those felt they lacked relevant work experience*
>
> *Nearly a third of new starters (31%) thought they did not have the appropriate work skills when they started their first full time role*
>
> *40% did not feel enough time and attention was given to acquiring these skills at school, college or university"*

Wow. "Nearly a third" in this instance, means 32 people. The 70% is 70% of those 32 people- TWENTY TWO PEOPLE felt that in their first job after college they wished they'd had more experience of work. "Many new starters" - I suppose it would be "many" if they were all in a phone box.

That's your world-beating press release leader right there. I wonder if Pearson College will actually manage to recruit 32 people this year? (I understand last year was around 60, 20 of those had their fees paid in full)

[APOLOGY: According to UCAS, the correct figure is 12, none of whom had Pearson College as their first or reserve choice.]

Pearson, as regular readers may know, have a history of looking for dodgy stats to support the argument that universities do not prepare student for the world of work.

At this stage I'd advise people to check ANY stats based press release on employability for spin and accuracy. If a real university used stats like these, they'd be laughed at.

OpenEd13 - Instruction To Deliver

I can say with some degree of confidence that Michael Barber has made my life significantly worse, not once (as a career public servant driven to distraction by metrics and targets) not twice (as someone who worked in the UK HE sector pre-Browne review) not three times (as an education technology specialist trying to pick the fact from the fiction in the MOOC movement) but an astonishing four times (as the father of a child who reads amazingly well but it utterly bewildered by "synthetic phonics"). Despite this, I can't quite shake a sneaking admiration for a man who has striven to make the world a better and fairer place in the best way he sees.

Barber's professional life is presented in a book that is part memoir and part manual, but I can't help but suspect he would be happier to see it presented as a series of graphs. Metrics and targets are the ideas that move his narrative forward, and the idea of routine and continuity pepper each chapter. He's taken ideas and damn well made sure they were delivered and stayed delivered, and that the numbers returned backed up the original ideas.

He began his career in the Hackney branch of the Labour Party in the mid/late 80s and early 90s(a few years after Blair), and described some of the acts of his party members of "silly", which to any student of Labour Party history is akin to someone living in Berlin in 1989 describing things as being "noisy". Hackney Council in the late 80s was an astonishing place. There were allegations of corruption and child abuse, budgetary crises, education crises- I'm not for a second implying that Barber had anything to do with any of these (though he was head of education at the council) but for him to mention none of this is bizarre to say the least.

> *"Meanwhile, in the council meetings themselves, I watched the madness around me and tried to vote sensibly. In fact, there was a minority of us in the Labour group whom the other described disparagingly as "the sensible caucus", which left me wondering about what they were" (p8)*

Equally bizarre is the way a rank-and-file history teacher could become a policy wonk at the notoriously militant National Union of Teachers and move from there to become a Visiting Fellow and then Professor of Education at Keele University. Barber describes these moves as a matter-of-fact; in reality they must have been driven by a great deal of work, publication, profile-raising and personal connection.

Regarding some of this - there is no mention of Barber's 1992 IPPR publication with Tim Brighouse " Partners In Change", his scholarly 1994 account of the 1944 Education act, his 1996 book " The Learning Game" ("arguments for an educational revolution", apparently - reviewed in Times Higher Education by none other than James Tooley!), the 1996 book on the National Curriculum he wrote with Chris Woodhead and Sheila Dainton- how did he make these contacts, and begin this research? It would greatly help the reader to know.

"Partners in Change" - in particular - would have been an interesting addition to ItD. *"In the minds of most educational-policy makers,"* it laments (p1) *"the image of school organisation appears to have barely changed in 100 years"*. We see the *"exponential growth in knowledge"* and a *"technological revolution"* (anticipating Avalanche) follow in quick succession.

A case study baldly states (p18) *"There is widespread acceptance that in the field of science and technology education the British education system has been unsuccessful relative to other leading studies"*, though this is not referenced. The pamphlet itself is a plea for the wider introduction of "Teaching Assistants" - para-professionals in the classroom supporting fully-trained teachers, and concludes in Austen-esque fashion: *"It is universally accepted that ways must be found of ensuring that standards of achievement rise substantially throughout the decade ahead [...] In this context, our proposals could constitute a major contribution to the development of the "learning society" Britain so badly needs to become."*

Teaching assistants became widespread throughout the Blair administration, and are generally seen as a supportive force for good. But form and nature of the argument, and a few of the saws to which Barber returns throughout his life, are of most interest to us more than 20 years later. One aside, *"- a political as well as a pedagogical pay-off could be anticipated"*, is particularly telling. And one footnote (the only possible reference) from Instruction to Deliver on the topic, *"a very young [David] Miliband had been through our draft with a copious red pen. [Tim] Brighouse [now Sir Tim, director of UK schools IT company RM] commented: "Do you know the most annoying thing of all is that he was right almost every time?"* is just plain amusing.

There are omissions too, in his account of the literacy (and numeracy) strategies on which his name was made in government. Despite his later "deliverology" claims, Barber used non-profit CfBT to drive the changes he was mandating into schools. Quoted in "Reinventing Schools, Reforming Teaching" (Bangs, MacBeath, Galton: 2010) he notes:

> *"Implementation- wasn't really what [civil servants had] done before- I don't regret having a relationship with CfBT (who delivered the literacy and numeracy strategies) it worked; it was much easier and more flexible than it would have been if it was in-house. [There was] a massive advantage to not having them as civil servants"*

When one is making broad claims about public sector reform, it may not be politic to mention that you brought in the third sector to push through changes as you were unable to work with the staff you had. My own experience of civil service policy-making suggests that they were, in fact, prefiguring Tymms and suggesting that his changes would not be effective.

Barber is noticeably absent from most of the major political biography from the early years of the Blair administration. Blair himself mentions Barber only four times in "A Journey", each only in passing. Alastair Campbell's voluminous diaries offer little: *"Michael Barber was impressive, and seemed like a really good bloke"* (p667) *"was impressive"* (p678) in volume 3 (1999-2001), and later in the same volume noting some of Blair's concerns about Barber:

> *"He (Blair) was still worried that even if Michael Barber's changes went through, and even if all the targets were met, would that actually deliver the first-class public services we had talked of. His approach though was still very top down" (p688)*

Mandelson offers only one comment in his excellent "The Third Man":*[...] Michael Barber was a zealously reformist academic, who advised Tony on education before the election"* (p227) and tellingly, Barber mentions the acknowledged architect of New Labour only three times. Little love lost?

Ken Follett, reviewing Instruction to Deliver in The Guardian, gets to what I think of the heart of the differences between Barber and Gordon Brown.

> *"What is missing from this picture? Parliament, of course. A completely different view is held by Gordon Brown, one of the few politicians I know who is as bright as Barber. Brown has been talking about returning power to the House of Commons."*

The latter part of Instruction to Deliver is a series of recommendations on enhancing the power of the Prime Minister via changes to the structure of the civil service. It is clear to me that to Barber, policy is something to be delivered, whereas with Browne policy is something to be debated. Parliament (and indeed, democracy) is almost entirely absent from Instruction to Deliver.

And this, to me, is the central point that I've taken away from this telling of Michael Barber's career. He displays surprisingly little interest in policy, he appears divorced from any conception of a grand narrative. Politics, to him, is about making the graph go in the right direction, and about ensuring that ministerial whims are carried out.

For an obviously smart man, this surprises me greatly. A large section of the book is entitled "routine", and deals with the day-to-day rounds of meetings and emails that bridge the gap between policy and statistical return. He takes a qu0te from Matthew D'Ancona as a mantra:

> *"There is no drama in delivery- only a long, grinding, haul punctuated by public frustration with the pace of change"* (p112)

He cites stoicism as his favoured quality in a sporting hero, a "constant sense of steady progress" as his favourite journey (the trans-Siberian railway!) and, most incredibly for the UK left:

> *"I remember watching with admiration as Denis Healy made his famous speech at Labour's 1976 party conference defending his decision to go cap in hand* [yes, he actually uses those words!] *to the International Monetary Fund and the cuts that ensued"*

Anthony Seldon, in his biography "Blair Unbound" writes about the beginning of the end of deliverology.

> *"Barber was resistant [to the Birt-led project on the cabinet committees in Blair's third term] believing the existing structure of stock-takes and informal exchanges with ministers suited Blair better, but Whitehall had the upper hand. After the [2005] election the new Cabinet Committee structure swung into operation"*

What was best for Blair was not necessarily what was best for government, and it took an outsider like Birt to see this. Barber notes:

> *"What happened in practice after the election was that the committees did have a value, particularly to other participants. However, they did not offer the Prime Minister what he really wanted [...] which was a sharp, informal, genuine exchange with a secretary of state about what was happening and what was planned. [...] After the first of the new Cabinet Committees, which took place shortly before I left, Blair exclaimed in exasperation, "What's happened to my stocktakes?" exactly as I had anticipated (p254)*

It is difficult not to admire Barber's tenacity, and his conviction that he is making a positive change in the world. I wanted to dislike him - I don't. But I worry about a culture that prides unquestioning loyalty over critical thinking - and I have seen at first hand the changes in the civil service that this brought about. To give Blair what he wanted was not to give Blair what he needed- and Blair's administration was marred by a pursuit of metrics over genuine change.

"Education is broken, somebody should do something"

no license given, but clear permission for sharing and adaption.

Presentation at ALT-C2013, Nottingham. This is the complete text of the presentation, with added links for clarity

As long as there has been education, it has been broken. For all the struggles of the finest teachers, for all the ingenuity of the greatest publishers, for all the grand buildings, the government regulations, the league tables and swathes of measurement and data - sometimes some people did not learn something that it was expected that they would.

This is not their story.

It is, in fact, the story of an entirely different group of people, many of whom have seen some significant success in their own education, others of which gave up on the whole thing as a bad job and have been grumpily poking it with sticks ever since. These are the people who go around reassuring us that - not only is education broken, but it is clear that somebody should do something.

In this group I would include several commentators, salespeople, bloggers, Sir Michael Barbers- but most of all I would include journalists.

Education, and the use of technology in education, has not historically been a subject to set printers rolling (except possibly in a purely literal sense with Gutenberg in 1439). There was a brief period at the turn of the century- words such as UK eUniversity and Fathom.com spring, unbidden, to mind; and a short blip back in 2010 when everyone got so impressed with their iPad that they assumed it would replace just about every living and non-living entity in the observable universe. But still, it was an "interesting aside on page 4" thing, not a "hold the front page" thing. Sandwiched between a gratuitous picture of a semi-famous woman with dead eyes in a revealing dress and 8 densely packed paragraphs of political speculation read by no-one and believed by fewer.

And then, in 2011, the world changed. George Siemens drew the link between experiments in online Connectivism mainly conducted in Canada, and a bold initiative from Stanford University to share advanced courses in Robotics. Of course, that initiative became what we know as Udacity, and built upon a great deal of now largely forgotten work at Stanford by John Mitchell, developer of their in-house CourseWare platform, and decades of earlier research and development across the world.

Do you remember where you were when you read your first MOOC article in a proper newspaper? For most I imagine it was when the comment section of the New York Times threw a spectacular double punch in May 2012 - firstly David Brookes' " Campus Tsunami", followed a week later by Thomas Friedman's " Come The Revolution". These articles were sparked by the launch of an unprecedented third MOOC platform, MIT and Harvard's EdX, alongside Udacity and Coursera which both spun out of Stanford.

These two early articles are in many ways emblematic of the way in which the MOOC has been presented. Monster-movie titles. A focus on millionaire rock-star entrepreneurs, who just happen to have done a bit of teaching and research. And each of these articles mentions the word "open" only once, the first in the context of the "wide-open" web, the second in the context of opening up opportunities to gain qualifications.

Interestingly, neither mention the word "MOOC".

I examined the first substantial main-paper MOOC-related article (not comment, where possible) from a range of mainstream sources on the web. Reuters. The Washington Post. The Daily Telegraph. The Guardian. (Interestingly the Daily Mail has yet to tackle the topic - do MOOCs cure or cause cancer? The ongoing obdurate online oncological ontology awaits urgent clarification).

- New York Times (02/11/2012) The Year of the MOOC
- The Atlantic (11/05/2012) The Big Idea That Can Revolutionise Higher Education: 'MOOC'
- The Guardian (11/11/2012) Do online courses spell the end for the traditional university?
- Financial Times (22/10/2012) Free, high-quality and with mass appeal

- Washington Post (03/11/2012) Elite education for the masses
- BBC News (20/06/2012) Top US universities put their reputation online
- The Telegraph (03/08/2012) Distance Learning: The Online Learning Revolution
- Time (18/10/2012) College is dead, long live college
- Huffington Post (05/08/2012) MOOCs From Elite Colleges Transform Online Higher Education
- Fox News (27/12/2012) Will college be free someday?
- Reuters (19/10/2012) Getting the most out of an online education

I used text mining tools to visualise commonly linked concepts in these articles. Text mining is a complex and multifaceted methodology, and I don't claim to understand it all. I simply plotted closely related words using a "communities" focused modularity, seeking words that frequently correspond. But just think of this as a slightly fancier wordle.

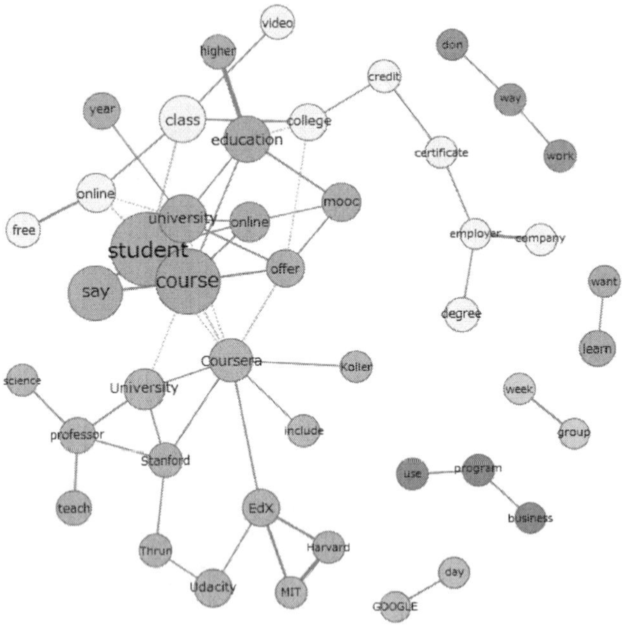

Again, one searches in vain for the word "open". The larger, purple blobs are the most common - they focus on the nub of the story, as perceived by multiple journalists. Students, courses, online higher education offers. You can also see a turquoise community of terms dealing with (for anyone with press training) what looks like your paragraph 3 background stuff, names, locations. Sebastian Thrun (famed for not inventing Google Glass, driverless cars, StreetView and online learning) looms large. And the yellow blobs seem to describe the student experience- a free online class with videos, where you can get a certificate to show employers.

In 2010, Henry Giroux was lamenting the dumbing down of education in the review of Education, Pedagogy and Cultural Studies. In a long and densely argued article of parallels and sympathetic resonances between austerity in education and the Greek resistance to what he describes as neo-liberalism (before George Siemens decided we couldn't do that anymore), the following lines really stood out for me:

> *"while a number of other institutions are now challenging the market driven values that have shaped [western] society for the last thirty years, education seems to be one of the few spheres left that is willing to enshrine such values and, with no irony intended, does so in the name of reform."*

Richard Hall extends a similar argument to the sphere of technology in education:

> *"This increasingly competitive, efficiency-driven discourse focuses all activity on entrepreneurial activity with risk transferred from the State to the institution and the individual. The technology debate inside higher education, including MOOCs, falls within this paradigm and acts as a disciplinary brake on universities [-]. What is witnessed is increasingly a denial of socialised activity beyond that which is enclosed and commodified, be it the University's attempt to escape its predefined role as competing capital, or the individual's role as competing, indentured entrepreneur."*

Or as Lesly Barry, of the University of Louisiana at Lafayette said just last week:

> *"Many of us know the situation first-hand. Universities nationwide are being forced to curtail programs. Students graduate with a debt burden that severely limits their horizons. Many faculty are part-timers without access to a living wage, let alone resources for teaching or professional development. Libraries have had acquisitions budgets eliminated, and journal subscriptions cut. Faculty and students are no*

> *longer considered primary stakeholders in the university, and administrators are tasked with repurposing our institutions to more commercial ends."*

These values are enshrined not, in fact, by the actors in the education system but by observers of it - namely politicians, policy-makers and journalists. And, the increasingly techno-deterministic educational discourse, bringing with it a focus on quantitative measures and whispers of "artificial intelligence (in reality, a simple set of algorithms and a great paint job) means that increasingly the first two groups are relying on a summary provided by the third.

This is why the quality of education technology journalism is one of our bigger problems, and why I expend such a lot of energy writing and talking about it.

One of a very small numbers of generally great Education Technology journalists, Audrey Watters describes the problem:

> *"Indeed, much of the hullaballoo about MOOCs this year has very little to do with the individual learner and more to do with the future of the university, which according to the doomsayers "will not survive the next 10 to 15 years unless they radically overhaul their current business models". [-]"Will MOOCs spell the end of higher education?" more than one headline has asked this year (sometimes with great glee, other times with great trepidation). As UVA's Siva Vaidhyanathan recently noted, "This may or may not be the dawn of a new technological age for higher education. But it is certainly the dawn of a new era of unfounded hyperbole." The year of the MOOC indeed."*

I've had the experience of speaking to a huge variety of journalists about MOOCs - I'm the chap you phone up if Martin Bean's phone is engaged and Martin Weller isn't answering email (I've no illusions). Each time I've patiently and carefully taken journalists through the history, the nuance of the term, the pedagogic underpinning, what we already know about learning online and learning at scale. Each time they've gone away and written the article they want to, full of hype and natural disaster metaphors.

But maybe that's just how to get page impressions. At least real decision makers get better advice than this.

It would be unfair to discuss the problem of MOOC hyperbole without a glancing mention of "Avalanche Is Coming". Sir Michael Barber - a very interesting gentleman whom time pressures forbid me to examine in more detail at this juncture - was the lead writer behind IPPR's much derided report into the "disruption of higher education". Sir Michael is not a journalist - he has a background in education and government, so has absolutely no excuse for feeding this beast.

In a similar way to my corpus of MOOC articles, I've also produced a plot of commonly linked concepts in "Avalanche":

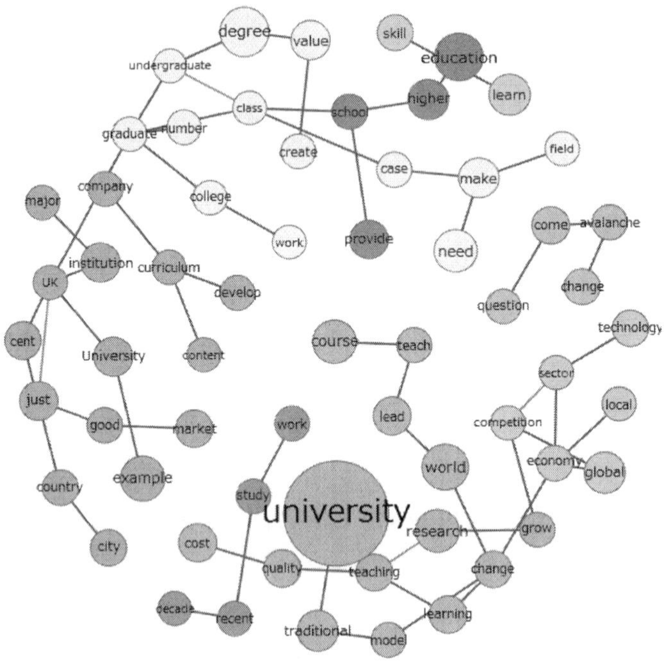

The repeated co-incidence of company, curriculum, develop and content was a particular delight (orange blobs). And open is nowhere to be found.

But, looking at the fine detail both of the co-incidence plot and the report itself we are looking at a superb example of the links between the MOOC hysteria and the commercial and instrumentalist unbundling project. The repeated emphasis on study leading to work, a need for change in order to facilitate competition and the internal dismantling and "de-organisation" that Deleuze and Guattari talk about before they get to the rhizomes in " A Thousand Plateaus".

"Open" was the first organ that we lost. From a nuanced and specific position in the world of the open educational resource, it is a word reduced to a synonym for two senses of free - free of cost (free as in beer) and free of prerequisites (free as in ride). Freedom, of course, is another word for nothing left to lose - yet somehow we have managed to lose it anyway.

Mike Caulfield puts the birth of the basis of conceptual machine learning at 1954 with Skinner- but novelty and the notion of a response to changes in society is another key trope. We've decades of high quality research in the field of learning facilitated by machines, yet to the op-ed crowd MOOCs are the latest thing.

We are really still in search of Newman's "intellectual daguerreotype".

> *"The general principles of any study you may learn by books at home; but the detail, the colour, the tone, the air, the life which makes it live in us, you must catch all these from those in whom it lives already. You must imitate the student in French or German, who is not content with his grammar, but goes to Paris or Dresden: you must take example from the young artist, who aspires to visit the great Masters in Florence and in Rome.* ***Till we have discovered some intellectual daguerreotype, which takes off the course of thought, and the form, lineaments, and features of truth, as completely and minutely as the optical instrument reproduces the sensible object, we must come to the teachers of wisdom to learn wisdom, we must repair to the fountain, and drink there.*** *Portions of it may go from thence to the ends of the earth by means of books; but the fullness is in one place alone. It is in such assemblages and congregations of intellect that books themselves, the masterpieces of human genius, are written, or at least originated."*

And our press have mistaken a restatement of this possibility for the thing itself. Our position, as educators and as researchers in this field is to be honest, even to the point of negativity. David Wiley's Reusability Paradox has not yet been solved, participation and engagement in online communities is still an exception rather than a rule, resources adapt to learners rather than the other way round, and fully online learning remains a niche. There is still so much work to be done.

Giroux, as cited above, talks of:

> *"a concerted ideological and political effort by corporate backed lobbyists, politicians, and conservatives to weaken the power of existing and prospective teachers who challenge the mix of economic Darwinism and right-wing conservatism now aimed at dismantling any vestige of critical education in the name of educational reform."*

As peculiar as it may now, seem, the open education movement began in opposition to this effort. Those of you who engaged with things like the SCORE project and the UKOER programme will remember the conversations with incredulous academics and managers. The range of benefits, exemplars, business models and rationales that we can all now rattle off - and the majority of these now have considerable evidence behind them, were far less clear in 2008 and 2009. The fear of "giving away the crown jewels" to the benefit of the world has been replaced by a huge eagerness to give away these same gemstones to private companies spun out of Stanford and the OU.

(and don't think that it is because of OER not being aimed at students - Audrey Watters wrote only last week about a swathe of commercial lesson plan sites and courseware directories being the unexpected commercial edtech theme of the year)

As Brian Lamb and Jim Groom asked: *"Has the wave of the open web crested, its promise of freedom crashed on the rocks of the proprietary web? Can open education and the corporate interests that control mainstream Web 2.0 co-exist?"*

To look again to the way the New York Times reported the initial OCW idea, this time with Carey Goldberg "Auditing Courses at M.I.T., on the web and free".

> *"Still, is the institute worried that M.I.T. students will balk at paying about $26,000 a year in tuition when they can get all their materials online?*
>
> *"Absolutely not,"* Dr. Vest *[then M.I.T. President]* said. *"Our central value is people and the human experience of faculty working with students in classrooms and laboratories, and students learning from each other, and the kind of intensive environment we create in our residential university."*
>
> *"I don't think we are giving away the direct value, by any means that we give to students"* he said. *"But I think we will help other institutions around the world.""*

Looking across a range of OER/OCW articles from the mid-00s onwards (using the same methodological approach as the MOOC articles above) I came up with the following corpus:

- **New York Times** 01/11/2010 *For Exposure, Universities Put Courses on the Web*
- **The Atlantic** xx
- **The Guardian** 17/01/2007 *The Great Giveaway*
- **Financial Times** 21/04/2008 *Adult Workers have a lot to learn*

online

- **Washington Post** 31/12/2007 *Internet Access Is Only Prerequisite For More and More College Classes*
- **BBC News** 23/10/2006 *OU offers free learning materials*
- **The Telegraph** 25/11/2010 *Why free online lectures will destroy universities - unless they get their act together fast*
- **Time** 27/04/2009 *Logging on to the Ivy League [UNABLE TO ACCESS FULL TEXT]*
- **Huffington Post** 10/08/2009 *Narrowing the digital divide*
- **Fox News** 29/12/2007 *Internet opens elite colleges to all*
- **Reuters** x*x*
- **Times Higher Education** 24/09/2009 *Get it out in the open*

And using the same plotting technique as above:

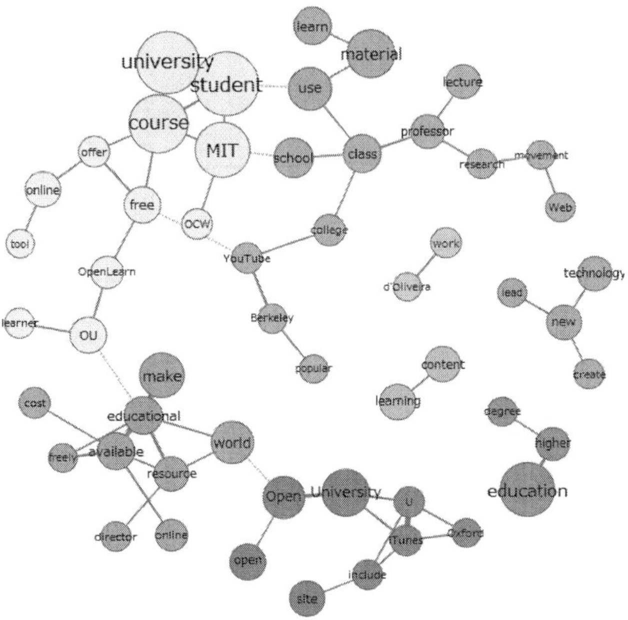

There was no talk here of “disrupting” education - if anyone was being disrupted it was the publishers who take the work of academics and sell it back to them. The concept of a “direct value” in on campus education now seems impossibly quaint - MOOC talk attempts to short circuit this by an elision of value and recognition in the offer of certification. These certificates, and the faltering attempts to link them to university credit, have entered what I’ve decided to call a Baudrillardian hyperreality of education, no longer signifying anything but the perceived importance of the processes that generate them.

Of course, the process (rather than the practice) of education is what drives the MOOC world. Writers without a critical perspective on both education and technology can be lulled into a simple skeumorphic model of replicated offline models re-established online. You can see large classes witnessing lectures by "rock star professors", simple quizzes to reflect understanding, discussion groups, assignments and required reading. The process ensures that all of this is measured, monitored and recorded - both (somehow) to accurately gauge student achievement and to refine the process.

Hand and Sandywell, in " E-topia as Cosmopolis or Citadel", suggest that:

> *"Adorno's conception of the administered society and Foucault's panopticon have been given digital wings, where societal regulation is seen as operating through the capillaries of information exchange. We shift from industrial to post-industrial forms of regulation. Where the original panopticon secured compliant bodies for the industrial process, the cybernetic panopticon of digital capitalism produces docile minds locked into their screens"*

Foucault's original point regarding Bentham's Panopticon (in " Discipline and Punish") was that it was the possibility of observation rather than the actuality of observation in such a situation that brought about obedience - "to induce in the inmate a state of conscious and permanent visibility that assures the automatic functioning of power". The process, however, induces in the MOOC inmate a consciousness of observation as a component of a totality - she knows that there is no chance that the superstar academic is watching her as an individual as the academic is not there, but she is painfully aware that the platform is watching her every move for its own, manifestly non-educational, purposes.

So, then, as anyone that has participated in an xMOOC will know, the game playing begins and the peer assessment becomes a lottery of either unsubstantiated criticism or a timid "that was great". The process is complete, the value is- well, that's not for me to say.

The thrust of "E-Topia" concerns the need for a refined theoretical language to properly situate the effect of internet technologies on the global socio-political discourse. And I would, of course, support such an aim. But I would argue that the construction of a language that can convey the realities of education, be it on- or off- line, massive or personal, open or "open" - away from the crumbling narrative of the market, is the essential first step. To close with more words from Audrey Watters:

> *"We need to get better at asking who is telling these stories. We need to ask why. We need to think about how we plan to tell our stories - our narratives and our counter-narratives. How do we make them "stick"?"*

At the very least, we need to begin telling those stories. We need the confidence, almost the arrogance to stand up with nothing more substantial than a compelling story. Because that's what every MOOC start-up under the sun is doing that, to journalistic applause and repetition, and it seems to be working very well for them.

You'll Never Hear Surf Music Again

"Strange beautiful grass of green
with your majestic silver seas
your mysterious mountains I wish to see closer-"

What is social media like? Speaking at the 2014 UCISA conference, Clay Shirky put the collaborative structures that have been built up around web technology in a category of their own. He asked: Is [Facebook] like other media? Is [Facebook] like a table? Or is [Facebook] like [Facebook]?

It transpired that we are dealing with a new category. Shirky argues that as information technology moves deeper and deeper into the world of human communication, it allows users to use the data trails they create to develop meaningful insights into their lives and interactions.

Social media, in 2014, is more media than social. Every organisation has a person or a team, usually in the communications department, with a contractual remit to be "social". There is a policy, not usually an entirely written one, which determines what constitutes "social" for other members of staff. Falling the wrong side of the line causes trouble. And believe that these lines are policed.

Just ask Thomas Docherty (a former Head of English at Warwick) about sharing and surveillance). At a conference celebrating the republication of " Warwick University Limited" - a book describing the levels of political surveillance of academic staff and students in the 1970s were subject to - he noted that:

> *"Academics and students, if interested in material research and*

> *learning, have to work in the shadows, in clandestine fashion"*

At least, had he been present at the conference, he would have noted this. I quote from a letter he sent whilst forbidden to enter the campus or make contact with his students.

As things stand, we know very little about his suspension, other than what has been released by the institution, which reassures us that his trenchant and freely expressed political views and membership of the Council for the Defence of British Universities are not the reason for this unusual punishment. At the time of [initial] publication Thomas Docherty is still suspended (some say indefinitely), and has been for 240 days [but see note]

Writing about her experiences at Worldviews2013 Melonie Fullick noted:

> *"Those starting out in academic life need to receive the message, loud and clear, that this kind of "public" work [new ways of engaging those outside of academia, primarily social media] is valued. They need to know that what they're doing is a part of a larger project or movement, a more significant shift in the culture of academic institutions, and that it will be recognized as such. This will encourage them to do the work of engagement alongside other forms of work that currently take precedence in the prestige economy of academe."*

Docherty is hardly the only example of an outspoken academic who has been censured by an institution, and there are many far, far more telling tales of social media and the way it reacts to outspoken opinions. I just use the example as it is a local one. But far more insidious is the kinds of self-censorship that many of us must participate in. "No religion or politics", as the old saying goes.

But our employers (and ourselves) are not the only critical readers here. The networks themselves monitor and respond to the emotions and ideas we choose to express. The recent Facebook research on mood contagion, though welcome in open publication, reminds us just how much attention platforms pay to what we share - and, almost as a given, how valuable this information can be.

Witness also the controversy around the migration to Facebook Messenger on mobile platforms. The New York Times suggested the backlash was "part confusion, part mistrust". Really, users have been spoiling for a fight with Facebook for a long time, a misunderstanding of how android permissions work (an application can record sound and take pictures, thus it needs to be allowed to use the microphone and camera-) feeds a building resentment of move fast and break things". Which itself has become the less quotable "move fast with stable infra".

Couple this with the dense web of connections that can be built up around a single persona and we see the true cause of the Nymwars- far from improving online conversation, as google claimed when improving YouTube comments, drawing activity together across numerous sites raises the value of this data. As our picture becomes more complete, we can be better understood by those who wish to understand us. To inform us. To sell to us. And to police us.

For the moment, an uneasy truce has been called. The real name is not required - the single identity remains. It seems hopelessly naive to think our real names could not be determined from our data if needed. By whoever feels the need to.

Compared to Facebook, we've always given twitter rather a free ride.

But this too, with the introduction first of sponsored tweets and then of other tweets we may find interesting, becomes less about our decisions and more about our derived preferences. This is made explicit in the new onboarding process. Twitter in 2014 is a long way from twitter in 2007.

There has been the beginnings of a movement away from this total spectrum sharing - platforms like Snapchat and Whatsapp connect people with their friends directly - the idea of the network comes through forwarding and very selective sharing. Networks like Secret and Whisper do away with the idea of "whole-person" media - anonymous "macros" (words+image) are shared based on location only.

Though each will create a trail, these are not publicly viewable and are difficult to integrate with other trails. Shirky sees the creation of a trail as being something that empowers the user - *"If there is a behaviour that matters to them, they can see it and detail it to change that behaviour"* - a position that tends towards to the ChrisDancyfication of everything.

We use social media trails (and online activity, for that matter) like we use cloud chambers, to draw and assert links between events that are visible only in retrospect. It's a big shift from sharing altruistically and to build connections, to sharing as a side-effect of self-monitoring.

I've rambled a little, but the central thesis I'm building here is:

As social media users, we are becoming aware of the value of the aggregated data we generate. Our interactions with social media platforms are characterised by mistrust and fear. We no longer expect these platforms to use our data ethically or to our advantage. We expect others to use what we share to our disadvantage. So - we share strategically, defensively, and using a lot of the techniques developed in corporate social media and emerging new media trends focus on either closely controlled sharing or anonymous sharing.

Shirky's position on the inexorable domination of the "social" clearly does not mesh with these trends - and this throws open the question of the place of social media in academia. Bluntly, should we be recommending to learners that they join any social network? And how should we be protecting and supporting those that choose to.

Social media has changed underneath us, and we need to respond to what social media is rather than what it was.

Alan (cogdog) Levine recently quoted from Frank Chimero:

> *"We concede that there is some value to Twitter, but the social musing we did early on no longer fits. My feed (full of people I admire) is mostly just a loud, stupid, sad place. Basically: a mirror to the world we made that I don't want to look into."*

I'd add, for the reasons above, "dehumanising" and "potentially dangerous".

Levine glosses this beautifully:

> *"Long long ago, in a web far far away, everything was like neat little home-made bungalows stretched out on the open plain, under a giant expansive sky, where we wandered freely, exploring. Now we crowd among densely ad covered walkways of a shiny giant mall, never seeing the sky, nor the real earth, at whim to the places built for us."*

He's a man that uses social media more than nearly anyone I know, myself included. And now he deliberately limits his exposure to the noise of the influence he has. He develops his own work-arounds to preserve and foster the things he finds important. Because he (and we) cannot rely on social media to continue acting in the same way. You can't rely on tagging. You can't rely on permanence. You can't rely on the ability to link between services. You can't even rely on access.

Tony Hirst is one of the most talented data journalists I know. In his own words:

> *"I used to build things around Amazon's API, and Yahoo's APIs, and Google APIs, and Twitter's API. As those companies innovated, they built bare bones services that they let others play with. Against the established value network order of SOAP and enterprise service models let the RESTful upstarts play with their toys. And the upstarts let us play with their toys. And we did, because they were easy to play with.*
>
> *But they're not anymore. The upstarts started to build up their services, improve them, entrench them. And now they're not something you can play with. The toys became enterprise warez and now you need professional tools to play with them. I used to hack around URLs and play with the result using a few lines of Javascript. Now I need credentials and heavyweight libraries, programming frameworks and tooling."*

After facing similar issues - with syndication, stability, permanence, advertising - Jim Groom (and others) are experimenting with forms of "social media" that are platform independent. Known, the webmention protocol, and similar emerging tools stem from the work of IndieWebCamp - a distributed team dedicated to providing a range of alternatives to corporate social media. They work to the following principles: your content is yours - you are better connected - you are in control

The first fits in nicely with ongoing work such as Reclaim Hosting, but for me the key aspect is control. One of the many nice aspects of these tools is that they are not year zero solutions - they start from the assumption that integration with other (commercial) networks will be key and that conversation there was as important as "native" comments. Compare Diaspora- which initially positioned itself as a direct alternative to existing networks (and is erroneously described in the press as a network where "content is impossible to remove"). With user-owned tools you own what you share plus a copy of what is shared with you, and you have final control over all of this. Publish on your Own Site, Share Everywhere (P.O.S.S.E.)

Of course, this doesn't lessen the risk of openly sharing online - these risks stem for the kind of corporations that employ us and that we entrust our data to. But it does help users keep control of what they do share. Which is a start.

But a start of what? We already seeing weak signals that young people (indeed all users) are drifting away from social networks, almost as fast as those who hope to talk to them are adopting the same networks. The quantified self is moving towards the qualified self, as users begin to understand and game the metrics that they are supposedly using for their own purposes.

People are more complex than activity trails and social networks suggest. The care taken to present facets (or even to perpetuate the illusion of an absence of facets). The ways they find to get answers out systems not set up to respond to questions.

Social media has changed. It's the same tune, but a different song.

Ben Werdmuller (Known developer) suggests, in a recent post:

> *"The web is the most effective way there has ever been to connect people with different contexts and skills. Right now, a very small number of platforms control the form (and therefore, at least to an extent, the content) of those conversations. I think the web is richer if we all own our own sites - and Known is a simple, flexible platform to let people do that."*

In 2014 suspicion about the actions of the super-social media platforms has reached fever pitch. Are we approaching a proper social media backlash? What does this mean for teaching online, and do projects like "known" offer another way?

> *"Your people I do not understand*
> *And to you I will put an end*
> *And you'll never hear*
> *Surf music again."*

(though the theme to Coronation Street, became "Third Stone From The Sun", which became "Dance with the Devil", which became" I'm Too Sexy"...)

[**EDIT:** 23/09/14 - Times Higher Education (£) are reporting that Docherty's suspension will end on 29th September, *269*days after it commenced. Warwick University (*"university of the year"*) have not made any comment regarding the reason for the suspension, or why it has ended, but it is understood that the disciplinary process will still continue. Because obviously he hasn't been punished enough.]

[**EDIT 2:** 21/10/14 - Times Higher Education (£) report that Docherty has been cleared of all charges]

Three strands of open education, or reading Open Education news.

This is something that originated in mine and Amber Thomas' paper "OER: A Historical Perspective", which I took to #opened12 with Sheila MacNeill. I never managed to write it up on here, and as I refer to it a lot and it is becoming increasingly apposite, I thought I'd rectify that.

Basically, there are three strands of open education.

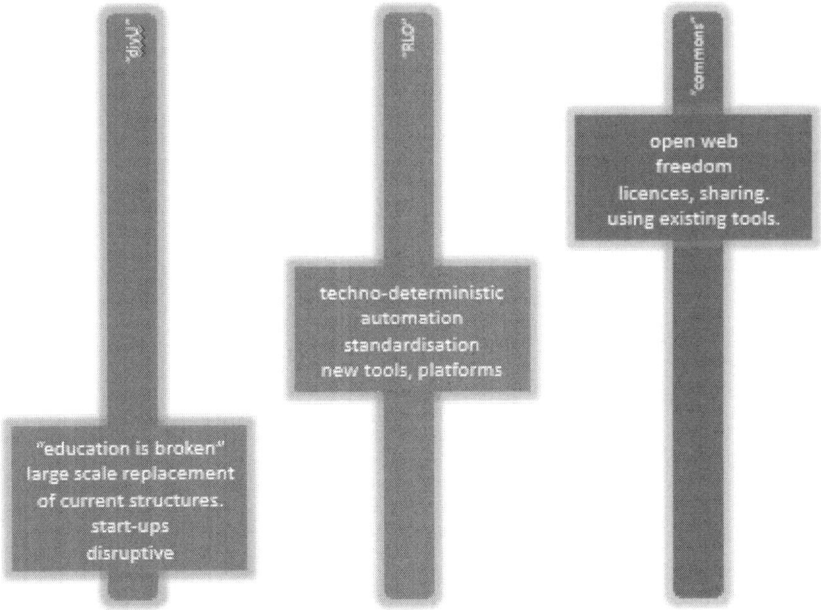

Firstly, what I call the "RLO" tendency, after the Reusable Learning Object movement where I think it is most purely expressed. This tendency is interested in providing an ordered and easily reusable collection of high quality materials for reuse - with corresponding interests in content packaging, interoperability, user metrics and automating discovery.

Secondly, I'd postulate the "Commons" tendency, which I associate with the Noughties OER boom. Release, and release under a creative commons license, is the key here, with less focus on quality or technical affordances, and an emphasis on learners as users rather than educators.

Thirdly, I initially called them the "DIYU" tendency but would now go for "disruption". These are the "education is broken" crowd, looking to sweep away and replace the existing education system. Their language comes from business rather than education, and there is an emphasis on private funding and new financial models.

So you can view the "Open Education Movement", such as it is, as a chimera, composed of these three strands, with different strands being in the ascendency at each time. For example, the current unpleasantness around MOOCs could be characterised as a mixture of the "disruption" and "RLO" strands, with the "commons" strand being a very tiny part of it.

In comparison, something like Oxford Podcasts could be seen as primarily "commons", with elements of "RLO" and very little "disruption".

I usually try to understand breaking news in open education by reference to each of these three strands. So, when I read today of the Pearson-owned OpenClass MOOC platform offering a collection of "high-quality" OER as a sign-up incentive, I consider it from each perspective: "RLO" - this provides use data to Pearson, who may use it for business purposes (e.g. via Knewton). The closed pool allows them to ensure compatibility and usability. "Commons" - this promotion of OER by a commercial publisher is a vindication of OER efforts in being "as good as" published material. But it may represent a landgrab of "open space" for a product offered in a closed environment. "Disruption" - by breaking the link to paying for academic content, this might undermine academic publishing models. But it does make it easier (and cheaper) to start building courses on the platform, rather than on an institutionally owned VLE/LMS

Often benefits and drawbacks for each strands are interlinked (as in this example). But in general significant initiatives (and significant commentators - for example you could easily link to a David Wiley blog post clearly situated in all three strands!) tend to be active across the spectrum.

I present this as a partial explanation of why it can often feel as if open education is pulling in multiple directions, and why initiatives too centred in one strand can become divisive. It is certainly instructive that MOOCs are now beginning to encompass the "commons" ideas of resources open to all, whilst letting go (a little) of the "disruptive" idea of destroying universities and the "RLO" dream of a perfect universe of resources and data.

And with the re-emergence of "blended learning" and "resource banks", maybe the future is beginning to learn from the past-

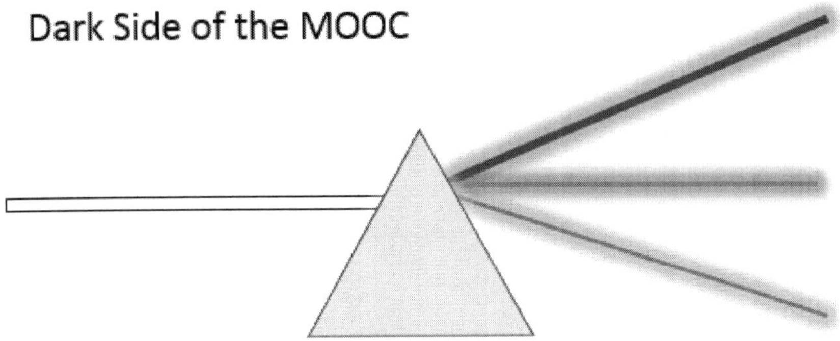

"And then one day you find
Ten years have got behind you
No one told you when to run
You missed the starting gun..."

(of course, Trey Parker and Matt Stone already did a much-swearier version of this post [nb not safe for work, consistent bad language from the start. Marvellous])

The Winning Move Is Not To Play: Game theory and the Willetts funding model.

The very little I know about the application of game theory on educational policy I learnt from my inspirational former colleague, Professor David Turner at the University of Glamorgan. The bits that I have got wrong are, however, entirely my own fault.

During a speech at the Universities UK Spring Conference, David Willetts (UK Secretary of State for Universities) reiterated his warnings about the high potential cost to the taxpayer of universities electing to charge fees reflecting the full range of that which is permitted to them. It is now an open secret that the new funding model for universities is certain to cost the taxpayer more within this parliament, and is very likely never to cost any less than the current model. Bearing this in mind, Willetts has warned senior university staff that money may be taken from other university income streams (for instance the research budget) in order to be able to fund the additional loans that would be required to meet these fees.

Tough talk. But it unfortunately betrays an inability to understand his own policies around competition and an "open market".

The Willetts conundrum

	Most or all institutions charge below £7.5k	Most or all institutions charge above £7.5k
Institution A charges below £7.5k	-1, -1 (all insts experience real terms drop in funding)	-2, -1 (inst A looks "cheap" compared to other insts & experiences real terms drop in funding, all insts experience drop in income due to punitive measures)
Institution A charges above £7.5k	**1**, -1 (inst a grows in income and prestige. Most other insts experience drop in income)	-1, -1 (all insts experience drop in income due to punitive measures)

The table above outlines my analysis of the situation. The only chance that institutions have of even maintaining their existing funding is to charge above £7,500 and hope that enough of their competitors choose not to in order to avoid triggering the threatened cuts in research funding. Were the expected lower levels a revenue neutral (including inflation and additional costs incurred for the move to the new system) situation, it may be rational to broker a sector-wide compact (or cartel, if you prefer) to ensure that no-one steps over whatever line the government has drawn in the sand.

But the minimum (and even the implied "normal" maximum) mean that institutions would lose money as against the current system. When you combine this with the decade of incentives encouraging the sector to compete, we are very likely to see a rush to the top. Based on my analysis, above, this is the only rational choice for institutional managers looking to maintain or increase income.

This is a "non-zero-sum" game, as there is no way to maintain a position. Institutions will either win or lose - and a lower price than the rest of the sector means that they will lose heavily. The same goes for private institutions, incidentally. What motive have they got not to seek the maximum possible income?

I've said it before (many times), I'll say it again. This model of university funding is unworkable.

You could make your own game theory analysis of the two models of HE. On one side you have the new model, where students, institutions and the tax-payer all lose out. On the other the current model, where they don't.

Scary monsters and super creeps

With my six-year-old son in tow I had the perfect excuse to view on Sunday what promises to be the Higher Education film of the summer - Monsters University.

Meanwhile, David Willetts was writing the foreword of the Higher Education Wonk strategy of – let's be honest - the morning, "International Education Strategy: Global Growth and Prosperity"

So on the one hand a knowingly grotesque fantastical parody of a higher education system based equally on fear and wishful thinking, mashed into an unrealistic linear plot and driven by non-human entities for non-human ends - and on the other hand (yes, you've guessed it-) Monsters University.

But, cheap LOLs aside, there is more to link the two than you may think. In Joseph Campbell's terms - both focus on a particular facet of the monomyth-**the crossing of the first threshold**. As "Hero with 1000 faces" puts it:

> *"With the personifications of his destiny to guide and aid him, the hero goes forward in his adventure until he comes to the 'threshold guardian' at the entrance to the zone of magnified power. Such custodians bound the world in four directions - also up and down - standing for the limits of the hero's present sphere, or life horizon. Beyond them is darkness, the unknown and danger; just as beyond the parental watch is danger to the infant and beyond the protection of his society danger to the members of the tribe. The usual person is more than content, he is even proud, to remain within the indicated bounds, and popular belief gives him every reason to fear so much as the first step into the unexplored. The adventure is always and everywhere a*

> *passage beyond the veil of the known into the unknown; the powers that watch at the boundary are dangerous; to deal with them is risky; yet for anyone with competence and courage the danger fades."*

Mike Wachowski (the little green one with the eyeball) marks this with a *fermata*-a pause at a clearly marked threshold, usually a visible line or change in terrain. It's a beautiful, character-defining shot which is repeated again and again throughout the film. He takes a moment to reflect - almost to say "I can't believe it!" at each stage of his journey. He's genuinely awed to have gotten as far as he has.

What was interesting in a storytelling sense was how little personal growth Mike demonstrates during the film. He arrives pretty much fully-formed at the start of the prequel - he's already thoughtful, diligent and supportive of others. In that sense the viewer is led to believe that he sees higher education as an opportunity for hard work.

Sullivan - the blue hairy one - starts the film with a broader sense of entitlement due to a natural talent and family connections. He sees higher education as a simple threshold, one where a completion affords him entry to the lifestyle he desires.

For David Willetts (the beigey-pink one with the glasses and the bald head), higher education is also a threshold. It is a gateway through which one must pass in order to succeed. Paragraph 2.2 focuses on the value of UK qualifications to overseas students - in essence the "payload" of the UK education offer. People apply to UK education because they value the qualifications they get - it's another "crossing of the first threshold moment".

In a way it is an example of linear thinking, education as a narrative arc, where you pay for a qualification which offers you certain benefits on completion. But as Joseph Campbell (or Mike Wachowski) would tell him, crossing the threshold is only a starting point, not an end point.

Sticking with Campbell's terms, you could see higher education as **a belly of the whale** moment, through **initiation**, **road of trials** and **atonement with the father.**

The idea of paying for a qualification is manifest nonsense. And advertising UK education as the best place to buy a qualification doubly so. Only twice in the BIS strategy does the student experience merit a mention - once in reference to studying in Australia, the other as a possible issue of incorrectly using student visas.

For all the "students at the heart of the system" rhetoric, what we are left with customers at the heart of the market.

Nowhere is money an issue in "Monsters University". Status - yes. Students with a certain pedigree or certain "look" are afforded a level of respect from others - but - as Sullivan finds out, this is not a substitute for academic effort, and the expectations of academic success end up weighing heavily on him.

Paying for a place in a course gets you precisely nothing, apart from a limited amount of status which is easily lost at the first point you actually have to do some work. Cartoonist Winston Rowntree illustrates this perfectly in an article about online dating on Cracked.com which is better than it has any right to be.

Mike Wachowski passes the initial threshold and keeps working - he's the epitome of a lifelong learner. But everything in the BIS strategy is aimed at the Sullivan approach to education - the consumer, the entitlement model.

I wrote a while ago around the model of student as labourer-consumer. What we see in the BIS strategy is proof that the purchase model of education is not just an aberration, but a deeply flawed ideology that goes right to the hearts of those charged with supporting and improving our universities.

In Monsters University, neither route is seen as the correct one, with both protagonist monsters being rusticated for contact that brings the university into disrepute. The implication is that the institution itself needs to change, to accept students as individuals rather than matching them to a profile. And, as Monsters Inc, made clear - the basis of the entire society, which is situated in the exploitative use of natural resources and a fear of outsiders, is open to question.

The black art of report writing and reading

It's been a while since I got involved in the strange world of government (or agency) report writing but I find myself back there again. For those who don't know, I wrote a bunch of stuff for and around HEFCE - an organisation that really sweats the drafting process- with documents going through a good 15-16 iterations/circulations before they reach either a senior manager or a comms team. In that process I'd been the one doing the drafting, staring at the same document day after day making microscopic changes in nuance and tone.

*[An example of one that I did a *lot* of work on was Towards a Framework of Professional Teaching Standards (pdf), ostensibly not a HEFCE document but I was lead drafter... I've re-uploaded it here to preserve my pain for future generations]*

Nowadays I seem mainly to be in the "expert panel member" role and find that my sympathies go out to those who are trying to draw our miscellaneous hobby-horses and tangents into a piece of extended text that: captures all of the things that everyone has said, without upsetting anyone who disagrees, meets the original remit, displays a respectable understanding of the issues, makes a meaningful contribution to the debate.

Academics, imagine writing a journal paper on a subject you know nothing about, based on nothing but three or four conversations with a group of people with widely differing views and levels of understanding, taking into account a whole world of political and professional pressures. It's like that. If you are thinking "that sounds exactly like the way I want to destroy my sanity!" I see that the wonk is strong with you.

But I have also become an avid consumer of these reports, and find that my experiences of writing them weigh heavily on the way I read them.

A report - I would argue - is not written to be read. It is written to be written. It is not written as a flowing single piece of text; it is written as a series of quotations and buzzwords, agendas and links to other reports. It is there to be decoded. Words in government reports do not behave in the same way as words in other parts of the universe.

In 2006, The Avalanches released their seminal album "Since I Left You". It is formed of thousands and thousands of short samples, some microseconds long. It is affecting music, but it is an odd non-specific nostalgia for records that you have never heard. The closer you listen, the less you hear the unity of the composition and the more you see the clashes between the individual parts.

Nick Hornby (who should damn well stick to writing about music), described in his "31 songs" one of the singles from the album as using:

> *scraps of things you have never heard in ways that you couldn't have imagined; the result is that they have, effectively, created something from nothing [...there is a] sense of undaunted resourcefulness, the same determination to make the incoherent cohere - and cohere into something new - through talent and a simple force of will.*

Just as a non-musician/expert would miss the entire artistry of such an enterprise, and react to the quality of the tune - the non-specialist reader (for which read journalists and inexperienced wonks, as these are the people who write the summaries that everyone else reads) will not understand the references and artistry, and simply react to the more easily understood aspects.

These are the aspects that are tweaked by press teams and such like to construct what used to be called “quotables” but may now be called “tweetables”- small micro-sections of the report that summarisers are expected to pick up on and talk about. The kind of things that would make the headlines in the parallel universe where education-related reports make headlines.

But these can often be used to distract from the real meat of the paper, which may indeed point towards different conclusions to the summaries. This is why it is essential to read reports yourself, as far as you possibly can - and ideally to have some experience in writing them.

Here’s a few things I like to watch for:

a vague recommendation usually implies a serious internal disagreement around that issue.

effusive praise for an organisation implies an unhappy or insecure organisation

a case study implies an absence of hard data.

an absence of an expected reference suggests an attempt to distance the new report from the older one, which has most likely been discredited.

a short foreword, or no foreword may mean a lack of genuine support at senior levels

a great deal of speculation tells me that there could be a lack of firm short/medium term plans- with the organisation writing the report effectively abandoning the issue to the market-place

strong dismissal of alternative ideas will, of course, mean that adversarial interests are suggesting that idea.

drawing on unpublished survey material generally implies that the surveys are very dodgy indeed.

Spinning a story: Gove, Klein, BECTA, Cameron and Murdoch

Allow me to tell you a story.

Once upon a time, there was a media organisation called News International. They owned a number of powerful media sources, including the Times, The Sun, The News of The World and a big chunk of BSkyB TV. And that was just in the UK. News International's parent company was News Corporation, which was run by a chap named Rupert Murdoch and also owned important things like Fox News, 20th Century Fox, HarperCollins and the Wall Street Journal.

Such was the power of this media organisation, many former employees went on to become members of UK parliament, and many former (and current) members of parliament ended up writing columns for News International papers.

A charming young man named Michael Gove was a leader writer at the Times. He subsequently became a member of Parliament, maintaining a useful contract (valued at £5000/month) to write for News International. Happily, whilst at the Times, he met and fell in love with his wife Sarah Vine - who still writes for the Times on important international issues such as advising readers " how to be a perfect housewife", including the delightful suggestion *"As to sex, you'll soon be down to doing it once a month while the children are at granny's, so really he should get accustomed to the idea now."*

Even after becoming the Secretary of State for Education, Michael - perhaps in gratitude to his former employers - found time to accept a contract from HarperCollins to write a book. His friend, David Cameron, became Prime Minister (after a troubled campaign where the greatest turning point was the accidental broadcasting of the incumbent PM's unguarded comments on a member of the public by Sky News), a cause of great delight for his neighbour and riding partner Rebekah Brooks, now Chair of News International, and also to his director of communications, Andy Coulson - who also used to work for News International.

Meanwhile, at News Corp, things weren't looking quite so rosy. The internet was rendering many of Mr Murdoch's business interests less and less profitable. Information was indeed turning out to be free, and an attempt to monetise his high-cost acquisition of the once-popular MySpace demonstrated that he did not understand this brave new world. So he and his son James concentrated on lobbying for tighter controls on media "piracy", building paywalls to hide behind (and ensuring I can't link to the sources I want to), and searching for a new revenue stream.

Late in 2009, he found it. Educational technology. Moving quickly, he bought a number of existing companies in the area, and brought in former head of the New York Public Schools System, Joel Klein, to lead this new initiative. Joel had left his previous job under something of a cloud, having sacked Columbia University academic Rashid Khalidi from his teacher training programme because he didn't like his views on Israel and Palestine. However Rupert (much like his friend David Cameron) believed in giving people a second chance.

Joel Klein became friends with Michael Gove, and in January 2011 Gove invited Klein to speak at his conference about "free schools" in UK education. Klein's also found time to give an interview to News International's "Sunday Times" during this visit - and this interview included the dynamic assertion that" *It's easier to prosecute a capital-*

punishment case in the US than terminate an incompetent teacher."

But speaking at the inaugural New Schools conference, he was clearer about his aims for education.

> *"Last, to shake up the system, we must change how we use technology to deliver instruction. (This is what I'm now seeking to do at News Corporation.)- [O]ne of the best things we could do is hire fewer teachers and pay more to the ones we hire. And, as in any other field, technology can help get us there. If you have 5,000 math teachers, many of whom are underperforming, significantly improving overall quality is nearly impossible. But if you get the best math professors in the world-who are great teachers and who deeply understand math-and match them with great software developers, they can create sophisticated interactive programs that engage kids and empower teachers."*

Happily, Michael Gove and David Cameron displayed the foresight to abolish BECTA in 2010, BECTA being the organisation charged with supporting schools in using ICT to ensure that they don't get ripped off by unscrupulous vendors making over-egged claims about the power of educational software. This was a controversial and unexpected decision, later criticised by the Public Administration Committee, and by experts in secure IT provision.

Parallel to this, Gove had set up the facility for parents to set up "their own" schools, with the support of the fine services offered by the growing private sector. So Joel's delightful dreams of breaking teacher union power and selling schools expensive software could come true here in the UK, and his friends David Cameron and Michael Gove had managed independently to do the exact things that he needed to move this dream forward - just like in New York!

Sadly, this is not a story with happy ending. In July 2011, it emerged that David's friend Rebekah, and his former communications director (but still his friend) Andy, were implicated in a major scandal involving bribing police officers and intercepting the voice mail message of terrorism and murder victims. Such was the outcry that Rupert had to fly over to visit his friend David, and Rebekah had to resign. Happily Rupert (and David) knew just the man to solve this difficult problem of Rupert losing lots of money and power: Joel Klein!

Selling a story

I suppose it started when I was reading about the UK government's plans to withdraw from the European Human Rights Convention. It's a stupid idea for a number of reasons, but that wasn't why I noticed it.

All the language used in interviews was about the right to deport terrorists, and how the EHRC was standing in the way. But the European Court of Human Rights has only ruled on around ten (pdf, p16) such decisions. Withdrawing seemed rather disproportionate.

Similarly, the media outrage around a family being "built" a "mansion" by the state to house their eleven children. And the calls for benefit caps to protect against the welfare spending effects of approximately 190 large families.

And all of the measures, including forced labour, aimed at addressing the so called "benefit culture" extending over multiple generations that recent research has found it unable to identify any examples of in one of the UK's most deprived areas.

And then I started thinking back further, about the bizarre unisnotforme.com site run by a mum who appointed her daughter as an apprentice in her PR company rather than see her take a degree. (all the other employees are, of course, graduates).

It didn't take much digging around to find that this was a front for a campaign to make 'A'-levels more closely align to the needs of employers(and also here)

And I'd wager that renegotiation of our adherence to international human rights law (longer working hours, less employee rights), cuts to the value of benefits (making low waged work the only option) and "free" employees" (obviously!) are designed to benefit private employers as well.

Private enterprise is clearly expected to solve all of the world's problem, armed only with large amounts of taxpayers money and gargantuan levels of media hype. I mean, just because it hasn't worked in the UK for railways, heavy industry, unemployment...

But what about all this "education is broken" MOOC nonsense? Have we proven that entrepreneurs are better at supporting young people in achieving their dreams?

You might remember Peter " floating cities in the sea" Theil gave 20 people 100k to spend a year doing start-ups rather than go to universities, in 2011. Two years on it appears that journalists can only track down one who is earning any kind of income. Those who have dug deeper have either found very little activity (quora link, needs a sign in) or try to say it is too soon to measure. It is not too soon to measure. These are 20 of the brightest and best, chosen personally by Peter Theil. He predicted, and expected, great things:

> *"Pundits and hand-wringers love to claim that universities are the only path to a successful life. In truth, an inquisitive mind, rigorously applied to a deep-rooted problem can change the world as readily as the plushest academic lab"*

I wonder when he was last in a university lab?

Katy Jordan at the Open University (UK) has put together all of the MOOC student statistics she could find (isn't it odd that they are not generally made public-) and demonstrated that you can confidently expect more than 80% of people who sign up for a course will not complete it. Some try to justify this by pointing at the thousands that still "graduate" - but these are almost always graduates already, generally rich, western and very well educated. I'll leave it as an exercise for the reader to work out how many MOOCs (at a generous 20% success rate) we need to meet the higher education demands of developing countries.

The wonderful David Wiley backed start-up "Degreed" (the "Education is broken, somebody should do something" people) is still looking for evidence of people using "jailbroken" learning to further their careers. If they can't do better than the wishful thinking and stock photography they currently have, the jig may be up.

Even when for-profits are given the so-simple-the public-sector-can-do-it task of running schools and universities, there is little benefit and often great detriment. Both in the UK (and again) and the US, academies and charter schools are not delivering any appreciable gain in student attainment. US for-profit universities are under constant investigation for dubious recruitment practices.

Despite a tsunami (TM) of hype, the new wave of education start-ups has actually delivered surprisingly little of mainstream benefit. They can point to mass access to learning opportunities, but that has been around since the birth of the web, and has been largely led by traditional institutions.

Yet the bandwagon keeps rolling. What are the hidden benefits that allow commercial education leeway to fail so many? Why are the public education sector constantly criticised whilst the corporates and the start-ups can do no wrong?

Is it benefits for the employment market, cross-media ownership, a talent for writing a good press release or something else?

One of my main personal projects for 2013 on this blog is to try to unpick the power behind the reasons for this continued attack on public education, from primary schools to universities, in the UK and beyond.

[see also: "Hacking at Education" by Audrey Watters]

The Campaigning Academic

So I'm sitting in a nondescript airport bar in Vancouver with Brian Lamb. We're at the end of an immense and amazing conference on Open Education (OpenEd12, which I'll be writing much more about). We've drinks in hand but have not yet reached the "gentle incoherence/blind rage" stage. And what are two supposed luminaries of the EdTech/edublogging scene talking about? The slow inexorable march of Coursera? The current consuming obsession with learning analytics? Gartner Campbell's amazing keynote?

No. We are lamenting, with passion and disappointment, the slow death of investigative journalism. Brian speaks of the end of his long-standing support for the Globe and Mail, I respond with my own lingering fondness for Private Eye. We discussed of the freelance work of Nick Davies in uncovering the News Corp phone-hacking scandal - the way that one single revelation (the hacking of the voicemail of a murdered schoolgirl) turned an astonishingly well-researched "niche interest" media story into an all-engulfing political and media firestorm.

-

Flash back six months to another pint of beer, this time in the home of an old friend and (currently) a sub-editor. "All my life I wanted to be a journalist", he tells me, "but the job I had dreamed of and trained for no longer exists." I worry that the job of his dreams is the one I've been doing in my own time, for free, here.

-

And back even further, as I nervously check and re-check the sums that crystallise the argument that the new model of funding UK higher education would cost the tax-payer significantly more than the then-current method. I was so terrified I was actually ill - bottled publishing myself and sent the whole story to another blogger who published it word-for-word-

-

Forward again to last Friday. I follow a link on twitter to read of Jennifer M. Jones' decision to quit her PhD. In the build-up to what I can only call the "'lympics" she blogged and tweeted from a range of bizarre and twisted 'lympic education events, about the pressures and the politics that defined not just the games but the planned public reaction to the games. It was mesmerising, it was chilling, and it was - I'm not sure whether she'd agree, but this is how I saw it - investigative journalism at it's very finest.

But the structure of a PhD meant that she had to keep engaging with the topic. I remember seeing her tweets from a cheap hotel in London, during the hysteria and suspension of critical facilities that was the Opening Ceremony. I remember how painful it was for her when the whole world seemed to get sucked in to the insidious machine that she had been documenting and understanding over a research project that had taken over her life.

And I couldn't help thinking that getting out then, getting out now should not be seen as failure. She's clear that it isn't - she's able to do the small community projects she really wants to. And for all those of us who benefited from the way she reported back from the belly of the beast and have since had chance to get to know an amazing person don't see it as a failure either.

-

So what am I drawing together here?

The realities of the media profession mean that investigative writers like Nick Davies are becoming increasingly rare, and that even the ones that do exist have to fit their findings into easily digestible nuggets for the 24 hour news juggernaut to graze on.

The realities of academia mean that, although sustained investigation and reflection are possible, they are constrained to the need to produce "academese" outputs, which are constrained to arbitrary lengths and timings, and a written in a language that is nearly incomprehensible to all but a small group of specialists. And that work outside of these constraints is not rewarded, or even stigmatised as failure.

There is a space - in the gap between academia and journalism, somewhere in the vicinity of the digital humanities movement - for what I would call the "campaigning academic", someone who is supported (in a similar way to traditional research funding) to investigate issues of interest and to report back in a variety of accessible media. Maybe this "reporting back" could build up into equivalence to an academic reward, maybe not.

These would be cross-disciplinary scholars, not tied to a particular critical perspective or methodology. And they would likely be highly networked, linking in both to the interested and the involved in any particular area - at times becoming both. They might have a high media profile and an accessible style (Ben Goldacre comes to mind). Or they might be an anonymous but fascinating blogger (whoever it is that does the wonderful Public Policy and The Past). Or anything in between.

But they would campaign, they would investigate, they would expose and they would analyse. Bringing together academic and old-school journalistic standards of integrity and verifiability.

Is academia the new journalism?

Increasingly the boundaries between the journalistic and academic professions are becoming muddled, with both embracing the practices and norms of blogging as the process of publishing and sharing are disrupted (yep, that's a correct Christiensen-referencing use of the word) by online platforms and social media. I've written about this idea before, with an particular focus on the way academia (and research funding) can adapt to facilitate this process.

Politics Inspires, an initially JISC-funded project based around the politics departments of Oxford and Cambridge, recently held an afternoon workshop on the practices and realities of academic blogging around politics. A superb set of panels encompassed the project itself (which has now been taken into the departments and is clearly established as an ongoing concern), LSE Blogs, Crooked Timber, and The Conversation- each using academic bloggers to respond to and analyse current events in politics and policy.

From the more traditional media end of things we had a speaker from the Guardian Politics blog, from the less traditional media OpenDemocracy. And from a more analytical end we saw speakers from the Oxford Internet Institute and the Reuters Institute for the study of journalism, with the whole event led by Stuart White of the Public Policy Unit at Oxford.

For such a wide variety of speakers there was an unusual consistency of message: everyone was very clear that the academic voice was one that could and should make a valuable contribution to public life, and that academic blogging (be this group or individual, mediated or not by news values) had a key role to play.

However, despite an increasing emphasis from research funders on public engagement, and from departments and institutions looking to extend their public profile - academia has been slow to engage, perhaps because of an unclear link between practice and measurable benefits. How can you tell when your blog is successful?

It seems clear that the journal article is no longer a primary means of research dissemination - even though expectations and funding do both provide a continued stream of articles. The blog has the potential to become this - giving the academic control over how their research is reported (unlike the traditional PR route) and sitting on the open web- often under an open license.

For newsrooms too the idea of a quick, lively and responsive medium has proved popular. Andrew Sparrow's Guardian Politics blog responds to (and occasionally defines) the news agenda of each day. And he often looks for and links to academic blogs (he gave the example of the wonderful revolts.co.uk as an academic blog source many journalist/bloggers use as background for stories of backbench insurrection in the House of Commons.)

So are academics becoming journalists? Clearly there is something special that an academic can bring to the reporting of any story, and that is a deep - lifelong - understanding of the micro-issues behind the headline. We've all had experiences where something we feel we understand well is reported badly - for me most articles (and frankly, many think-tank reports!) on higher education are largely unreadable for this reason. Academic blogging offers a chance to add a knowledgeable and historically nuanced voice to the public understanding of a story.

But journalistic values - being able to react quickly, write accessibly and promote your work - can be incredibly helpful for academics looking to drive interest in their work and enhance their own profile. Blogging, of course, is astonishingly addictive: especially when it starts conversations and helps you make connections that lead to collaborations and friendship. For work that links to public policy or current affairs this is coupled with a real chance to inform, and maybe shape, debate. One speaker wondered whether "direct influence on policy-making via blogs could be counted under the REF" (in which case maybe I'll be expecting HEFCE QR to flow direct to followersoftheapocalyp.se?)

From a theoretical perspective Bill Dutton of the Oxford Internet Institute postulated the existence of the Fifth Estate- a citizen publishing revolution based around the communicative and knowledge generating power of networks-. "sourcing, creating, distributing/leaking, networking and exhibiting collective intelligence.". Very connectivism, which for me emphasised the range of academic positions that were converging on the idea of online communities as learning communities.

Of course, something like this fifth estate doesn't get to stay an emergent, commons-focused space for long. Organisations like the advertising-led Huffington Post, and (specifically) the government and foundation funded "The Conversation" are capitalising on this willingness to write purely for recognition and building businesses on the back of free blogger content. And in a lesser, but somehow more insidious way, those institutions who are supporting academics in blogging are seeking a bewildering range of metrics and impact measures. (But -again- what *is* success for a blogger?) In both cases, the commodification of free labour is foregrounded - prompting one to question why the writer should not profit from their own work.

[that last part about The Conversation spawned a whole other twitter conversation with some of the editors there, which I have storified - A Conversation about The Conversation]

Stylistically, the spectre of "buzzfeed" hangs over both academia and journalism - the temptation to ramp up hits can lead to the listicle and the headline tricks that bloggers like you don't know you are missing out on (etc.). What buzzfeed evolves into may be interesting- I like especially the way that sites like UsVsTh3m play with the format to sneak a distinct leftist politics and social commentary into the memes and nostalgia. But whether articles are experimental or long form essay, accessible or specialist, they represent a willingness to share and communicate that is laudable and useful.

For instance - as the event unfolded in Oxford bloggers, academics and citizen commentators around the country were converging on the twitter hashtag #caredata- critiquing the use of NHS patient data from a range of expert perspectives. The focus was a parliamentary committee questioning ministers and civil servants - an otherwise routine event that was amplified and expanded upon by the Fifth estate in a perfect illustration of the way journalism and academic engagement are informing and shaping an ongoing national debate.

A blog should have a voice - it should be personal, conversational and there should be less concern for complete accuracy than there is for having the confidence to test out (as the writers on crooked timber sometimes do) half-finished ideas. And - I would add - it need to be confident in the space it wants to fill. One contributor suggested that a blog is the first rough draft of journalism is the first rough draft of history- but is the blog not an oral history where a newspaper article is the official version?

The first ebook collection of "Politics Inspires" posts, "Democratic Wealth", is freely available as is a podcast of the "Academic Blogging" event - with both released under an open license. Also, keep an eye on the @PoliticsInspire twitter account.

My favourite part of the HEFCE teaching funding method, and how screwed we are if we lose it

The current HEFCE funding model has a number of quite marvellous features which I would be happy to expound upon at great length, but my personal favourite must be the "tolerance band".

This is technically defined as an allowance for the difference between the standard resource (the funding available for the number of students enrolled on particular courses that the institution has indicated to HEFCE each year) and the assumed resource (which is the funding available for the students that have actually enrolled on particular courses each year). Because HEFCE is wise and noble it allows a 5% difference either way between these amounts before it starts either clawing back funds or reducing student numbers for the following year.

This 10% band of tolerance is the thing that keeps institutions stable. It allows for fluctuations in student numbers, and permits an institution to receive an expected amount of funding every year, allowing for an accurate budget and long term planning.

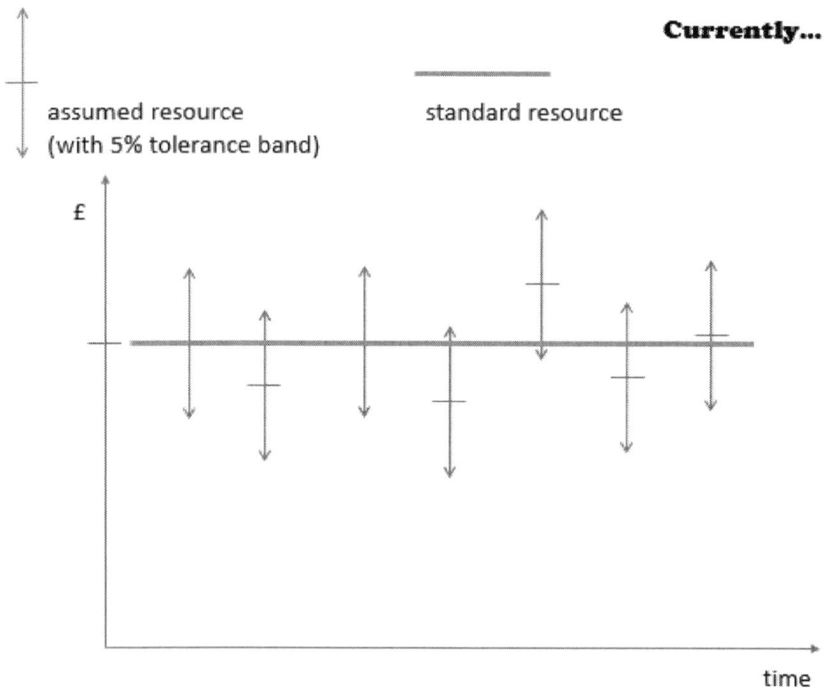

Under the new funding model, the majority of the financial support (80%+) that used to come from HEFCE will come from a new organisation, Student Finance. This allocates funds based directly on student choice, and - crucially - does not include a compensatory function. So the stability of funding levels, year-on-year, is lost.

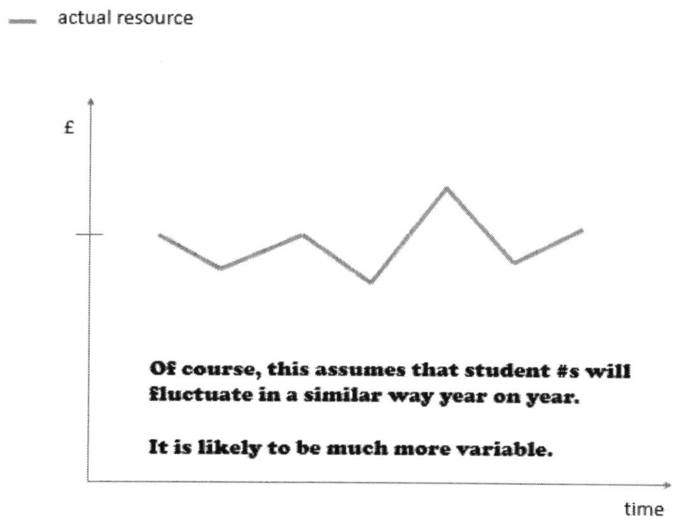

The graph above shows what would happen if the fluctuations in student number are uncompensated, assuming the rate of fluctuation linked to student choice remains similar to what we see currently. Already, you can see that a reliable level of funding is not possible, and that an institution must take a lower level of funding as its basis for budgeting.

But, of course, other factors come in to play in a purer market, the most significant of these being the enhanced importance of marketing and communications for institutions. Though marketing can offer great recruitment gains if done well, it must be remembered that there are multiple actors in the market, all of which will be engineering their own enhancements. You could imagine one-year-only cut-price deals, collusion and horse-trading, marketing "blitzes" on priority areas.

Possibly?

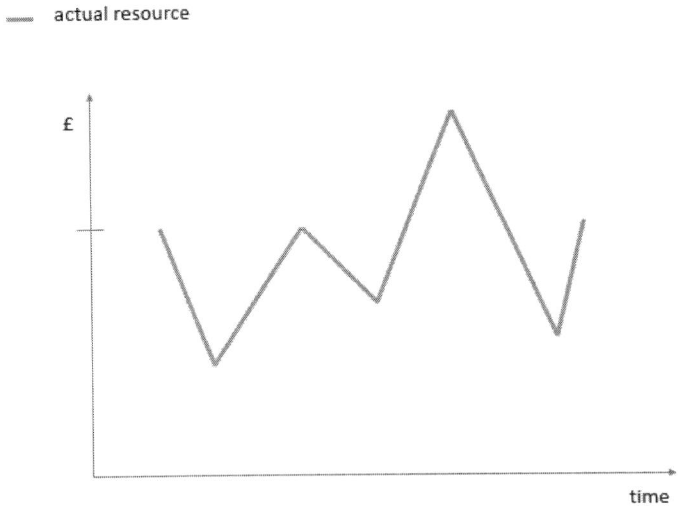

So something with much higher peaks and deeper troughs would be expected, meaning that the "base" level of institutional resource is substantially lower, and that the institution must be capable of quickly scaling particular courses substantially up or down depending on recruitment.

This is a similar scenario to seasonal changes for demand in manufacturing, and manufacturing companies have responded to these pressures in one main way.

The casualisation of labour.

Rather than keep enough staff permanently on their books to meet peak demand, it is more likely that a factory would keep only the staff that they would need for periods of low demand, and draw on a pool of casualised (short-term contract, hourly pay, semi-skilled or unskilled) labour to cope with peaks.

Universities are already starting to do the same thing. Staff on "atypical contracts" (a lovely HESA euphemism) already make up more than a third of university staff - and return accuracy for this category of staff is notably poor - it is likely to be far, far higher.

Universities as employers, England 2009 (HESA)

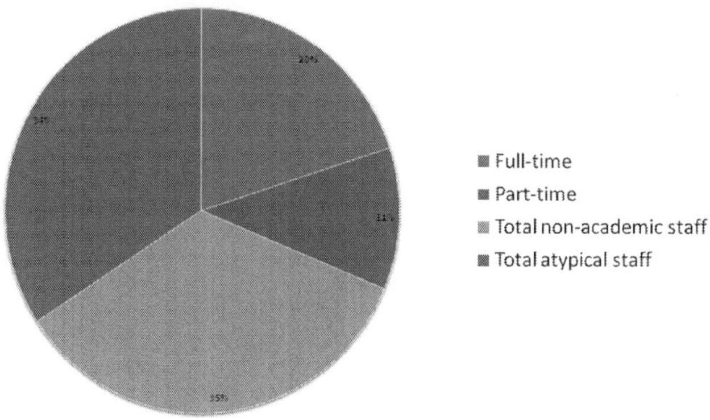

The new model of funding only makes this situation for staff more likely. It may be that the age of the "career academic", of tenure and of teaching plus research contracts is dead.

It is possible that this is simply an unintended consequence of a policy that has been notoriously poorly conceived and understood. But (and I am moving into tin foil hat territory here) we have already seen how the new model costs the taxpayer more than it saves, adds a significant extra burden to students, and (at best) offers institutions a similar amount of funding to what they get currently. So what is it for?

Is it this? A straight-ahead attack on the academic profession? A new world of casual, teaching-only, HE tutors, juggling multiple short-term contracts just to stay afloat? I dunno. But if it quacks like a duck…

The inflatable cathedral and the carnival.

It's rare that a blog post manages to implicitly offer a critique of itself, but this one by Ewen Le Borgne at the International Livestock Research Unit does so in such a mesmerisingly symmetrical way that I can only assume that it is intentional.

As a late 90s lit-crit student, I was of course introduced to Mikhail Bakhtin's legendary "Rabelais and his world", taking from it the central conceit of the carnivalesque in literature - you'd expect to come across this in any literature course. But what was maybe unique for me and my generation is that this discovery coincided with sudden and rapid growth of the world wide web. To me, as a precocious undergraduate, the web and the discourse of the web was a carnival, in the Bakhtinian sense that here was a place where social norms and hierarchies were shifted, where anything was fair game for reuse and parody, and where the marginalised and reviled found a new confident voice as their "superiors" were embarrassed, scared and tongue-tied. What no-one predicted was the way in which, over the following decade and a half, this discourse would become mainstream, the geek would (sorry, horrid cliché) inherit the earth, and the practices and protocols embedded in our early use of the web would come to define the way in which my generation and the ones after it expected intellectual property, publishing and knowledge management to work. This unexpected carnival radically re-conceptualised ideas of property, of the nature of the idea, of the idea of education and knowledge, of reputation and authority - we thought we were just downloading lost albums from Napster and writing about them on our Geocities pages, but it turned out we were living through the opening years of a revolution similar in scope to the advent of mechanisation.

Writer Cathrynne M Valente recently described the impact of this rather better than I could:

> *"Now that the internet has settled in to being a massive and integral part of our lives on Planet Earth, we are starting to see how it changes our culture in the medium to long term, how profoundly it skews even comparatively young predictions from 10-15 years ago. The internet is not a Singularity with a capital S, but it is a sea change sharing more in common with the industrial revolution than simply a new device."*

And the carnival is still here, it is just that we have forgotten it in a rush to import pre-digital ideas of authority and property online. And Le Borgne's post, with a call for a limited academian feast of fools, carefully constrained so as not to have any danger of disrupting anything, takes me back once again to Jim and Brian's high water mark. But this is not my point.

These days, we are complicit in selling the carnivalesque back to ourselves. Keynote talks and online seminars codify disruption as something that happens on a stage with a wireless headset mic and stock photos that aspire to the symbolic without ever quite reaching it. Andrew Orlowski slips this idea into a very amusing rant about Malcolm (Tipping Point) Gladwell:

> *"You could say these [Vertical Marketing Bureaucrat roles] are non-productive jobs in non-productive companies: the skills required to prattle on about "horizontal marketing segmentation" have very little to do with traditional sales skills, or R&D. But what they rely on are the same things the New Bureaucrats rely on: measurement and*

> *monitoring.*
>
> *[...] For want of a snappy description, and because it traverses the public and private sectors in a kind of League of the Clueless, I'll call this new class the vertical marketing bureaucracy, or VMB). These are people whose ambition is to speak at, or at least attend, New Media Conferences. Gladwell is their passport. And because TV and posh paper executives are now essentially part of the same vertical marketing bureaucracy (VMB) too, they're only too happy to report on Gladwell, the Phenomenon."*

There's now an established pattern for disruptive thought, a set of tropes and reference points that alert a bored audience that they are about to have their minds exploded by someone saying that learning is, like, all about people - and here are some numbers and graphs to prove it. Look, here's a picture of a poor person I saw on my holidays. LOOK AT MY HOLIDAY SNAPS, PEOPLE. FEEL MY SOCIOCULTURAL TOURISM! So instead of the full-on feast of fools, we get a feast-lite: a hierarchy of fools- largely white, largely male, largely middle-class, largely Euro-American at the top doing TED talks, with a slightly wider pool of similarly attributed VMBs beneath them aping their styles at things like Learning Without Frontiers and other futurist conferences in exciting inflatable spaces with stages and lighting rigs. And below that, the general seeker after truth - a conference-goer often at public expense - who gets- what?

They are no longer participants in the carnival. They are a backdrop to the official feast. A means of signifying to the Gladwell-esque that they have arrived. Whoop and holler, people.

I don't mind as much for New Media Conferences. I mean, people who voluntarily go to new media conferences deserve all they get. But when this Apple-toting licensed court jester approach sneaks in to serious conversations about education, I reach for my (metaphorical) revolver. Education (and the struggle for the soul of education) is far too important to trivialise with this cut-and-paste, cut-and-dried approach to disruption-by-numbers.

There are a small but significant number of education keynotees who may read this, and I have annoyed them before. But to anyone contemplating a large scale public address in this sphere, I point you to these three words of advice from Rob Englebright.

Purity. Truth. Beauty.

(the other rule of keynotes is always to use other people's ideas. Though to be fair, Jim should absolutely use this slide and Rob would be delighted)

Some words in conclusion from Prof. Michael Holquist (introduction to my 1984 edition of "Rabelais and his world"), Mikhail Bakhtin, and

Francois Rabelais.

> *"Those who lived through [the Russian revolution of 1917] were willy nilly thrown into the work of history. No one was allowed the luxury of a spectator's role. Those who normally seek the safety and anonymity of the gallery, such as peasants, workers, and - perhaps especially - intellectuals, to watch the kings, generals, prophets, and other public figures who occupy center stage go forward to volunteer their blood at Hegel's "slaughter bench of history," discovered they could not sit back and eat popcorn-or read books. The revolution gave a particularly Russian twist to Joyce's line, "Here comes everybody."" (Holquist)*

> *"[...] the official feasts of the Middle Ages, whether ecclesiastic, feudal or sponsored by the state, did not lead the people out of the established world order and created no second life. On the contrary, they sanctioned the existing pattern of things and reinforced them." (Bakhtin)*

> *"Friends, you will notice that in this world there are many more bollocks than men. Remember this." (Rabelais)*

The tyranny of iteration, or feedback in the age of noise

"This flower is scorched

This film is on

On a maddening loop

These clothes

These clothes don't fit us right

I'm to blame

It's all the same" - Michael Stipe

There are some musicians who can "play" guitar feedback as if it were a musical instrument - Neil Young is the usual citation (though I like to cite Peter Buck's work on " Automatic for the people" and " Monster"- there are thousands of other notable examples from all over the musical spectrum).

Without going into any great depth, guitar feedback happens when the sound coming out of your amplifier makes your guitar vibrate. This vibration moves your strings, this movement is picked up by your guitar pickups and send back to the amp, where it manifests either as a sustaining of the sound you were already playing, or a new sound that is related in a variety of ways to the existing note you were playing. This comes out of the amplifier, makes the guitar vibrate and so on/so forth.

Guitar amplifiers amplify a whole bunch of stuff that isn't the note you are intending to play (mains hum, handling noise-). A part of the terror and delight of "playing" feedback is that you don't know whether you are going to be re-amplifying your signal or the noise - and this unpredictability (being on the edge of having control over the sounds you are making) is - to me - what makes guitar feedback exciting. You have agency, but not complete control.

Engineers and cyberneticians describe this form of feedback as "positive feedback", an existing signal is strengthened by the process. Mark Johnson uses the idea of a "caress" to describe an interpersonal instance of positive feedback - a signal (be it physical or intellectual) generates a response that reinforces the signal and may also add new aspects to the signal. Hysteresis is another name for this modulation of the present state by the state of the system in the immediate past. Mark's use of the "caress" here is useful, as it adds in a range of other inferences - repetition, expectation and (yes) desire.

But the position remains that in most situations feedback cannot be reliably predicted without some kind of a model of the system in question, and even then predictions are patchy and limited.

In education management feedback has a different meaning - it suggests a single loop where learners respond to managers about their experience with educators, the latter of whom are pressured to modify their practice to "improve" feedback. This process is repeated at the end of every arbitrary chunk of learner experience, and in some circumstances a digest of this "feedback" is analysed alongside other data around what learners actually achieve, demographics, previous attainment and any other categorisation that is attached to either money, prestige or both.

In this respect it is barely feedback at all, as it doesn't naturally self-perpetuate. (I'm separating out the way in which an educator and group of learners actually respond to each other and modify their responses iteratively as this largely happens below the radar of institutional managers). There is no direct link between the modification of the initial signal and what is returned (not least because it is a different cohort of learners each time!) so it is impossible to play the feedback. In Mark Johnson's terms:

> *[I]t is performance which I am particularly interested in with teaching. We perform our knowledge with our bodies, artefacts, our institutional context and tools. I might start talking, but then reach for a resource to amplify what I am saying; or use the resource in conjunction with a tool, or turn the class situation around and get learners to do the talking. The ebb and flow of all this seem to have a family resemblance to musical and sexual examples.*

That paragraph nicely illustrates the idea of a performance that incorporates the "playing" of feedback in education

Modification of activity based on activity-derived feedback is an idea is often seen in the little-known(!) world of Big Data, where algorithms supposedly learn from the effects of their previous actions. Google use a variety of activity data streams to feed you things that you might be interested in, and one of these is the way you respond to recommendations such as this. But this works because the data is available near-instantaneously, so a fast pace of iteration gives the illusion of personalised responsiveness.

In contrast Amazon recommendations rely more on the overall volume of user activity rather than your personal activity, so you are in to the realms of "nudge" theory (people like you who like x also like y-) rather than personalisation. I've always been sceptical of the value of these suggestions, but you often see them cited as a good idea when people talk about learning object discovery! You can't really "play" this feedback, which I'm arguing is why it is less interesting.

So in order to "play" feedback fast iterations appear more effective than slow ones, and proximity to the individual adds to this sensation.

I've tried to map various "responsive" systems across these two axes: speed of iteration and proximity to the individual, and indicated a "playable" zone (where any autonomous agent in the system would feel that they had some control over the system as a whole) with a nice orange blob.

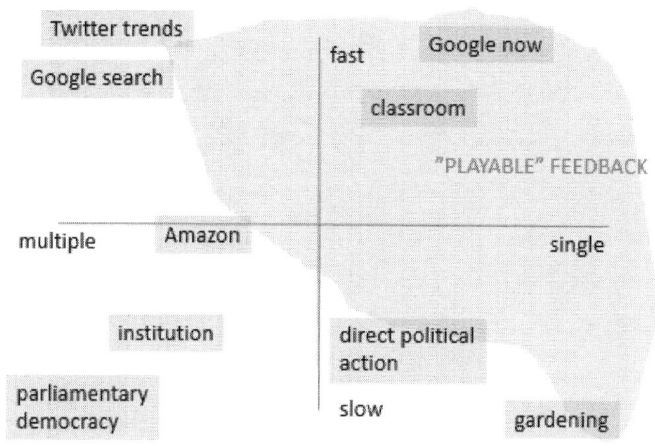

You'll note I sneaked "parliamentary democracy" and a few other wildcard ideas in there. I'm not the first to see big data systems, education and government reform on the same continuum by any means (and indeed, I've identified it as a trend for 2014!)

Eugene Morozov (the link above) sees a tendency towards individual "play" with feedback systems as a de-politicisation of engagement:

> *If Participation 1.0 was about the use of public reason to push for political reforms, with groups of concerned citizens coalescing around some vague notion of the shared public good, Participation 2.0 is about atomized individuals finding or contributing the right data to solve some problem without creating any disturbances in the system itself.*

The use of individually responsive systems is argued:

> *to redefine participation from something that arises from shared grievances and aims at structural reforms to something that arises from individual frustration with bureaucracies.*

Now, as usual with Morozov (the Michael Moore of big data skepticism, if you will), he's half-right and largely overstated. You can get playable feedback in both large scale system change and petty bureaucracy, though only one runs the risk of losing control.

The issue comes when the combined force of all the data that has been gathered swamps any meaningful impact your activity can have and you no longer feel like you are "playing" the system - we're moving here into self-oscillation where the overall noise swamps your original signal entirely.

In educational terms, these big student feedback initiatives may be doing something similar, and to put the student at the heart of a self-oscillating system seems like a particularly cruel joke.

On Slow Policy

It was Paul Kingsnorth (poet, scythe-mower, recovering "green") and Pope Francis 1 (pontif, misogynist, Argentinian) who between them set this particular hare running. Paul (you might know him as the co-founder of Dark Mountain) was noting on twitter with evident glee the frustration of the massed press in St Peter's Square, being offered nothing to report on but the occasional puff of coloured smoke.

A bored and restless press was kept waiting by a seriously "closed" process, and responded with irreverence and irritability. For once, the news wasn't moving to the tempo they were used to.

But the news didn't always move at that speed.

Here's the first paragraph of a Time magazine article on the papal coronation in October 1978 (there's more behind a paywall). This article represents the entire coverage of Time concerning the conclave. It is thoughtful, resonant, conveying more of a sense of the occasion than this entire Daily Mail article on the 2005 conclave, which though short and poorly written, at least captures the main points in a comprehensible manner.

Compare the Metro's "live blog" from the Vatican City. Or any one of the millions of other articles from the day, from bloggers, journalists, analysts and columnists - from canon law experts and militant atheists. Even from an advocate for livetweeting from within the conclave.

I'm not sure that this is the fault of the news industry, or the fault of our constant access to "new media". These are the things that get blamed for a lack of detailed comprehension, for a disengagement with the news and for a focus on trivialities rather than that great cliché, the "real issues that hard-working families are concerned with". Me - I blame policy making.

A while ago former government wonk Damien McBride wrote a lovely eye-opener of a blog post about "The Grid". This was the UK government's media management toolkit from 1997-2010.

> *"The 'grid system' initiated by New Labour - transferred from their 1997 election campaign - is commonly considered to be a news management tool, with a series of announcements plotted to dominate each day's coverage and provide occasional cover to bury bad news"*

The key word is "dominate" - the idea was to super-saturate the news ecosystem with controlled news items. The idea of "burying bad news" was taken to extremes by another government advisor of the day, Jo Moore, who suggested that the 11th September 2011 was a good time to release stories that were unlikely to offer the government flattering coverage. This scandal led to perhaps the greatest modern political quote, which I repeat with unbridled delight, from Permanent Secretary Sir Richard Mottram:

> "We're all fucked. I'm fucked. You're fucked. The whole department is fucked. It's the biggest cock-up ever. We're all completely fucked."

This is not the language of someone making good public policy. This is the language of panic.

To dominate a media that is skilled in identifying and disseminating key news angles government press officers attempt to overfeed journalists. The thinking appears to be that if you continually keep them reacting to events instantly, there will be no time for any analysis of the implications of the announcements in question - either taken singularly or cumulatively.

Jeremy Porter, the editor of the "journalistics" blog, estimated in 2009 that around 4,000 press releases- from government, industry and pressure groups - were sent out every single day.

I've worked in policy for most of my working life, so I see the other end as well - desperate, quick, attention-grabbing initiatives that make little or no sense given the wider swathes of policy history in a particular area.

Neither policy making nor policy analysis has any sense of history, despite the sterling work of blogs like Public Policy and the Past, and initiatives like the KCL/London "History&Policy" pages. In a way the system is such that there is deliberately no time for this indulgence.

And the increasingly hysterical attitudes of lobbyists and pressure groups, setting arbitrary targets before some great cataclysm occurs - campaigning for immediate action on some newspaper-fed flash fire of public concern - is little help to this. Knee-jerk policy is not a victory for a campaign- it is bad policy that unravels over the following weeks and months.

Slow policy would start with a fallow period - a fast - by both sides. An end to all policy announcements. For at least 12 months. This time would be used to commission and conduct, in public, proper research on the problems people face.

From policy makers, this would require a retreat from their fear of deep public analysis and their need to make headlines. And from commentators, a retreat from the need to reduce every policy decision to an act of political warfare. And from all of us, from the idea that everything requires immediate action.

Watching the smoke might be the best thing that ever happened to public policy.

[postscript: I've just been worrying that it is a year or so since the conclave, and that I'm too late with publishing this post in a book... none of us are immune]

Press one to graduate (and Clay Shirky again)

I love rights. They're a great measure of how much western civilisation thinks of you.

If you're a low-paid worker, an immigrant, disabled, or just unlucky enough to be poor your rights are an unaffordable luxury. They are an extravagance, a throwback to a bygone age, a toxin that destroys your profitability.

If you are a member of the global 1% (and if you are reading this you most likely are), your rights are inviolable and must be staunchly defended. Especially your consumer rights, and your right to choose to give large corporations money. Those ones are especially important.

Recently, a group of wealthy educators (though not the ones that actually do any educating), leavened with a few writers, commentators and others came together to defend a new bunch of consumer rights - your rights in the emerging market place of high-capacity online learning.

There is much to agree with, both in the initial draft and the document as it currently stands. You can still contribute to the google doc should you wish, and many others have done so. But it remains, at its heart, equivalent to the rights you have to return your malfunctioning MacBook and have it replaced. Or it would if it actually conferred any rights.

It disappeared on later drafts, but one of the telling phrases on the original Bill of Rights was "the right to have great teachers". Language like this echoes that of people like Joel Klein at NewsCorp:

> *"Last, to shake up the system, we must change how we use technology*

> *to deliver instruction. (This is what I'm now seeking to do at News Corporation.)- [O]ne of the best things we could do is hire fewer teachers and pay more to the ones we hire. And, as in any other field, technology can help get us there. If you have 5,000 math teachers, many of whom are underperforming, significantly improving overall quality is nearly impossible. But if you get the best math professors in the world-who are great teachers and who deeply understand math-and match them with great software developers, they can create sophisticated interactive programs that engage kids and empower teachers."*

Those "many of whom are underperforming" teachers are your adjuncts. Also known as regular folks doing a difficult job well for too little money. And this kind of idea is being smuggled under the cover of reaching new groups of students. Automating marking, signature track typing-style recognition, superstar lectures streamed online- all of these ideas represent a way not to employ an adjunct professor.

Simultaneously, "adjunct" professors (or part-time hourly-paid early-career teaching-only-contract staff, as we call them rather less snappily in the UK) are asserting their own right to withdraw their labour. Adjunct Project's "Quit" initiative feels like the beginning of the HE equivalent of Colony Collapse Disorder, where hives become unviable as masses of worker-bees disappear without explanation.

Across the world, academic tenure has shifted from an expectation, to a dream, to an unheard of state of employment for anyone under 40. And unsurprisingly, young academics are tiring of being exploited and patronised ("many of whom are underperforming"), and moving elsewhere. Out of academica. Into a career where they can one day aspire to rent their own home.

This is the aspect that Clay Shirky (yes, him again) misses entirely when he defends himself against detractors in The Awl. He's comparing MOOCs to mass education (specifically mass lectures) without contemplating that mass education is only like that because we are unwilling to invest in human resources to provide a better experience.

And the MOOC difference. It's cheaper. Initially. While the venture capital lasts. And that's it.

There's no increase in the quality of the experience, it's not a better product. Just a subsidised one. If you want a comparison from another industry, it's what happened when call centres realised they could replace swathes of staff with an automated attendant.

In that case, as with what is happening in education, it was a cost (salary) saving that drove the change. Swathes of skilled and knowledgeable staff could be replaced by an inflexible system and scripted (but untrained) low-paid offshore staff. But this led to a drastic lowering of customer satisfaction - these days the trend is to bring back the old-fashioned call centre - with major airlines and banks promoting the chance to speak to a real person to solve complex queries.

The almost one hundred million google results for "speak to a real person" bear this out. There is a demand for human intelligence in solving complex banking and ticketing queries - it is bizarre to believe that there would not be a demand for human intelligence in supporting learning.

So what of the humans in question - the adjuncts? If we are not spending the money on proper jobs for educators - if we literally cannot afford to grow the professors, provosts and vice-chancellors of the future -what exactly are we spending ever rising student fees on?

Openness

'We need to find a new model of supporting the work of academics.' - TOUCANS interview

I'm just adding this to preserve the interview I did with Gabi Witthaus of the TOUCANS project, which is examining attitudes to the OERu initiative. It's a very interesting project, and it's worth having a look at some of the other interviews that she's done - in a laudable instance of open practice they're all preserved as blog posts!

'We need to find a new model of supporting the work of academics.'

GW: I'd like to start by asking you, in very general terms, what your views are on the OERu.

DK: In very general terms, I'd say I see it as part of a cultural trend around the changing nature of higher education and around the way in which open education is becoming a part of that. I think I see it as having the same strengths and weaknesses as models such as Udacity, Coursera or MITx, that it is - and I think I'm on record as saying this previously - fundamentally a parasitic model. Basically all of the content is coming from academics and volunteers who are employed by traditional institutions, and the aim of these kinds of initiatives is to draw students in who might otherwise participate at the host institution. So that slightly worries me in that it's not a sustainable intervention; it has not solved the problem of how you actually reward academics for the work that they're doing.

GW: The term parasitic is quite negative and that obviously portrays your feelings about it. I'm not trying to sell the OERu but I think people within the OERu might refer to it as symbiotic, not parasitic, and certainly the way they are seeing the business model is it shouldn't be undermining existing provision. They're saying if each participating institution offers a little bit based on OERs they've already produced, and assessments that they're already running for their existing learners, and they recoup the costs of that assessment and accreditation, then the more institutions that participate, the bigger the offering can be. I don't think your point about it taking paying students away from mainstream provision is the way they would see it either. They would see the OERu as reaching a whole new audience that is currently unable to pay the fees.

DK: I can take that on board. Certainly, symbiotic is an interesting choice of word. I would query however, precisely what the contributing institutions are getting out of it. They seem to be contributing resources and staff time, and not actually getting any benefit at the end of it. I would say that clearly there needs to be a range of models for the delivery of higher education to a growing population. You could argue I suppose that this is actually about a wider cultural issue; I mean, exactly why is higher education so unaffordable at the moment? Why is it that we need to fit higher education alongside work? Why is it that academic work needs to bring in revenue? As an idealist, I can see completely the aims of what they're trying to do. But unfortunately when it comes down to it across the Western world, academics are kind of under attack in terms of their conditions - the contractual nature of their relationship with the institution. We're moving towards the idea of short-term, hourly pay. The idea of academic tenure or an academic career is basically dying off. We need to address these issues if higher education is actually going to be sustainable. There is going to need to be some way of paying academics so they can afford to live. I can see that these models are good for students if they can cope with online learning, they can cope with independent learning, and they are comfortable with self-directed work. A small group of learners, I suspect mainly in the post-graduate area, would be suited to that kind of learning. I used to work in the University of Glamorgan, Wales, which is an institution that does a lot to drive up participation in the Welsh valleys - some of the most deprived areas in Europe. A lot of the time it's very intensive on staff time and support. These students need a lot of support and guidance. They need a lot of introduction into academic ideas, ways to interact with information, and it's incredibly intensive. I would query as to whether online learning is the answer for those people.

GW: The OERu is hoping to get volunteers to support students. They're hoping to get retired academics, graduates who've been through an OERu course and others who are just interested to join as volunteers.

DK: That's a potential, but it's still limited to people who have got the private means to afford to volunteer in this way. It's like the Big Society idea - drawing on people who can afford to give, in Marxist terms, their labour. I'm probably one of the people in that target market. As you know, I'm involved with DS106, working with students around that MOOC. But it's still a self-selecting group. It's people that can afford to do this, and its people that can afford to be academics because they're interested in being academics. That's starting to happen already. Most postgraduates have got private means; most new academics have got some kind of resources outside of their academic employment just because it's paid so, so badly that you couldn't really do it otherwise. I suppose you could compare it to journalism as a profession that is essentially dying, because there are lots of people like me who are interested enough in micro-issues that they'll happily devote their time to research and writing about those issues. And I think you can see the same kind of thing with academics. Now in many ways you could see that as positive. It's democratising journalism, meaning you've not got the ideas of the proprietors and owners, and their friends and contacts being the thing that actually drives the agenda.

GW: A lot of people are concerned about quality when the question of volunteers comes up, whereas your concerns are more of a socio-political nature.

DK: I think so, yes. I mean I love academics, I think they're fantastic and I think they do amazing, amazing work. We need to have some way to pay these people so that we have a meritocracy for people who have reached academic positions because they're talented teachers, because they're great researchers, because they're basically just bright, interesting people. I'm not certain that a volunteer model is the best model in terms of academia as a profession.

GW: Now if we were just talking about a model for the UK or for a single country, we could proceed with that debate and say, well what should the government be doing? But this is an international model and it's based on the premise that-

DK: It's an international problem.

GW: Yeah, it's an international problem, and it's really aimed at, the ultimate point of it is a kind of altruistic attempt to support people in developing countries who have few resources, without hurting the better-resourced institutions in any way.

DK: Yes, it's a noble aim isn't it, that you are trying to provide higher education to people that wouldn't otherwise have access to it, but to my mind, that should be an aim of core academic practice. That's something we should be directly paying people to do, rather than expecting people to do it in their own time.

GW: When I interviewed people in the OERu network institutions, one person said: "The ideal OERu learner is a self-contained student who is going to resolutely keep persevering-"

DK: There are quite a lot of students and quite a lot of independent learners outside of institutional system that are doing that, but I don't think it's a model that's typical, especially not for those with previous experience of learning in this particular way. It's quite difficult. I mean, even coming from compulsory sector education into higher education is a really difficult job. From having someone else being responsible for your learning to you being responsible for your learning is really difficult, even with all the peer support, the library, the study skills support that you get in a traditional campus university. I think online learning is a similar step. Going from campus-style learning to that, I think it's a similar jump. And to expect people to make two jumps, if we're talking about people who haven't even completed compulsory education, that's a big, big step.

GW: Yes, I'm really curious to see if this model actually works. Going back to what you said earlier, that academics should be paid by their institutions to support students who can't afford to pay the fees of mainstream universities, someone's still got to pay for that - it's either the student or the taxpayer.

DK: Absolutely. It used to be a core part of what was expected of an academic. If you go back to Cambridge in the 17th century and look at contracts, the only tangible output that an academic was supposed to give was to offer a public lecture every year, and that was the reason they were employed, so they could provide a public lecture. Even these days in universities, there is a lot of outreach activity, which is what academics are at least partially paid to do. That can be really effective. If you look at what Viv Rolfe was doing in the DMU open day, just standing on a soap box and shouting about Biosciences OER - that was fantastic. If you look at the likes of Dr Alice Roberts on Coast on the BBC talking about geology and local history and biology, all the amazing stuff that she does, this kind of activity has long been part of an academic contract. A lot of the wonderful things about higher education have happened because academics have had it in their contracts to do that. It's slightly fading away because increasingly we're putting young academics onto hourly paid contracts or just paying them for the contact hours they do; they're doing the preparation and marking in their own time, and they've just not got time to do the wider collegiate, as it used to be called, activities. Bringing in a model like this would work if we still had widespread academic tenure in the US and the UK, if we still had academics employed full-time to do academic "stuff", but we don't have that any more. We're looking for efficiencies and that seems to be the priority rather than maximising the benefit that we get from the people that we do employ.

GW: There's something horribly ironic in that isn't there: it's because of the recession which is worldwide, we're cutting down on our own institutional staff capacity, and this is exactly the time that people in less-resourced parts of the world are even more disadvantaged than before.

DK: Absolutely.

GW: Let me come back to something you mentioned earlier, when you said you couldn't see what the benefit was for the institutions that joined the OERu. The people I interviewed who were in senior management were partly looking at it as a marketing exercise. They want to be seen to be out there, being innovative. But all of my interviewees, without exception said they had some curiosity about the OERu and they wanted to 'dip a toe in the water'. They felt it was a relatively low-risk way of experimenting with taking OERs to the next level and seeing what would happen. Wayne Mackintosh, in particular, emphasised sustainable educational practice. You know there are statistics that show that India would have to build something like two universities a week to meet the demand for higher education. For me that raises a whole separate question, which is, do these masses of people actually need and want a higher education?

DK: Yes, and if they do want higher education, do they want the kind of higher education that is sitting in front of a screen for a couple of hours in between shifts? Is that really what they actually want, or is that what we as the West have deigned to give them? I mean why shouldn't India build loads of universities? Unfortunately we've decided that the expansionary stage of higher education is completed now, and so therefore we have to do something else. It kind of feels like we're letting those people down in a way.

GW: That's an interesting way of looking at it. OK, something else that all the OERu members said to me when I interviewed them was that it was about social inclusion and widening participation.

DK: It's a nice easy way to meet that goal, isn't it? They don't have to go out there and engage with people. They can just tick the box and say this is for learners who are savvy enough and motivated enough to be online, be curious, to sign up for an online course. But I suspect those people would have found a way to get some kind of education anyway. It's not actually widening participation; it's just a cheaper way of reaching a student body. I mean, cynically, they could say, 'Maybe this is a good way of exposing ourselves to the market. We can eventually bring the best of these incredibly motivated people back as post-graduates.'

GW: A few people have said that.

DK: The way we sell higher education at the moment is that if you're not actually moving up in your career, there's not much point in getting your degree.

GW: In your slightly cynical view-?

DK: It's not *that* cynical-

GW: I find it quite depressing! But there might be something in it. Most of the people I spoke to in the OERu network were at the grassroots, academics within their institutions who are making this happen, with a few exceptions of senior managers. I think that the people on the ground who've been tasked with implementing this are incredibly focused on the social agenda. I believe that if you get a critical mass of people like that in an institution, you can achieve things that you wouldn't really imagine. You don't really know what's going to come out of it because of that.

DK: Well, it's a research project!

GW: The OERu not really a research project; it's an implementation project.

DK: Shooting first and asking questions later?

GW: OK then, it's an experiment! Once you've put your hypothesis out there, you've got to pour all the stuff into the test tubes and see what happens-

DK: Yeah- but, I suppose experiments usually start with thought experiments and then right at the end you can actually go in to the wet lab and start playing with stuff, but you've got some kind of a model of change in your head that says well this active group will combine with this active group, which will give the chemical in question the following pharmaceutical properties, wouldn't you?

GW: You would, yes.

DK: You wouldn't think, well let's just pour some of this in and some of that in and then say, well let's see what happens, and then drink it. That's not science.

GW: Well no- The hypothesis includes many ifs: if the OERu gets enough institutions involved, if they manage to recruit learners who are willing to give this a try, if the learners have got the staying power, if there are people willing to support the learners in the various ways that have been suggested, then who knows? Then- even if out of the hundred million people, one percent of them actually succeed, that's a million people.

DK: I think that the Open University might reach that number in China as well. You've also got the likes of Nottingham. You should see the university parks that they build out there in China. You've got, say, Sheffield Hallam and next door you've got Lancaster. It's just about sending academic staff out there, having people on the ground. That seems to be the way a lot of institutions are going, although unfortunately the Chinese and Indian economies are starting to slow down now.

GW: Something else the OERu people said about the benefits: there was a lot of talk about the collaboration between member institutions in the network as being valuable. There are what are perceived to be world leaders in PLAR/ APEL/ RPL in this network. For them PLAR is matching up what a person can do against a graduate profile.

DK: I remember working with a project looking at APEL in the University of Derby, and it takes substantially more time, for students and academics, than doing the course. There's been a lot of defence of APEL because of the degree mill argument - you know the ones that send you these emails saying you can get a PhD now for 6,000 GBP without doing any work.

GW: Otago Polytechnic in New Zealand and the North American institutions are doing a lot of APEL work. They didn't see it as being overly labour intensive. One person I interviewed was really happy that the OERu would provide a structure for PLAR applicants to prepare their portfolios that could then be mapped against course outcomes.

DK: Then again, it does actually drive up their income. It means that they don't have to employ many full-time academics to do full-time teaching.

GW: That's another question for me: if it is ultimately successful, imagine if every student could choose to do absolutely any programme either the mainstream way or the OERu way: then what do the institutions do - do they become licensing offices?

DK: There has been a lot of talk about this around JISC and CETIS. The link http://www.jisc.ac.uk/blog/mooc/ contains a short video showing an imaginary university called Universality that I invented back in 2010 to explore these models. I presented this at ALT-C 2010 (http://followersoftheapocalyp.se/oer-futures-and-universality-inc-altc2010), and what that suggested was basically a model largely based around peer support with extras like direct academic support, practical weeks and the exams and accreditation actually paid for. I didn't like the idea at the time and I still don't like it, but it appears to be becoming true. I mean, it's a slightly over-the-top, slightly tongue-in-cheek investigation of that kind of model. Something in that model that I did like was that they actually employed academics. They paid academics so that their primary goal would be creating OER and recording lectures that would drive hits, and then students paid directly to have one-to-one tuition with them, or to attend intensive courses. I suggested that they would be paid according to the number of hits their courses got. So there was the anthropology lecturer that was making millions and millions of pounds- I'm not going to speculate on what exactly she was doing - it could be anything- That is one potential model. When I see Udacity, Coursera, the stuff that is starting to happen around TedX, not so much the OERu, I see elements of that coming in.

This is slightly prefiguring mine and Amber's presentation for the ALT conference this year, which is that there are a number of sub-cultures within the open education movement. One of these is the "education is broken" DIY movement that says nothing in traditional education is working; it's all broken and we need to tear it up from the ground and start again, which largely for some reason involves the private sector. I think they can see a massive new market expanding. Much like what is starting to happen in the schools sector with academies and the New York state school system. I think there is a component within the open education movement which is directly antagonistic to traditional education, and that differs from the people who are just saying knowledge should be out there, should be shared, should be free - basically dodgy old hippies such as myself and the likes of Alan Levine, that kind of crowd. Brian Lamb as well has talked a lot about this. Then you've got the likes of David Wiley that are coming from the old tradition of reusable learning objects (RLO). It's all about making the existing model more efficient; it's using technology as a way of designing courses. It's the old RLO dream of automatically populating a course with the required material, seamless sharing within a VLE framework.

You've got all those different traditions that are kind of mashed together in the open education sphere, and the tensions in there are really interesting.

GW: You mentioned ALT-C - I'm also preparing something with Jonathan Darby and Megan Quentin-Baxter. It will be a symposium/ debate pretty much about these issues. One more thing I wanted to ask your opinion of. This slide has generated some really interesting comments from people I've interviewed. The image is based on a paper by Norm Friesen and Judith Murray.

DK: I think that ties in with the argument I was making earlier; it's a fantastic way of not providing student support and saving costs, and not paying academics and saving costs. So I could see institutions really going for that because it lowers their recurrent outgoings substantially.

GW: I suppose, going back to the business model, which is that no institution in the network should put out more than half a percent of their total offerings through the OERu, this would only apply to that half a percent.

DK: If these are the institutions leading on APEL, this could actually be their business model. There's no reason why there shouldn't be hundreds and hundreds of OERus.

GW: I suppose so, but a single OERu means more collaboration towards a single goal-

DK: And branding. You can imagine. I think the big untapped market for higher education expansion is the kind of people that are posting on particular interest forums and blogs and tumblrs etc. If you think of the man-years, and I think it is actually 'man' years, of the stuff going on wookipedia, the Star Wars fan site. People are experts in camera choices, scripting and sets, and they're contributing all this stuff because they love Star Wars. There's no reason at all why you couldn't put together something called the University of Alderran that would directly market itself to people are contributing in this way. 'Come here and learn about the musical principles in John Williams' scores!' By the way, I'd like to immediately dissociate myself from that idea.

GW: [Laughs.] To some extent isn't that what's already happening with the P2P University and so on?

DK: Yes, in the same way that people used to share on Slashdot in the old days, it would be Github or Stack Overflow now, that kind of thing. You can see Stack Overflow saying you're doing all this incredible learning, why not get a badge for it? A qualification that people could actually use on their CV might be of interest to them. I think we could go for the Star Wars model - there'd be a big market for that one.

GW: Yes, possibly even on other planets - we could really expand!

DK: Absolutely: A long time ago in an institution far, far away- That's no moon; it's got degree-awarding powers!

GW: (Laughs) Is there anything else you want to say about the whole concept of the OERu?

DK: My primary concern is finding ways of paying academics. I think we need to find a new model of supporting the work of academics. This is probably going to be the big defining struggle of the next ten years of higher education. I mean, how do we support academics in the early years; how do we get the people who are best at teaching and researching actually doing the job?

GW: Good question. I think there are some people who are a bit fatalistic about that and they're saying, well if the market shrinks for the kind of support for students that universities have traditionally offered, then academics must be creative and use all their grey matter to think of ways to move forward.

DK: Absolutely, because it's already starting to happen; I was writing about this in my blog. It's a future designed by entrepreneurs that were brought up on pulpy fifties science fiction; it's like a culture reaching back to the certainties of the black and white and the government as the Empire, free enterprise as the rebels, and shooting down the red tape. You look at the mainstream cultural growth of the likes of steampunk, looking back at previous ideas of the future rather than having new ideas of the future. There's a big gap here in defining what the world is going to be like, and academics need to step into it.

GW: I think I've taken enough of your time, although I'd love to continue! Is there anything else you want to say?

DK: I think I've been quite cynical in places, but I'm absolutely not saying we shouldn't try it. I think we should try it and see what happens but we need to be really self-critical in the best sense, and really aware of the politics and the implications of what we're doing.

David Kernohan

Venus in OERs

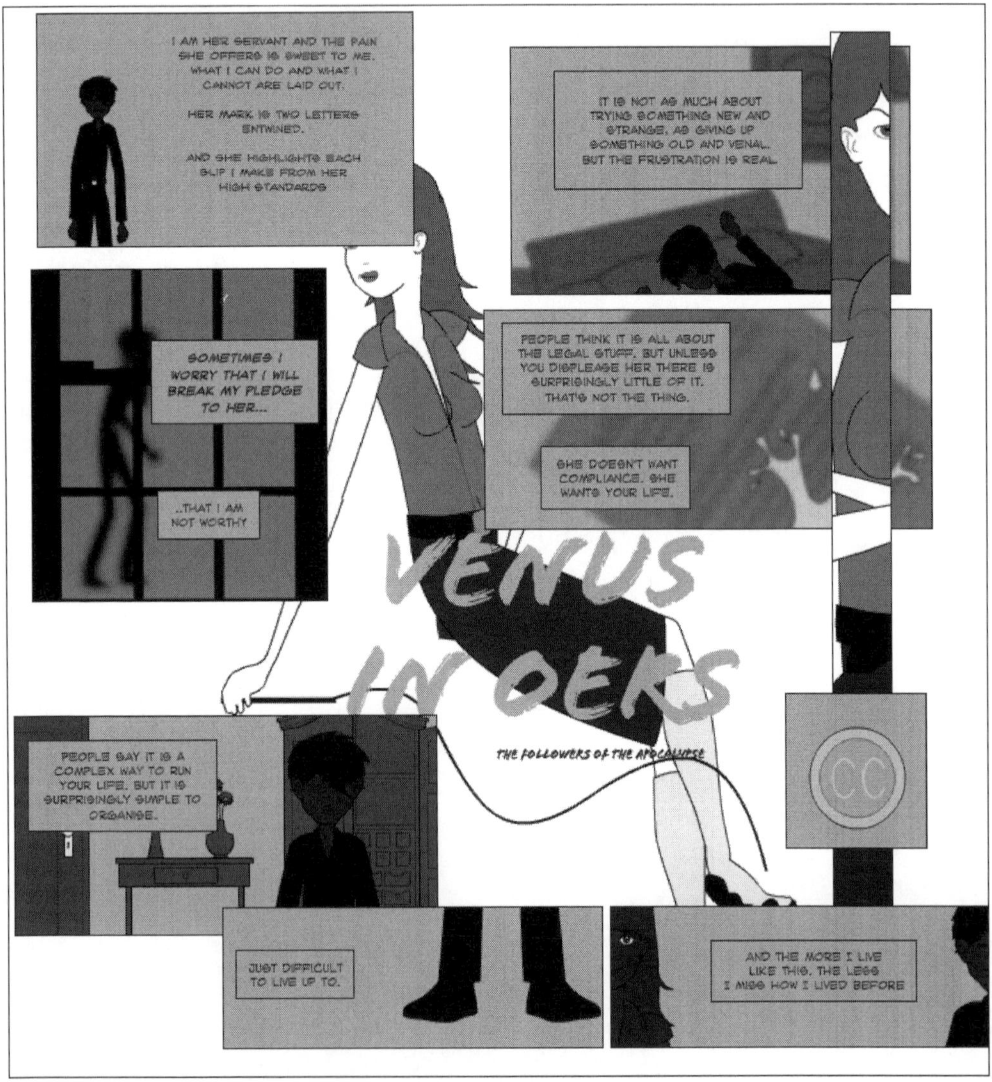

Okay, I've been thinking about doing this for ages, and Pixton (the comics thing I played with a few posts ago) seemed like the best way of presenting it. @ambrouk's "My story of O(pen)" was a wonderfully positive look at the benefits of open, so here I am drawing both on this slightly one-sided view and her very interesting choice of title to realise that openness is a discipline, and like every discipline it can be both beneficial, enjoyable and very difficult to stick to.

Brian Lamb expressed this rather well with his "frustrating misconceptions" on openness, the fact that people outside of "the lifestyle" have very odd ideas of how it actually works in practice - the things that seem to be the "point" when viewed from the outside are not the day-to-day benefits. And the huge elephant in the room, that Creative Commons is all about making better use of your copyright rather than abandoning it.

Hope the comic is gnomic enough to be interesting without being incomprehensible!

The existence of this post and Amber's does not mean that there is a secret BDSM fetish scene at our mutual employers. As far as I am aware. All the bits of the comic I own are available under CC-BY, though note that the good folks at Pixton also require attribution and that their property is not used commercially.

Small print

So Amazon, that well known global e-commerce company based in Seattle, doesn't pay any corporate tax in the UK and avoids VAT on various products by having a "corporate centre" in the thriving metropolis that is Luxembourg City (twinned, apparently, with the London Borough of Camden Town). This revelation has spurred a great deal of hand-wringing in the UK, but has also introduced the subtle distinction between a vendor and an "order fulfilment operation" to our ever-evolving sacred texts of business-speak.

@Stebax (the Enemies of Reason bloke) set a hare running in my mind on twitter by suggesting that, as his business in Britain was merely "blogpost delivery", he would henceforth be basing himself in Luxembourg. I wondered if he, along with many of us, are in fact in the business of idea delivery and thus were only taxable within our own minds.

I blog[ed] on Posterous, which is based in San Francisco and is now owned by Twitter which is split between SF and New York. Both organisations graciously allow me to retain ownership of my "work" (such as it is!) which is hosted by their platform. To be more specific, I voluntarily supply ideas to Twitter and Posterous, granting them a global non-exclusive and transferable royalty-free license to publish my work. To put this another way, I have entered into a contractual relationship with both organisations to provide them with content that I permit them to monetise as they see fit, and in return for this they provide a stable hosted platform for me to publish on to.

In both cases the model is either to use my content to sell ad space, or to use the promise of their ability to use my content to sell ad space to raise venture capital. These ads are bought (or will be bought) by global companies, who hope that they will be seen by a particular demographic of viewers filtered by earnings, interests, geographic location, gender or a million other variables.

In simple Marxist terms I create value via my labour which is exploited in return for profit, but all of this happens on a global basis. I sit at a desk in the UK, some guy sells ads from a desk in the US, some woman buys ads space from a desk in China but all of these transactions are actually stateless.

Corporate Tax law, as it currently stands, levies a charge on net profits relating to a trade conducted within a particular country. Section 6 (4)(a-b) of the 1988 Income and Corporation Taxes Act defines this:

> *"(a) "profits" means income and chargeable gains; and*
>
> *(b) "trade" includes "vocation", and also includes an office or employment or the occupation of woodlands in any context in which the expression is applied to that in the Income Tax Acts."*

Trade is here seen to include " Goods, Services, Income & Transfers", all of which concern the exploitation of commodities ("the products of human labour", after Marx).

Regarding posterous or twitter, the person producing the commodity in all this is me. My remuneration (as above) is the free use of the platform - a benefit which is not taxable, and/or is also the means by which the commodity I create can be exploited. You could imagine if I was C19th homeworker I would produce a certain number of ladies undergarments without pay in order to cover the cost of a sewing machine. This is the same, except I never get to own the sewing machine or get any wages.

[Going deeper, am I actually creating the commodity at all? I've been inspired by news on the Guardian, commentary on twitter and content from the UK government, Wikipedia and the town twinning association so far. So, in the same way that I'm adding value to what Posterous do, all these people are adding value to what I do. And what about the likes of Google selling ads alongside search results and aggregation...?]

So trying to locate where the "trade" happens, who is "trading" with whom and where profits are taxable is by no means a simple matter. I'd be tempted to argue that, as we move to increasingly global business models, that we need a global corporation tax collected by an international agency and spent for the benefit of the entire world - which in the short/medium term would be primarily aimed at the developing world in order to reduce global inequality. Eventually we could move for a global minimum wage and then some kind of sustainable and controlled use of natural and human resources. But I'm just a smelly hippy and I don't understand finance or business.

"Please, don't be educational!": Waste, Civilisation, Learning

After a tip-off from Charles Stross' always-excellent blog, I've been very struck by Karl Schroeder's reflections on a paper concerning the Fermi Paradox by Keith B. Wiley at Washington U. The paper offers a range of considerations concerning our lack of contact with alien civilisations, and (almost in passing) considers the range of expected signals that we would have expected to find from such civilisations.

Schroeder's take on this is that all of these signals - be they electromagnetic "noise", self-replicating deep space probes, the construction of orbital computing resources - are by-product (or waste) expressions of essentially wasteful civilisations. And that truly advanced civilisations would not produce waste. I like his re-statement of Clarke's Third Law, that "any sufficiently advanced technology is indistinguishable from nature". In other words, we wouldn't see it because we wouldn't have any way of knowing it wasn't natural.

Our own Western Civilisation bases itself on a presumption of resource scarcity, and I would perhaps paradoxically argue that waste is a by-product of scarcity: both in terms of "process waste" (the stuff we create incidentally whilst trying to get to scarce stuff) and "use waste" (the scarce stuff that we don't actually bother using after we get it for various psychologically and sociologically interesting reasons). The philosophy of the Zero Waste Institute (ZWI) is well worth a further look in this context, as the website states with impressive clarity:

> *"How has humanity dealt with the excess goods it generated?*
>
> *First generation (immediate satisfaction)- DISCARD and DUMPS = GARBAGE*

> *Second generation (short term)- POST-DISCARD REUSE = RECYCLING*
> *Third generation (long term)- EXPLICIT DESIGN FOR REUSE = ZERO WASTE"*

Schroeder seems to be putting genuinely advanced alien civilisations at a postulated "Fourth Generation" within this system, which I could perhaps state as:

> *"Fourth generation (eternal) - GOODS INDISTINGUISHABLE FROM NATURE = NEGATION OF WASTE AS CONCEPT"*

We open all kinds of bio-engineering cans of strawberry-flavoured worms here - but you could argue that microbes designed to produce drugs or food designed to be resistant to rot are the beginnings of a movement that could end with all technology becoming indistinguishable from nature, and thus within a natural cycle that has "waste" as one of several interim stages. (I'm assuming here, of course, that humankind manages to sort out this nonsense about patenting such things-)

Anyway, I'm fully aware I'm on dodgy ethical ground here, so let's talk about David Wiley's idea of " Open Educational Resources (OER) as classroom exhaust" - learning materials being shared as the by-product of learning. In ZWI terms we appear to be in the second generation here, perhaps beginning as OER becomes a more mainstream idea (and, we hope, practice) to edge in to the third.

Wiley is clear that he's taking the concept from the idea of the "data exhaust", which I would argue is actually a different beast entirely. A "data exhaust" is **process waste** - we've not deliberately set out to create user data, it just happened whilst we were trying to get to those resources we wanted to use. In contrast, learning materials are **use waste**, it's stuff that we deliberately put together to use for learning that didn't get used up.

A fair chunk of these learning materials may actually be in ZWI generation one (and therefore not in Wiley's virtuous classroom exhaust), so we dump it because we feel it is neither recyclable nor reusable outside of the immediate context that we have just been using it in. So what do we do to learning materials to make them so context specific?

An article I've had on my "to think about" stack for a long while is by writer and concert pianist Stephen Hough. In "Please, Don't Be Musical", he laments the way that musicians in training internalise so many conventions around the expression of musicality that we hear musicality rather than music. He quotes and reflects on the words of an old piano teacher:

> *"I remember very clearly a certain lesson with Gordon Green when I was about twelve years old. I was playing the opening of the first movement of Beethoven's sonata op. 110 and, just as I reached the decorative arpeggios at the bottom of the first page, he stopped me:* ***"My dear boy, this music is not beautiful*** *[pause for a deep draw on his smouldering pipe]-* ***it is sublime".*** *I was responding to the superficial charm of the melody instead of reaching inside the flesh and bones to the very soul of the music. It is a lesson hard to learn because it seems as if at the very moment when we have built up an impressive arsenal of interpretative trinkets we need to start getting rid of them. It is allied to life itself: as soon as we've learned how to behave as an adult we need to start to rediscover our childhood again."*

I wonder if educators preparing materials for learning are themselves guilty of "educationality" - you could see the "interpretative trinkets" as being conceptions of educational intent in a particular context, based around various theories of learning or environmental variables, manifesting themselves as tangible on an otherwise reusable resource. And it could be this "educationality" that gets in the way of reuse? Is "educationality" an indicator of waste? Is "educationality" what we have in the limo?

I've been around ds106 long enough to know the difference between mere beauty and the sublime (is there a plaisir/jouissance thing here?) and the latter tends not to have an implicit learning intention. Indeed, it could also be argued that "learning materials" from ds106 are generally shared because they are (a) learner-created and (b) awesome. And because, if you didn't know the source, you wouldn't think they were learning objects.

On the web, they are indistinguishable from nature.

Neither owt nor summit

UNESCO is an unusual organisation with a particularly unusual relationship with Britain.

We left, of course, in '84, following the US out in an early War on Press Accountability which handily prefigured the results of the Leveson Inquiry. The "New World Communications and Information Order"(properly known as " Many Voices, One World", sometimes the MacBride report) attempted to address the balance between the perspectives of the moneyed western mediarchy and those of the ordinary folks in the developing and developed world, and did so with the thoughtfulness and elan that you would expect from a group that originally boasted Marshall McLuhan amongst its members.

But clearly any idea that stops our noble news and media industry doing whatever the hell they want (as long as it pays) was an idea too far, especially to the Reagan and Thatcher administrations. Rather even than be party to a non-binding declaration, they walked, taking funding that had been used to preserve sites of global historical importance, for instance those in Iraq that they destroyed in 2004. The UK eventually crept back on board the UNESCO train with Blair in '97, another of those far reaching events of the momentous first 100 days of Labour power. And, again, after the US (this time in order to lower our subs by a couple of £ billion).

The Paris UNESCO building itself is a venue designed for such deliberations. Huge hallways, armies of support staff, priceless artwork lining the walls and a (very good) restaurant on the 7th floor serving wine with a thoroughly decent lunch, it couldn't be more colonial if it tried. From the balcony you look over the carefully

maintained Ecole Miltarie to the familiar shape of the Eiffel tower; you see the European enlightenment and you see the Industrial Revolution - science, beauty, business and marketing, empire and military force.

The OER declaration, newly signed into being last week, takes us back to a similar set of arguments to those that caused all that trouble nearly 30 years ago today. Are we in favour of corporations in the developed world seeing the developing world simply as a new market? Or are we looking to encourage and support new voices and structures growing indigenously around the world?

It's a line that the OER movement has walked nervously, with the first rumble of concern being from Leigh Blackall over the cultural suppositions implicit within structured learning resources, usually at the low granularity end of the spectrum. But it is also a line that open-as-in-door MOOCs seem still to pass without thought. One of the most common statistic-oids thrown into presentations was that to cater for projected global growth in HE enrolment, we'd need to build X campuses, holding Y students every Z weeks (the actual numbers here are extrapolations of guesswork and are entirely unimportant. The important thing is that they should be greeted with incredulity. That's the pitch, see. The inevitable economic logic of OER.)

Clearly developing nations should be buying into experimental Western tuition models, rather than developing their own infrastructure and academic traditions. We don't want them to become too competitive, after all. Why shouldn't growing economies be building universities at such a rate? We've built a fair few during the 100-odd years we were a growing economy.

The language of the declaration (which, I should note, is non-binding on signatories) is very much "traditional OER". The virtues of open access to knowledge, supporting the world. You know the deal. But everything in the surrounding seminar was OER plus. How can we offer accreditation, testing- to OER users. How can we make our materials more sticky, get more views, get more feedback (or "improve the experience", as the pitch goes").

Don't get me wrong, to push OER to UNESCO declaration status is an incredible achievement - testament to the work of a small team based around Sir John Daniels of the Commonwealth of Learning. It remains to be seen what use is made of this opportunity - I know I've already benefited myself in being able to refer to a codified international policy statement around OER. But there again, I come from one of the great spiritual homes of Higher Education - I used it to prop up claims about the importance of the work I'm directly involved in.

For me the OERu undercurrent is a key indication of the way OER is moving, as my colleague Amber Thomas put it in an interview as part of the TOUCANS project led by Gabi Witthaus:

> *"One of the things that annoyed me about the OERu was this pressure to join. That's commissioning universities to join - saying we need specific stuff from you. That's moving away from the talk about OERs being voluntary at the institutional level if doing that makes sense to you. If it's about commissioning educational practices, I think it's OK*

> *but I think you can extrapolate out of normal OER models too far. They're sort of trading on the good will and momentum of OER under existing levels of release, and they're saying if you don't join in you're a bit selfish. It's the difference between sustainable development and commissioning."*

The OER declaration is a great opportunity to begin the growth of the next great wave of human thought. But if we just use it to take money out of developing countries in order to add another funding stream to support our institutions competing in an emerging market, it would be a profound loss.

OER - Supporting the student experience

We are, as we are continually told, in a new era of higher education management. The student is at the heart of the system, and all the decisions are based on a need to improve the student experience above all else. Because funding directly follows the student, plans are necessarily short term and thus unstable.

But what could have more impact on the quality of the experience than the staff that institutions employ who deal directly with students. Every aspect of the much-fetishised student survey returns to this need - calls for "better feedback" are calls for more time with academics, calls for "better resources" are calls for the employment of staff to enable and support access to resources. But staff - good staff, motivated staff, secure staff - represent a long term institutional investment.

People are expensive, but what people can do is beyond price.

This is in contrast with the nearly £700m that UK HE spends annually on commercially published resources. To be clear this is an annual figure - covering journal subscriptions, updated textbooks, access to digital resources and general academic and source publications. It doesn't, however, include the time that academic staff spend writing, updating and peer reviewing these resources (about another £130m just for the peer review).

These figures keep rising (I use 2010-11 figures in the paragraph above) - it is now fair to assume that UK universities contribute more than **a billion pounds** to commercial publishers. Each year.

I couldn't argue that we should cut all spending on library resources (and some of these are very very good resources indeed) - but clearly something has gone wrong here and we need to consider alternate models.

Enter Open Educational Resources. A way of replacing resource spending with investing in and empowering staff to create and share their own. Thus improving the student experience. For staff:

> *Engagement with OER release generally has fostered reflection on existing teaching practice, increased technical skills, improved understanding of IPR and legal aspects, improved use and application of licenses and changes in content production processes.*

Or so an independent report into three years of UK OER activity claimed. They make powerful and direct evidence-based claims about the impact of the work on registered (and non-registered) students:

> *Evidence suggests that registered students and other learners are gaining confidence through their engagement with OER, including greater confidence in their learning, increased use of online 'open' resources (e.g. YouTube views/followers), enhanced student projects, collaborations and shared initiatives, including internationally, such as blogging and OER editing/production.*

OER-related activity carried out by students alongside their tutors has been shown to be a truly transformative experience.

> *[O]ne of the most significant impacts of the UKOER Programme was evidence of the changing relationships between academics and students. This was also echoed during our interviews with selected stakeholders following the detailed survey and was highlighted by many as one of the more exciting and challenging aspects of change emerging from their activities. These changes have the potential to*

> *flatten the traditional hierarchy and change the balance of power in learner/teacher relationships.*

There is much more on this, and I would recommend reading the amazing report written largely by Lou McGill and Allison Littlejohn.

So, to conclude - OER (and UKOER) has been - and continues to be - an enormously positive experience for academic staff and students. It is breaking down traditional boundaries, supporting independent and project learning, and offering staff the confidence and respect that their amazing work deserves.

All this on around £5m each year for three years. Funding which has now ceased, though the activity and associated benefits continue to be realised.

If I were asked whether OER or commercial publishing has had a more positive impact on the student experience - there is only one answer I could possibly give.

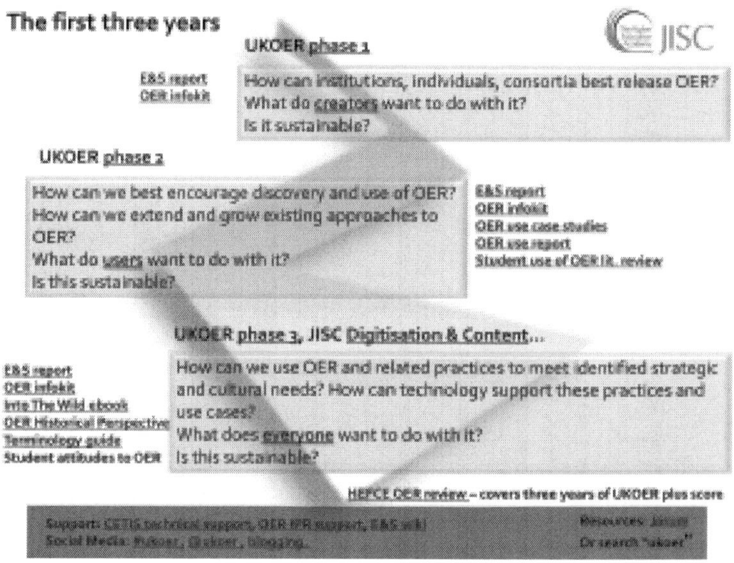

For a few dollars more? - OER, reuse and value.

Allow me to start with a (deliberately) controversial statement: "**The resources themselves are the least valuable aspect of OER, and academic reuse is the least valuable aspect of these resources.**"

I don't propose to be able to defend that entirely - but it is indicative of the way my mind is moving after reading a wonderful post by Tony Bates yesterday, and continuing to reflect on David Wiley's position and the findings of the UKOER Evaluation and Synthesis final report.

As someone who is involved in a major funded programme of OER release, **I want to be doubly clear that I don't think that this work has been a waste of time - or that the content created is without merit, or that current investigations into content reuse are worthless.** Far from it. I'm more inclined to believe that that what we have gained from our work is not what many people have argue that we have gained. It is far, far, more.

OER is interesting - as a **concept**, as a **process**, and as an **entity**.

(image credit: cybermule [from personal archive] - obvious nod of the hat to Sergio)

As a **concept**- and as Joss Winn and Richard Hall have argued- it poses serious questions for our understanding of what education is, and what institutions should be doing. Both in grander terms, concerning our understanding of knowledge and the value our society accords to it, and in less radical everyday thoughts about attribution, and how we discover and use material. I think that the volume of critical thought that OER has already created is immensely valuable - it has served as a genuinely new contribution to the age-old "purpose of education" debates, which are becoming increasingly essential in a higher education sector dealing with rapid transformational change. As a **process**, OER pushes consideration of intellectual property and pedagogy into the creation of materials for use in teaching. It makes us consider how much effort we put in (or don't) to ensuring that we have the best possible teaching aids for use with our students. And it engages what used to be the sole academic - working on their own to produce a hand-out, slides or a complex tool - with both the idea and the actuality of a community of practice, doing the same and similar things. This is the theme that I don't think many have focused on (though the OPAL project is a visible and notable exception) but it is where we are seeing a lot of movement. If you are engaged with OER creation, it becomes a part of your use practice. From properly citing images used on PowerPoint slides, to automatically searching for open resources as a preference, to thinking "could I create this in such a way I could release it openly" - involvement in or engagement with OER "release" fundamentally changes your "use" practices.

As an **entity**, an OER is available for use and inspiration. It can be modified, it can be altered, it can be used within agglomerations of material from a variety of sources, modified and republished. It can be linked to as part of a course. It can also be read and recreated (partially or fully), or read in order to inspire work in a particular direction. And all these things can be done by everyone, not just academics and students.

And, as David Wiley says- most of the "entity" points are also true of content that is simply visible. Not all (not the ones in the first line), but certainly the most common ones. I've been around the loop before concerning the long term (10yr+) goal of the UK government to see academic sharing as common practice, and (outside of a few excellent examples around community based projects like Humbox and Connexions) this has not been a resounding success. I don't go as far as

David does regarding openness being an additional production cost - academics produce resources anyway (which is where the cost is) making these resources OER at this point of creation is trivial - at most a few dollars more for 5 mins checking a license. You could even argue that making resources that are not usable by the whole world is a (substantial) additional production cost!

But I do agree that it is an additional attention cost. And I think that this is entirely a good thing. OER creation focuses attention on IPR and pedagogic choice. Precisely what we want academics to be thinking about when creating resources, and if we are connecting people together as they create (through a community like #ukoer on twitter, Humbox or something else), even better. And if we are contributing to discussions on the future of HE by doing so - fantastic. Note that none of these benefits require the actual availability or find-ability of OER - this is almost like a potential additional benefit. And this potential additional benefit is primarily to people outside academia entirely, or students new to academia- people who otherwise wouldn't have access to that knowledge or that opportunity for learning. Wikipedia (and similar projects) fulfil a lot of these needs, and the growth of academic input (rather than hostility) is welcome. But sometimes actual academic resources - short paper, annotated diagram, lecture recording - can go further than that.

Academic reuse - its long-tail, at best. There is a chance that there will be something useful, but as the needs of educators are so varied, no more than a chance. It's worth looking - but it's equally possible that building your own materials is the best option. As Tony Bates concluded: OERs need skill and hard work to make them useful [to others], and selling them as a panacea for education does more harm than good. OER reuse will make some things easier for some academics, some of the time.

But is this our only reason for releasing content openly? The concept and process benefits are already being seen, as are (increasingly) the benefits to independent learners and new students - the entity benefits to academics are too but on a smaller scale, and will take time to become fully understood. Have we got the luxury of the time needed to make that argument, and explain why it may be of lesser impact than many initially suggested?

When the chimes end, pick up your gun.

MOOCs are dubstep: how big money changed a small scene.

Those big "M" MOOCs, xMOOCs, "open-as-in-door" MOOCS, call them what you will are not going to go away, but neither are they going to take over the world. They're a bit like dubstep (bear with me here). Basically:

- A group of early pioneers based around a local scene begin interesting experiments.
- Via the web it influences like-minded people globally.
- Certain influences seep in to the mainstream
- Big business sits up and takes notice, they attempt to sign up and create people who are more marketable than the early pioneers
- The most obvious and striking features of the original underground are copied, over-used and drained of meaning. The subtlety and mood is forgotten.
- People are ashamed to admit they like the style, because in most people's heads it is associated with a multi-million-dollar product which has nothing to do with the early stuff they fell in love with.
- the now-mainstream style percolates into other areas

(if you want to an easy intro around how that happened in dubstep, try the BBC R1 "Generation Bass" documentary. Here's the trailer.)

When, in February 2012, Global Industry Analysts Inc. suggested that e-learning would be a $107bn global market in 2015 (a little under half of the UK national deficit), they were examining a sector that seems far from the " cottage industry" derided by Sir John Daniel

(Commonwealth of Learning) in 2010. In a segment that extends from traditional higher education, through corporate training, to every aspect of adult learning and compulsory sector tuition, it is little wonder that one start-up has generated $16m of venture capital without even having a defined business model.

That start-up is Coursera, spun out of Stanford and now offering more than 30 classes, in partnership with big names like UC Berkeley, U Michigan and Princeton. The catch is: the courses are offered for free to anyone in the world who wishes to take them. And Coursera are just one of many.

Udacity have secured significant venture capital and private investment around a similar model. Sebastian Thrun initially led an experimental open course (again out of Stanford), before moving to a start-up phase.

The Khan Academy is a not-for-profit that has secured $150,000 in donations alongside a $2m grant from Google. The initiative was kicked off by one former hedge fund manager making cheap videos for YouTube, and is now expanding faculty, offering summer schools, and accrediting learning - supported by a $5m grant from the O'Sullivan Foundation in Ireland.

Harvard and MIT have sunk a combined $60m into EdX, a not-for-profit online learning collaboration offering open learners free high-quality materials and tuition alongside the option to seek certification for successful completion.

StraighterLine does not offer free content (there's a $99 fee for "all you can learn"). But it boasts content from many notable private US institutions and Pearson, infrastructure from Blackboard, and easy transfer of credit gained into a range of accrediting partner colleges. It aggressively markets itself as an alternative to traditional university study - "the shortest distance between you and your degree". It has already raised $10m in venture capital.

The OER University (OERu) is a collaboration of a number of institutions internationally, intending to offer free materials and volunteer support, alongside supporting paid-for assessment and accreditation. It has not (yet) received venture capital, but has worked to closely integrate itself with influential international bodies.

Browser company Mozilla are developing a system of "Open Badges", allowing learners to reliably "show what they know", as validated by a range of non-education experts including NASA, Intel and Pixar/Disney.

And there are many, many other examples of initiatives attempting to short-cut the existing Higher Education system using online tools.

So the question is not "how can open online learning succeed?" the question has become "given open online learning, what should we be doing?"

But for all Peter Theil's dire warnings, there's only one group of people chucking millions of dollars at start-ups with no viable business models.

In the words of Cathy Finn-Derecki: *"It looks like the anxiety-provoking media coverage about "the latest web thing that the cool schools are doing" speaks louder to these business-types than the actual business of teaching and learning, and that's pretty darned sad."*

However, if money does talk - why do we hear so little in the mainstream press about the MOOC that raised hardware costs and more via voluntary contributions from course adherents?

Traditional higher education needs to be involved in experimenting with and analysing this model. But no one would recommend a wholesale adoption. The business-backed MOOC movement may change the higher education landscape, but it will not obliterate it.

And even if you don't think you like dubstep, you're probably hearing the influence and effects of the early pioneers in the new music you *are* listening to.

Misattributing cyber-lawyers, Wilde on twitter and a TINA turn - free culture and value

Like most memes, it's difficult to trace the source of "if you are not the customer, you are the product". Often linked, vaguely, to google, the earliest citable source I can find is a 15 June 2011report of a conference at Harvard on "hyper-public spaces". Jonathan Zittrain, director of the Berkmann Centre for Internet and Society is quoted as saying "If what you are getting online is for free, you are not the customer, you are the product.". However, an earlier (23 Nov 2010) Lifehacker article cites a Metafilter user, blue_beetle, as the 26 August 2010 originator of the idea, simply stated as "If you are not paying for it, you're not the customer; you're the product being sold.". His real name is Andrew Lewis (@andlewis), and - wonderfully - he now sells t-shirts with his much retweeted comment on, possibly having given up on the idea that free culture colossus Zittrain would send him some money/beer/whuffie.

[of course, awesome scholars such as Brian Lamb and Jim Groom- writing in EDUCAAUSE! - have traced the source of the meme back even further, to a 30 April 2010 tweet from Steve Greenberg (greenbes)]

It's one of those tilt-shift ideas that offers a new perspective on an old way of seeing the world, and as such has spread quickly through the twittersphere, fitting as it does neatly within 140 characters. One of the many things I love about twitter is the resurgence of the bon mot - should Oscar Wilde ever be reincarnated he would utterly kill twitter, the entire opening essay to Dorian Gray is pretty much the best tweetdeck column ever, as far as it appears to me.

Blue_beetle's comment began one of those long interminable metafilter threads about the redesign and adaptation of a then-popular web2.0 thing, in this case the user driven news aggregator, Digg. He got first comment too, itself pretty braggable. But fundamentally, the context was our right, as users, to complain about changes to a service that we are paying for by indirect (participation, personal data, unpaid creative labour) means rather than directly (subscriptions and such). If one user gets so annoyed that he tweets *"@kevinrose way to go ruining digg, now it's gay and ur a fagg."* (source of info about this erudite tweet: stavrosthewonderchicken), does the fact that he is not paying for the service with money mean that he doesn't have the right to speculate about the sexuality of the site and founder?

However, as the quotation has spread across the internet, it has taken on a number of utterly polarised inferences. It can be read as a cheesily alternative hipster *"corporations are, like, really terrible"*, or a neo-liberal *"you freetards gotta learn that you're still paying, just in another way"*. Like Wilde's bon mots (or his US near-contemporary, Mark Twain), it is used by just about everyone, to back up just about any position concerning Stuff on Teh Internets and the Paying For It thereof.

Which brings me to @ambrouk giving "The OER Turn" a spin on the JISC InfTeam blog. For the non-believer, Open Educational Resources are an excellent microcosm of the wider debates about free and libre online, debates I've touched on in my attempt on the old post-scarcity warhorse.

Simply put, the idea of someone putting the byproduct of their intellectual labour online for people to do stuff with for free breaks pretty much everything we think we know about economics. Not just bends, or challenges, actually breaks. The two generalised responses to this are:

(i) the paper-over-the-cracks model where we sprain pre-frontal lobe-strings talking about the place of value within a system with the whole customer-or-product thing (or arguing that the system itself constitutes value) and start pretending advertising as a revenue model makes any sense whatsoever.

(ii) the "OK, this is something new" model where we realise how little we "get" about human motivation. And start watching. And learning.

People in the west tend towards (i), bowing to another staple un-citable "it is easier to imagine the end of the world than the end of capitalism". This is especially true within the OER movement, where people are acutely and uncomfortably aware that somebody somewhere, be it Hewlett, Gates or the Government, is paying for all this. Therefore, goes the rhetoric, we need to show them that the practice has impact: so we firstly skew our practice to be somehow measurable, and secondly we spend time, energy and (someone else's) money measuring it. And if we show them impact, then they will give us more money. Apparently. This is also where the customer/product idea comes back in too - if in every interaction we are either a customer or a product then - hooray - we've saved capitalism for a few more months.

But if you look at, say, university funding in the UK (just to pick a topic at random), you'll see that the sector has done a sterling job in demonstrating return on investment. This has not stopped lead funders (the UK government) from screwing the system up like an old fag packet and bringing in something a bit more, y'know, private sector. Funders do not listen to return on investment arguments - which is good news as it allows us to build for genuine long term change under the guise of doing whatever it is they are fleetingly interested in. But bad news for people who want to build return on investment arguments based on ideas of what funders might want to hear - especially if they are wrapped up in TINA arguments of "valourise or die".

Polishing this off in my usual apocalyptic mode, we've really not got long left with this old free market stuff. If you want a tweetable from me: it's not a recession, it's the real end of boom and bust. I guess we've got to start using any resources that we have to think about alternatives, and the open availability of the knowledge and expertise that humankind has developed during this failed market experiment is an essential starting point. As Brian Lamb puts it "it is almost criminally irresponsible to hoard knowledge" - now, more than ever. Put simply, what if during our online lives we were neither customers, nor products? What if we acted like we were human beings?

Disruption over before it began.

After I write a paper, or a blog post, or a tweet even - it is common practice to read it through. Not just to pcik up typos, or to rethink my legendarily - and, infuriatingly to press office friends, needlessly - complex sentence structure: but to ensure that what I have written actually makes sense and doesn't contradict itself.

It is the latter of these that Clayton "Disruption" Christensen omits in a recently published screed over at the Boston Globe. CC, for those just joining this ongoing tale, has form in pivoting away from his ideological love-child and declaring that the future of education is "hybrid".

"Hybrid" - in this context, is using technology alongside traditional classroom based instruction. It's a retreat from the wider "disruption" idea that lower-quality, low-cost provision will undercut existing courses and institution, in that it sees the institutions as being complicity in their own disruption. (again, we're in Von Hippel territory, where innovation is driven by actors already in this space.)

But anyway. Read it through and answer this question: does Christensen think that MOOCs have failed or succeeded in disrupting education?

He starts of suggesting that it is too early to say - a fairly weak claim that "[the MOOC] *potential to disrupt is only just beginning to be seen*".

But a few paragraphs later we have "*Without even competing directly as true low-cost substitutes, MOOCs have managed to generate price competition previously unheard of among traditional campuses*". MOOCs, apparently are responsible for all cost reductions in higher education.

That's a hell of a claim. MOOCs did all that? But it gets worse:

> *"Free access to content from prestigious institutions revealed that content didn't need to be proprietary"*

Let's ignore, for the sake of clarity, that this is proprietary content, owned jointly by said prestigious institutions and MOOC platforms. Let's also ignore the fact that it is not reusable content, in that you need to seek permission to reuse a MOOC video (and why, seriously would you want to - it is not what it has been designed to do?). Let's talk textbooks. Let's talk academic papers.

Proprietary content is, like it or not, a part of education despite the efforts of the likes of David Wiley and David Porter to develop OER textbooks. And, most likely, it always will be. Different content formats and ownership structures will likely establish themselves - but all of these are windows into the decidedly non-proprietary sum of human knowledge. Unless we get the wholesale IP reform I am hoping for, we're stuck with paying (at some point, in some way) for the efforts of those who curate and display this knowledge.

Same paragraph:

"Despite the intense trepidation that technology would somehow replace teachers, it became clear that MOOCs didn't pre-empt interaction; instead, they forced more contact and accountability on both the student and the teacher."

MOOCs actively pre-empt interaction, contact and accountability between the student and the teacher! This is why there's all the (nonsensical) talk about AI, and all those experiments with peer assessment. MOOC courses are pretty expensive to develop, but the one key cost saving as against traditional provision is that you can run much higher staff:student ratios because students cannot contact their tutors. (Let's leave whether or not this is a good student experience to one side for now). So a completely false statement.

> *"Faculty have also been forced to reassess how and why they teach the way they do. Some professors began experimenting with alternative models, such as flipped classrooms and other blended-learning techniques by taking advantage of readily available, open, online materials."*

Forced to experiment. Forced. Again Christensen displays a terrifying ignorance of the actual reality of modern academic teaching, which has been using flipped-classroom (seriously- "do the reading, come to the seminar" and blended learning are widespread) and related techniques for a long time. This experimentation comes largely from academic teaching staff taking pride in their work and seeking to improve.

> *"Udacity, for its part, should be applauded for not burning through all of its money in pursuit of the wrong strategy. The company realized - and publicly acknowledged - that its future lay on a different path than it had originally anticipated. Indeed, Udacity's pivot may have even prevented a MOOC bubble from bursting."*

applauds Udacity for totally burning through a hell of a lot of other people's money in pursuit of the wrong strategy and getting Thomas Friedman to hype it out of all proportion.

I'm not sure that the #thrunpivot has prevented a MOOC bubble from bursting. Enough people seem to be investing time and money in ensuring the bubble does not burst to keep it inflated for a few years yet before venture capital moves on. But here Christensen is implicitly agreeing that Udacity was right to move away from competing directly with institutions, not saying that the MOOC movement has been successful at anything other than generating blog posts and sarcasm.

> *"Oddly, bubbles occur when too many people are too right about the potential of something like MOOCs. The personal computer bubble of 1984 and the dot-com bubble from 1999 to 2002 epitomize what's known as "capital market myopia," when investors ignore the logical implications of their individual investments in the same business category. MOOCs could have easily fallen into a similar trap - it's difficult to imagine all the organizations receiving the enormous, collective investment in online learning ultimately succeeding."*

This is too good. Because everyone was *right* about the potential of the MOOC the MOOC did not achieve this potential. So if we all stop being *right* about the need to end the adjunctification of education and raise state funding for HE then it will happen?

I'd say there is - maybe - a space for one or two "MOOC "platforms offering adult-learning style course and selling tat alongside to pay the hosting bills. Maybe. But it is not a disruption simply because it is not attractive enough an offer to draw customers away from traditional education.

> *"In all likelihood, companies like Coursera and Udacity - Harvard and MIT's offering, edX, operates as a nonprofit - that started out as MOOC providers will eventually move away from certain qualities of the unfortunate acronym. "Massive" and "open" are not particularly conducive to viable or sustainable business models."*

Well there we have it, the Massive Open Online Course is the future.

This, if we are honest, is an admission that the MOOC does not work in this arena. What we are left with is the less exciting proposition that "if prestigious institutions continue to give us lots of exclusive content we can sell it cheaper and to more people than the institutions can."

Christensen tails off with some nonsense about courses not meeting the needs of employers, as if that were somehow the reason that wages are stagnating and opportunities drying up for highly trained and skilled graduates.

For all of the bombast around disruption as a theory it is a pretty bleak prognosis. Consumers make choices primarily driven by cost, it goes. Education is all about future benefit in employment. Employment in 3-4 years will look pretty similar to employment now, and employers are best placed to identify any changes.

Maybe the time has come, in these less than certain times, to replace the theory of disruption with something less certain of a future that looks much like a more miserable version of the present. Maybe employers - currently engaged in hiring less, laying off more and deskilling elsewhere, are not best placed to consider the future of employment. Maybe tuition fees are high by political choice, and we need a change of politics to lower them.

Bricking against the clicks?

> *"[There is] only one answer: really fix public education and give everyone equal opportunity. Present situation a crime against young."*
> *"[C]urrent technology-and its increasing diffusion among people in all countries-makes it possible to drive the marginal cost of each new unit of education, effectively, to zero"*
>
> *"Technology has transformed how we live and play and will transform how we learn."*

Not the words of inspirational keynote speakers at a recent open education conferences; the words of (in order) Rupert Murdoch (the CEO of NewsCorp), Michael Saylor (the CEO of Microstrategy) and the Governor of Florida, Jeb Bush. Murdoch had recently been visiting the Harlam Village Academy, a poster child" of this new wave of education and a favoured project of his (and Michael Gove's) friend, Joel Klein. Apparently, to become a "poster child" you need a 75% churn rate of teaching staff within one year - who knew? And you'll recall, of course, that Jeb and George W. Bush's brother (Neil) set up Ignite! learning: a digital content solution for learning.

The highest educational "marginal cost" is not, despite the efforts of many academic publishers, materials: it is salary. This is true in both compulsory and post-compulsory sectors. So all of those wonderful, inspiring quotes about technology "fixing" education above actually relate to the casualisation and de-professionalisation of educators.

This is a neat illustration of the bizarre educational confusion that the political right seems to find itself in. On the one hand we have the kind of techno-determinism above, on the other we have David Cameron's calls for a return to " real discipline", with pupils standing up when teachers enter the room (sorry, Daily Mail link). And you get the bizarre target-driving literacy drive via the medium of synthetic phonics, which is the favoured Conservative reading methodology for no adequately explored reason that anyone can see - indeed as far as I understand it most serious educational researchers see Whole Language and Phonic approaches as complementary. In higher education you see the split between railing against mickey-mouse courses like Golf Course Studies and in favour of vocational courses like, er, Golf Course Studies. Or the push for higher and higher academic standards, and the push for higher and higher profits and lower costs. With one foot in the imagined past, and another in the corporatised digital future, the only possibility is confused and ill-considered policy.

You'd be hard pushed to spot a unifying link between these seemingly diametrically approaches, and I've struggled with it for a long time. You can also add to this mix the emerging "sound-bite" culture of disruption and educational revolutions - easily grasped obvious interventions that can give the impression of activity where none is needed.

George Siemens' post from ASU Skysong Education Innovation Summit brought this all together for me. The whole post demands to be read, but one key point that stuck out for me:

> *"The best way for me to kill a conversation was to say "I work in a university". That would pretty much end things. The correct answer, apparently, was something like "I work for [foundation, bank, VC] and I want to allocate funds to this market""*

There's clearly little or no place for actual educators in this gold rush.

Which I guess is the point: all of the expected profits in this "market" would come from either employing less educators or from cutting the pay and conditions of existing staff.

Gary Matkin touched on these wider issues in his should-have-been-a-keynote at the OCWC/OER 2012 annual conference in Queens' College, Cambridge. His characterisation of the commodification of education shifting the value proposition from product to service a parallel to Cable Green's vision of a pay-to-graduate future which was (@dr_neil) Universality in a nutshell - and that he seems bizarrely proud to have had mentioned in Money Magazine.

I commented on this trend in my write-up of the OCWC11 conference as the "search for a new model" and the "growth of private sector competition". This is no longer a trend, this is mainstream open education.

Panagiota Alevizou in my other favourite conference presentation (excluding of course, the amazing #ukoer stuff), looked at the way academics are reacting to the commodification implicit within open release using the language of mediatization. Clearly the role and language of the consumer of free "online learning media" sit uneasily within education:

> *"[E]ducators' prior knowledge and familiarity with Web 2.0 or technical skills, as well as wider OER advocacy agendas or general familiarity with openness and crowdsourced education, are also high in the motivational threshold." [but] "The sharing of one's own materials and the reuse of others' OERs is less expansive"*

Whereas the rhetoric of openness is superficially attractive to those committed to sharing knowledge, there are also concerns around precisely this kind of commodification within mainstream educational discourse. As nearly all the presenters at cam12 conceded, in an atmosphere that at times seemed more like a revival meeting than a sober gathering of academics from 21 countries, open educational resources are inevitable; however this is much more so than the institutions that sustain the academics responsible for releasing them. The developing business models around "open" and "technology" need urgently to take their own parasitic nature into account.

The student as labourer-consumer

One of the odder beliefs that our culture seems to have developed about markets is the idea of market efficiency. Specifically, the idea that - given the publicly available information presented at the time of action - the actions of any given player in a market are unable to offer greater efficiency than the average of the actions of all players within that market. Or, to stick this in non-economist language, if everyone has access to the same info then no-one has an advantage.

Prices are "imagined" (there really is no better word) to reflect the sum of relevant available information. So, if we know that over the past 10 years, graduates have earned x times more than non-graduates, we would make a choice of whether or not to invest in a university course based on that knowledge - thus the price of university education (in a free market) would reflect the availability of this knowledge.

You can already spot where this falls down. Firstly, as they used to say on the radio adverts, past performance does not indicative of future returns. Secondly, I (as an uber-HE geek) would be making my decision based on a substantially greater set of information, and more importantly a substantially greater understanding of the relative value of said information, than someone with no access to that level of geekery - so I get an advantage over someone like my 17-year-old self who was the first in their family to attend university.

Government action in England has so far attempted to address the second of these issues - committing to the provision of a "key information set" (KIS).This covers vital stuff such as reported student satisfaction with teaching, course contact hours, accommodation costs and the average graduate salary. Let's leave aside the practicalities both of collecting and comparing this information - issues that are being worked on assiduously and carefully by staff within institutions, HEFCE and the government - and ask the fundamental question of whether this is good information to base an investment decision on.

There's a whole (and scary) field of study around the idea of "human capital", which suggests ways of making decisions concerning precisely this kind of personal investment. Broadly speaking, you can contrast the idea of potential labour (one's ability to do something considered useful to a person who may want to give you money to do it) with actual labour (getting on and doing stuff to get paid). Education - within this model - is an investment in potential labour, giving one the ability to achieve greater benefit from actual labour. It's vanishingly rare that I get to write a paragraph that both Adam Smith and Karl Marx would agree with, but there we are.

Where I would depart from both is to postulate that the accumulation of potential labour is in itself actual labour. Education, I would argue, is an active process, and one of the great tragedies of the contemporary marketisation of learning is that it is widely assumed that it is passive.

Passive accumulation of benefit is easy to price - it's like restaurant food. A price is stated, I pay the price, and (usually) get the pizza as specified. If I pay more for my pizza I get a better experience, either better quality, larger quantities or more convenient delivery. Nothing I personally do (within reason) affects the experience I pay for, or the benefits I get from it. So I can make a decision based on my needs and requirements, taking cost and other relevant information into account, and I'm happy and pizza-filled. And the pizza restaurant owner can decide what to offer me, and at what price, drawing on similar historical information.

Active processes are more difficult to conceptualise, and they are problematic to assign value to in marketised systems. You could see exercise (to exercise off all this pizza) as a potential worked example. There are a whole range of gyms I could join, using everything from price to available equipment to the relative attractiveness of the clientele as criteria. Or I could not bother. The amount of my financial investment in exercise is markedly less relevant to my success than the amount of personal effort I put in. I could join the most expensive gym in Bristol and sit around drinking smoothies and ogling, or I could pay nothing and go for a brisk walk every morning. Gym owners can tell me all kinds of stuff about the historical success of their clients and the facilities available to me, but if I only use the juice bar I don't get any of those expected benefits.

So the best I can hope for from university education is that it gives me the tools I need to actively get myself to the place I want to be. I can't blame the university if I don't get there - I can only blame myself for not putting the work in, or for not choosing to buy the tools and support I needed. But what information would I need to make an informed choice regarding which tools and what support I needed?

The information set I would need would be wide-ranging, and quite possibly unique to me. I'd want to put a lot of faith in my own aptitudes (and would be interested in ways of measuring these to gain a better understanding of what these really are), and ways in which the labour I would be undertaking is matched or not to these aptitudes. This is not to trivialise the aptitudes I would gain during the course, indeed these would be brought more closely into focus by my knowledge of any disparity between the two - I would also have a clearer insight into the support I would need to be offered to support these.

But labourer-consumer also works as a passive model. Within the late-capitalist conception of higher study students are indeed paying to work - to work after graduation in a more remunerative (or, less often, a more satisfying) role. But this higher payment is a speculation - more simply, a gamble - in that a student will have no way of knowing whether such a role will be available to them at such salaries at the point of graduation. This is also seen in other careers where candidates are expected to pay for their own training, most notably with commercial pilots. New pilots are paying to be exploited by prospective employers (little info is available online, but £50,000 seems to be a frequently quoted figure on fora), without any personal growth that would be attractive within another field (a pilot's license is pretty useless to a bus driver, though rates of pay are fairly similar.) This is the danger of seeing education as passive, it becomes the accumulation of competencies linked to actual (or perceived) employer needs.

I'm far from convinced that paying to work is a helpful development within the history of labour relations. Whether Higher Education can make it work will be linked to how far away they can move from a passive model of education and towards something that offers active personal benefits.

Open as in door or open as in heart?

A note on the end of Steve Carson's post about MOOCs and the liberal arts prompted a brief conversation about the two different meanings of "MOOC" with Brandon Muramatsu. Steve's original post drew (based on his conversation with Brandon) a distinction between the Edx/ Coursera/ Udacity "MOOCs" and the Change11/ ds106/ wileyMOOC "MOOCs" - he suggested using MOCs as a description of the former (as they are not, in the strictest sense, open). But Brandon felt, on reflection, that the real distinction concerned how massive the courses were.

As a primer for those of you who read this but don't live it (you lucky people!) MOOC stands for "Massively Open Online Course", basically a big global chunk of online learning that doesn't cost you (the learner) any money. It's the big noise in university-level education as it's got that game-changingy disruptive innovation feel about it right now.

At the basic level, you could just take your standard online course (crappy managed learning environment, some professor doing a video lecture, discussion forum with tumbleweeds (*) and take off the paywall. Obviously everyone involved still needs to get paid (because isn't that what game-changing disruptive innovation is all about?) so there are a range of models around to ensure that this happens. Most commonly you'll see lots of advertisements everywhere, because that's totally a sustainable business model, or the "open" students getting to pay for accreditation or similar extras.

These get called MOOCs because of some earlier work (Siemens/Downes/Cormier/Wiley and so on) that also involved learning for free, coined the term, and the four words in the acronym seem to fit. But really there is not much else in common. The earlier MOOCs were built around the ideas behind connectivism, which could be (slightly controversially) unpacked as the suggestion that much valuable learning happens because of the connections and networks that learners build during a course. If you want to disappear further down this rabbit hole of networks and educational theory, check out rhizomatic learning.

So - for your first version above you could see something like:

learner ->guy(**) in a suit who used to lecture in the ivy league ->knowledge

and for the second an unASCIIable mess of learners connecting to each other and discovering knowledge in all kind of places, with a smelly hippy educator generally helping out and making sure it all stays lovely.

But fundamentally there are two kinds of MOOC because there are two competing cultural conceptualisations of the learning process, both of which have value and relevance but which have become politically (small P) polarised. The first, I guess, is easier to monetize as it treats the idea of an expert as a saleable resource.

Hence my categorisation, drawing on Stallman's legendary "free as in freedom/free as in beer" (libre/free) dichotomy.

Some courses are open as in door. You can walk in, you can listen for free. Others are open as in heart. You become part of a community, you are accepted and nurtured.

For many the first is and will be enough. For me, having tried the second, I'm not sure I could go back.

(*) no. not your online course, that's great. It's just all the other ones.

(**) and it is always a guy

The OER spin doctor on the wheels of steel.

As @josswinn frequently reminds me, OER is political, in terms in how it stands both within and against the prevailing ethos of marketised education, and in the way it is (at heart) a personal choice with wider political ramifications, taking in debates about work and labour, intellectual property and ownership, and the nature and purpose of the institution of academia.

As an essentially transformative political idea, it needs help to gain ground in areas where diametrically opposed opinions have long held sway. I've been wondering if we couldn't be doing a better job of getting our key messages across using a well chosen metaphor in the grand political spin-doctor style.

Our Coalition overlords provide an awesome example of what I am looking for - how many times have you heard, in the context of the national debt, the UK compared to a poorly managed household budget, where belts have to be tightened? Hundreds, thousands? It works because it connects something theoretical and abstract with something real and concrete which many of us will have experienced.

It models a response in a new situation from a response to an old one.

However metaphors work both ways. You could argue that this choice of metaphor tells us more about the background of Gideon Osborne and colleagues, multi-millionaires who have never had a mortgage, much less a personal cash-flow problem. And you'd maybe suggest that a family having difficulty paying a debt may look to earn more money, or restructure their loan, rather than going without food and clothes.

There's a whole other blog post to be written about how wrongheaded and dangerous this concept is as applied to this situation. But despite this, a cursory glance at any set of comments on a Guardian editorial, or at Gideon's dire opening to his CSR statement suggest that it has had and continues to have a huge effect in shaping public opinion, and public responses.

The situation around the (re)use of OER in formal is slightly more obscure. What common experience do we have which models a useful response to OER by a teacher or lecturer?

Breaking it down, do we need to demonstrate that:

> * reuse is preferable to the creation of new content?, or
> * reuse is a part of the creation of new content?
> * reuse is valuable because of the nature of the content, not the cultural frame of references?
> * reuse saves time and/or money?
> * reuse adds value to existing practice?

The CSAP OER team compared sharing and using OER to sharing and using recipes in cooking in a recent blog post, other responses to a request I made on twitter last week have included:

> *The Roman Catholic Church(?), ebay ; freecycle; comedy (parody / mimicry), music/theatre/dance, the use of the reference break in hip hop (the funky drummer), environment/energy areas, cooking, museums/ libraries (providing access to limited/rare things); (unhelpfully) teaching, mash ups (both in the hip-hop and web app senses), coding, books, crosswords, videogames (in jokes / references), boardgame design-.*

(hat-tips to the PatLockely/ xpert_project mindmeld, deburca,

BasCordewener and especially KavuBob)

There's some great (and very off-the-wall!) suggestions in there, but - to me - nothing that really captures what we hope OER reuse could be. Coding, the idea of code reuse being better than starting from scratch and the existence of stuff like Google Code, perhaps came closest - but is hardly mainstream to most academic staff. Music is another interesting idea, especially the use of famous sounds and loops(gratuitous link to what may well be my favourite website ever, mid-nineties HTML tables and all) - but how much of this is the musician remembering how a particular sound or style makes them feel in another context.

So much of cultural reuse is about the associations and resonances that a particular artefact has within popular imagination. I remember being in equal parts distressed and cynically impressed when I first came across DJ Yoda, cutting and pasting enough of any given genre or meme to allow an audience to recognise and respond to it, but without ever being anything other than a stream of references without a meaning. But OER isn't about the greatest hits of teachers, I see it more as an educational Pandora, where (unexpectedly) you find just the right thing-

The idea of "teacher as DJ" has been popular for a while, using images of bringing in materials from various sources to keep a thematic flow going. It's perhaps the closest we have come, but it may take a few more years in western culture before the DJ and the musician are seen as equally creative (though I'd argue the case for people like DJ Shadow as being worth several thousand limp-wristed indie kids in the creativity stakes). And are DJs not more concerned with entertaining their audience than in getting them to "understand" what they are playing?

"Teacher as DJ" says a lot about us too - the DJ is (very much) the "sage on the stage", setting the mood, introducing themes, calling for responses. The audience have little control over the experience, except to walk out in disgust. And the DJ (in popular imagination) has that insouciant air of unstudied cool that commands attention and respect without attempting to earn it. Is this how we see ourselves?

But somewhere out there is *the* killer OER metaphor, which would allow us to explain to people that "it's just like x", where x is a situation that prompts desirable outcome "y": which is a close analog to our desirable OER outcome reaction.

Cor baby - that's really free?

There's a new market price for learning resources. **Free.** So say (in the UK) the Guardian, the TES and now mobile network operator 02.

That's free as in beer, which is substantially better than £30 for a textbook. Isn't it?

For the uninterested end user (the same group who couldn't care less that Wikipedia is mostly CC-BY-SA), yes.

Unless they happen to feel that their personal information, contact details, browsing history and stated preference actually do have a market value beyond access to materials that are largely taxpayer funded anyway.

Unless they want to use the resources in unexpected contexts, excerpt from them confidently and stay "legal" whilst doing so.

Unless they have nagging suspicions that materials may be filtered, censored or altered by commercial entities who essentially see them as marketing tools.

Unless they want to share materials they have found with colleagues and friends outside of the provisions of the provided service.

Unless they don't want to advertise the likes of O2 in their classroom, feeling perhaps that learning and the support of learning is not a branch of marketing or PR.

Unless they happen to live or work outside of the UK, or whatever jurisdiction the material they want to use is available in.

Unless they happen to think that maybe, the knowledge build up by centuries of human endeavour belongs to everyone and does not need to be commodified and marketised for consumption.

This is the first great victory for free education. We've won - the open education, open everything, filthy-hippy team eduBeard have vanquished all before us. Yeah! We've broken publishing. The new model of knowledge sharing is here.

Now, do we need to get on and break marketing? Maybe take a few pot-shots at capital and the creation of value on the way?

Some would say that we don't. If there is no "value" in openness other than availability, we've completed our job and got the achievement badge. You can now get to learning materials at no cost to the end user. Sure, you may need to sign in, sign over your most valuable commodity (your information), abide by arbitrary rules, and surrender any thoughts of ownership, personal control or even long-term availability of resources. But that might be OK. That might be enough.

For those on the other side: You're going to be unpopular. The "no cost" argument is a strong one, as is the "reputational benefit to the provider". One has been lost entirely, the other needs some serious analysis. And some unattractive, almost counter-intuitive politics need to be communicated, jargon- and assumption- free, in an attractive way. Oh, and some of the best funded and most able marketing professionals will be ranged against you, as you attack the very basis of their value assumptions. It's going to be trouble.

My wife (a huge inspiration both professionally and personally) shared the following quote from Hunter S Thompson with me recently:

> *"So we shall let the reader answer this question for himself: who is the happier man, he who has braved the storm of life and lived or he who has stayed securely on shore and merely existed?"*

If we can't do it for the truth, and we can't do it for our rights, if we can't do it for the future, we should do it because it is going to be the loudest, lairiest, mind-blowing headfuck of a ride in the end of civilisation.

Because if this is what winning feels like, then I've been playing the wrong game.

Death Star Library

So Downes (and via Downes, Jim Groom) are hankering after the "subversive" roots of a MOOC movement that currently feels as edgy and relevant (and as exploitative and dull) as Starbucks. Reminding us that the original gameplan was to shake up those nasty elite institutions and bring new (and non-broken) education to the delighted and grateful masses.

Which might be true. In North America.

Some of us live in countries where Higher Education was free to those who could benefit, in living memory for someone in their mid-30s.

Here in the currently free nation of the United Kingdom (to give one example), the corporate hype behind MOOCs looks (and smells) the same as the hype that is pushing us to build a system just like the one that spat you out. The original wave of MOOCs (your connectivism stuff- well the ideas at least) felt like a reconnection with the earlier ideas of a system that could offer education to all. They felt like the tradition of university outreach and public lectures that have informed the UK system since before America. As in, before the European discovery of America.

We see the outsourcing of key activities, the encroaching managerialism, the flashy marketing that our institutions are beginning to undertake as just another wing of the ideology that brings us Udacity and Coursera. Maybe because other universities in other countries sold out so long ago it is easier for us to see.

What we had - what I benefited so much from - in the 80s and 90s has been under sustained attack ever since, by a shared ideology surmising that this education lark would be a nice little earner with a few little tweaks here and there. Every reform since then has been about making it easier to funnel government and student money to the private sector. Student experience is getting worse. Staff experience is getting worse. But that is not the point, it seems.

And when we see these VC-backed ex-academics, telling us that in 15 years there will be five institutions of higher education left, when we see journalists and analysts jumping on an easy answer that does away with academia almost entirely, when we see the very notion of "superstar lecturers" being taken seriously - we see the completion of this cycle.

It is easy to fall into the trap of assuming that your bad experience makes the system worthless. Your bad experience sucks - this is both true and lamentable - but it doesn't make the system wrong. It makes the influences and ideas that are slowly colonising the system a great risk that allows the same experience to be repeated again and again. This is modern neo-liberal education policy writ large - my experience was unsatisfactory, therefore the system is unsatisfactory, therefore the attractive shiny and hyped to the gills idea that is suddenly everywhere is the future. And education is fucking broken. Yes.

Modern-day universities suck. But *why* they suck has more to do with the same people that are selling us the new model than the people who are trying to maintain the old one.

Work needs to be done. But I am unable to agree that the answer lies in trying to subvert what already exists, because there is already an entire industry that has been trying to do that for 20 years, and they have already succeeded in destroying a lot of what was great about the old system. When we see academic conditions fall again and again, when we see new PhDs earning less than they would tending bar, when we see learners treated like numbers, we know that it could be better because in living memory it has been better. Maybe it is our memories we need to share with you.

Even the Death Star had a library. It was on Deck 106.

Roll your own university

One really positive outcome of the strife and argument around UK HE funding is the development of a number of prospective independent centres of Higher Education, such as the Really Open University and the Lincoln Social Science Centre. Coupling this with detailed cultural critiques of knowledge and education such as the University of Utopia and Dark Mountain - and the worldwide Alternative University "movement" - we seem to be living through a time when a serious contender to the traditional HE institution is emerging. (Indeed, for those who think an alternative movement is not truly established until it is co-opted by marketing practice, take a look at NotGoingToUni!)

However, one stumbling block that these otherwise excellent initiatives face is the currency of the degree itself. No matter the criticism that the "degree" is constantly under (arbitrariness, contentions over value and significance, increasing co-option by consumerist narratives, and over-emphasis on summative assessment as a measure of a formative process), it is still a legitimising agent for what is essentially a sustained focus on radical critique for its own sake.

Traditional universities discuss and promote radical and subversive ideas (alongside the vocational world-of-work stuff) but the fact that this leads to "a degree" gives students and staff the space and authority to do this.

So how could an alternative to University access this hegemonic legitimacy whilst not changing one single iota of their academic practice?

Why - by applying for UK degree awarding powers, of course!

BPP did it, as did Ashridge Business School. London Business School are doing it, also Pearson, Kaplan the London School of Management and Science-.

But there's no rule to say that you need to teach Business Management to apply. It's actually fairly easy to apply. The QAA have published some handy guidance to help you, as have BIS.

What it comes down to is 4 years of teaching to Higher Education levels, a robust system of management and quality assurance (including external examiner processes), availability of appropriate staff and learning resources and (sorry) £30,000 of cash, £40,000 if you want to award research degrees (MPhil, PhD) too. I can only imagine that the fee exists to deter speculative/poorly prepared applications - but I can appreciate that it will deter a lot of people who may not be able to raise that kind of money. The best one can imagine happening is some foundation or fund being set up to support this process.

Ignoring the payment requirement, I could imagine a lot of groups being in a position to apply:

- FE Colleges already delivering HE.
- Recently-closed (or under threat) departments and faculties from mainstream universities.
- Established collaborative (cross-institutional) entities.
- Social (peer) educators - such as School of Everything and P2PU.
- Global educators, if they can claim to be "based" in England or Wales (though the growth of online learning would suggest that this may need to be changed-)

- Trade Unions or charities

And broadly what they need to have in place (appendix A of linked document) is:

- A good quality system of academic governance
- Mechanisms of internal and external quality assurance
- Good staff with relevant experience.
- Availability of learning and teaching resources/infrastructure

I want to come back to this, and try and pick out in detail what would be needed for an application with a fair chance of success, drawing on publicly available and open documentation and resources where possible, and proposing potential alternative models. And I note that new guidance is expected imminently - probably in the forthcoming HE White Paper - so I will comment on these changes as well.

But the key message is that **you don't have to behave like a mainstream university to have degree awarding powers**, you don't even need to charge students any fees! - and that recent funding changes mean that new models are not only possible but inevitable. Let's hope that some of these new models are resilient and meaningful enough to do some genuine long-term good for UK society.

Investment analysis: Coursera or UK Higher Education?

It was with much fanfare that xMOOC big-beast Coursera announced that it has turned a small annual income, equivalent to a little over £140k, from its own activities. This represents the first gleanings of a return on venture capital estimated at around £10.4m($16m) over one year of operation.

However, Coursera also claimed an enrolment of 3.2m students worldwide, putting it at a similar size to the entire UK HE system. It was with this in mind I started on the partially insane task of doing a direct comparison of the two systems for investment purposes.

Throughput

The primary business of both systems is deliver courses (delineated units of learning) to students. UK HE claims just under 2.5m students - lower than the 3.2m students claimed by Coursera - but boasts a drop-out rate of just 7.4% (giving a total of 2,311,893 course completions). On the other hand, the drop out rate of Coursera is estimated at 95%, suggesting that around 160,000 students are successfully taught to the completion of a course of study.

These successful Coursera students are spread across 313 courses, which compares with 51,116 courses offered by UK HE. It is also worth noting that the average "course" of study in UK HE is three years in duration and leads to an internationally valued qualification. In comparison, Coursera offers courses lasting around 6 weeks, which do not currently lead to any recognised qualification.

The primary difference is in cost - Coursera offerings are largely free, whereas UK HE can charge up to £27,000 for a three year course (though this is paid via a government backed loan). The huge price differential (coupled with differences in the nature of the courses) suggests that there is little, if any, market overlap - despite many inflated claims about Coursera in the press.

Profitability

UK HE ran an operating surplus of £1.1bn in the year 2013, most likely down to a non-core income of £2.9bn from businesses and charities. This is based on a total income of £27.8bn from all sources, including students and government.

As discussed above, Coursera achieved £143,743 of total operating income outside of venture capital injections. For the purposes of this comparison we will call it an operating surplus, even though it does not take into account the return on investment expected by existing venture capital contributors.

UKHE therefore makes an operating surplus of £481.78 per successful student, compared to 90 pence per successful Coursera student.

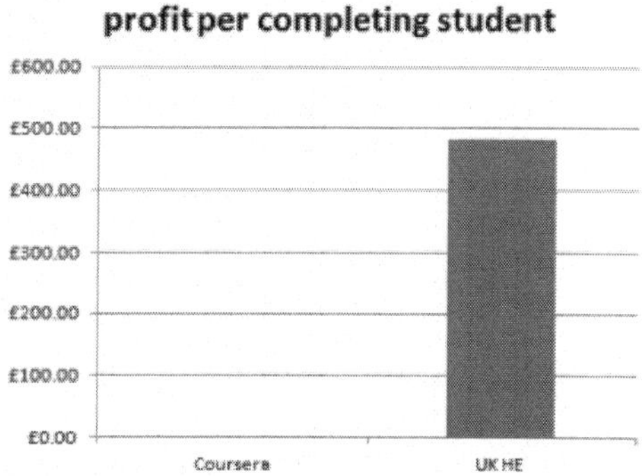

Product quality

Assessing the quality of higher-level learning often uses a staff:student ratio as a proxy for quality, drawing on decades of research. In employing 181,385 academic staff, UK HE can offer one educator per 14 students.

In examining the Coursera staff list, I was able to identify two (2) members of staff that I would consider to be academics - Prof Ng and Prof Koller. This offers a slightly less impressive 1 to 1.6m staff:student ratio.

UK HE is ranked highly by many global university rankings. Indeed, it contributes 11 courses to Coursera (which is famously selective concerning contributing institutions).

Product diversity

Coursera has begun to move into paid learning certification, and has partnered with ProctorU to provide paid proctored examinations which may lead to university credit. Income streams are limited to the purchase of additional premium services by students. But its primary assets are a bespoke teaching platform and the range of user data generated by its students (the latter may be monetised by selling to future employers, though this is not yet a proven market)

UK HE offers a huge range of courses at undergraduate, postgraduate, pre-university and professional development levels - both on and offline, along with a range of free courses aimed at community outreach. It has a substantial estate, which is used to generate income via event hosting and management, and is also active in research and development - winning contracts from private and government sources. Primary income is from tuition, and numbers and investment remain steady despite recent funding method changes.

Return on investment

On the basis of the figures presented above, for every pound of the operating surplus generated by UK HE, £25 has been invested (primarily by government)

For every pound of the operating surplus generated by Coursera, £73 has been invested (primarily by venture capital, who will be seeking a return on their investment). It is notable that Coursera must also return a percentage of any profit to institutional partners, as compensation for their investment of brand goodwill and staff time.

Other analyses

Financial ratings agency Moody's has recently downgraded the ratings of two UK universities (De Montfort and Keele) to Aa2, in line with their recent downgrade of the UK more generally. A third, Cambridge, maintains a triple-a rating. Despite this, the UK HE sector is clearly perceived as investment-worthy by Moody's - concerns are related to the activities of the current UK government rather than any failings within the sector itself.

Coursera has not been rated by Moody's as it has not issued - and is unable to issue - any bonds. It would be unable to raise money via this means as it has an insufficient credit history.

Venture Capital Analyst Sramana Mitra notes:

> *"What worries me about Coursera is that a high-growth business model has not emerged yet. How long will VCs continue to support the business under those circumstances?"*

Conclusion

I stand shoulder-to-shoulder with David Cameron (did I just write that?) and the rest of the UK government when I conclude that the UK HE sector represents a far better investment in this market. It is more efficient at providing courses of education - providing a wealth of diversity and choice, and an industry standard accreditation product.

It also has a greater diversity of income streams, and has shown long-term sustainability.

By comparison, Coursera appears to have significant issues with the viability of its core product. Student attrition rates suggest that although their courses are initially attractive, they have very limited long term appeal. Attempts to generate further income have centred on enticing completing students to pay for premium services rather than improving their core offer. I would see Coursera as a very high-risk investment, and one that already has a number of prior investors (financial and in kind) with a call on any ongoing profit.

I need hardly add that anyone taking investment advice from Followers of the Apocalypse probably needs to have a chat with a grown up first.

Screwtape opens up

I don't know why (Christian apologetics are not generally my bag), but during my break I picked up the classic " Screwtape Letters", by CS Lewis, and as I dropped off under the influence of a large glass of Old Pulteney I started to think about OER. I'm not entirely sure that "openness" is as black and white as theology, but if nothing else it was an interesting writing exercise. This is what I wrote:

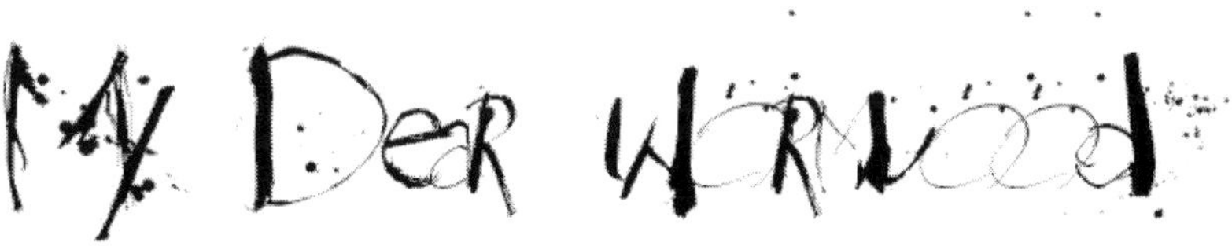

I note your concerns with interest. For the last century the Groves of Academia (such as they are) have been ours, and what delights we have tasted because of it! The twisted and confused soul of a pro-vice chancellor, whipped into a frenzy of self-importance both at his own cleverness and low cunning, the nutritious sin of a "star researcher" smugly full of contempt for his fellow toilers - what feasts they have provided, as I'm sure you recall from your late visit to Our Father's House.

Already, we are heightening the flavour of our next batch - pitting institution against institution, scholar against scholar, subject of study against subject of study; such delicious conflict, such fear, such snobbery, such self-immolation and despair! If all goes well we will feast again on your return, as richly and as lip-smackingly well as we ever have before, washed down with the finest Administrative Whines and accompanied with our latest delicacy, tweetbreads.

When seen against these plans, your worries about "openness" seem at best misplaced. Every time Academia have tried to "share" what they have learnt and what they know, for the good of humanity (and how sickening the thought of the Enemy's pleasure at such a disgustingly noble aim!) we have managed to distort this into the same old anxieties to lead them back to Our Father's arms.

Remember the worries when they started to publish their research in learned journals? We convinced them to sell the journals to our expert friends in the publishing industries. So they could be managed better - and so prices would be such that they could only be read in Academic Libraries. Then, with the growth of their Internet, we ensured that sharing and learning would be behind paywalls and authentication. Even when the Enemy caused them to rise up and demand to own the fruits of their own labour, we hid these "open" resources inside repositories of astonishing complexity and scale - this, coupled with our uplifting purification of the Academic language to ensure impenetrability meant that that a merely interested member of the public would have next to no chance of finding an academic paper, and next to no chance of understanding it if he did.

But to make certain our victory, we started to reward scholars based on the amount of impenetrable research they published on the "right" subject in the "right journals". The mechanics of human greed and aggrandisement are the most beautiful structures in the universe, and the savour of supposedly intelligent souls brought down by such supposedly base tools continues to spice our repast daily. Ah, such days!

I am certain you can adapt such tactics to your concern around "open educational resources" or "OpenCourseWare" (already a division - could you exploit this?) and that the list of suggestions that follows is superfluous.

1. My understanding is that a common worry in this endeavour is that of "sustainability". You will know that our disguises have meant that this once-innocuous word hides a hoard of potential - do ensure that your Openers think only of the sustainability of their work, their projects, their roles. To do this once again means competition, the very highway Below. If an Opener is to chance to reflect on the wider sustainability of society or what they thrillingly call "culture" and the need for academic knowledge to support this, a new call for funding or conference papers will soon remove that unprofitable line of argument from their mind.

2. Speaking of funders - it is essential that you cement within their minds the concept of "return on investment". Get them measuring, measuring, measuring! - who interacted with which resources, when, how and why. With luck you can get them to cancel the whole area of work as unprofitable - at worst you will be directing the majority of their attention to work that is of use to nobody and is never-ending (something that we have excelled at within so very much of Academia.). Never for a second allow them to dwell on serendipity or longer-term goals - you could easily ensure that funding is short-scale and must be re-argued for each year, for example. A deadline does much to allow us to work, as does the bringing of other pressures (such as the sterling work of our man Willetts) to bear. I am aware that

you and your fellow Tempters have found great cause to rejoice within the Browne Review - but unless we push on with the idea of continued crisis it may cause our Subjects to pause to contemplate the nature and purpose of what Education is for. Such thinking is seldom to our benefit.

3. If you are unable to do this, think instead of quality and the "student experience". Our project Apple - ah! that name! such rich symbolism- - has done much to conflate quality with a shiny appearance (and your cousin Grub has found much favour here Below for his part in this). As you know, there is no end of money that can be spent on getting the images, and the fonts, and the narration "just" so. Surely much of what is currently devoted to the fashionable cause of "open education" can be steered into this cul-de-sac - much more if you included the niceties of "pedagogic design" and "context". As above, your goal here should be to ensure that the least possible amount of funding is devoted to the release of dangerously simple resources.

4. Licensing, IPR - such sweet words to all of our kind. Imagine our delight to see that already there are more than a handful of mutually-incompatible open (and semi-open) licenses, and that confusion and concern are already sown. I hear in many places actual lawyers - often our most devoted servants - are involved in what was meant to be a simple and cheap initiative. Legal issues can be made as utterly impenetrable and eternal as the works of the Enemy, and I trust that you (after your sterling work with academic contracts of employment) will need little instruction here. Remind them of the specialness of their circumstances, feed their naïf insistence that nobody should ever profit from their work, and with the stroke of a pen they are yours.

5. As I have said before, *"We live in the Managerial Age, in a world of "Admin." The greatest evil is not now done in those sordid "dens of crime" that Dickens loved to paint. It is not done even in concentration camps and labour camps. In those we see its final result. But it is conceived and ordered (moved, seconded, carried, and minuted) in clean, carpeted, warmed, and well-lighted offices, by quiet people who do not need to raise their voice."*

Hence, naturally enough, my symbol for Hell is something like the bureaucracy of a middle-ranking Russell Group University. You may see this as an occasion for complacency, but stay on your watch - should one of these "Openers" get the idea of sharing knowledge into one of these interminable minutes the whole game is lost. Universities do what they do because of inertia and a misplaced love of tradition. If you can keep the emphasis on sharing as something new and alien you should effectively marshal opposition and prevent a decision being reached or recorded. Ideally we need working groups, if not consultants.

6. Most powerfully, of course, you have the sweet smell of hubris. If you can convince your subjects that their work is special, and unique, and most of all separate to other ways of sharing online we can ensure this potential movement becomes little more than an academic pipe dream. I do not need to underline the need to avoid, at all costs, the obvious mental link between sharing these resources and sharing other things. Separate conferences, separate funding streams - and above all a separate language - these are the tools that have brought about the successful fragmentation of academic knowledge. We would delight to see them work again here. Encourage also the "edupreneurs" (how I wish we had invented the word!) to see

openness as a means of profit, a means of fame and a route to further power.

Dearest nephew Wormwood, there is little to worry about here. What at first seemed a great defeat of so much that we have worked for is simply an opportunity for a greater victory. Vice is best disguised as virtue, and the clearest virtues hide the oldest and basest vices. Philanthropy (and is this not what we have here, simple, old-fashioned, disgusting, philanthropy?) is often selfish and nearly always public. And we can generally benefit far more than the intended recipients.

Your affectionate Uncle,

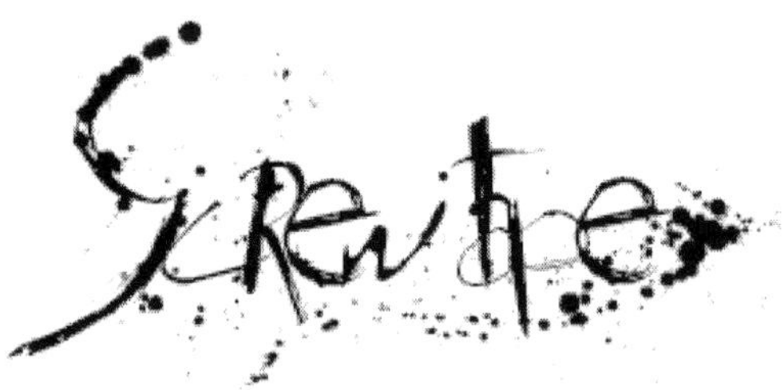

P.S: It also occurs to me that Screwtape would have made an excellent Programme Manager.

My openedspace

Just what is "Open Education"? How does it fit with everything else? This post is one of three exploring the same issue from the perspectives of Amber Thomas, Lawrie Phipps and myself (and hopefully, others-) as a part of Open Education Week.

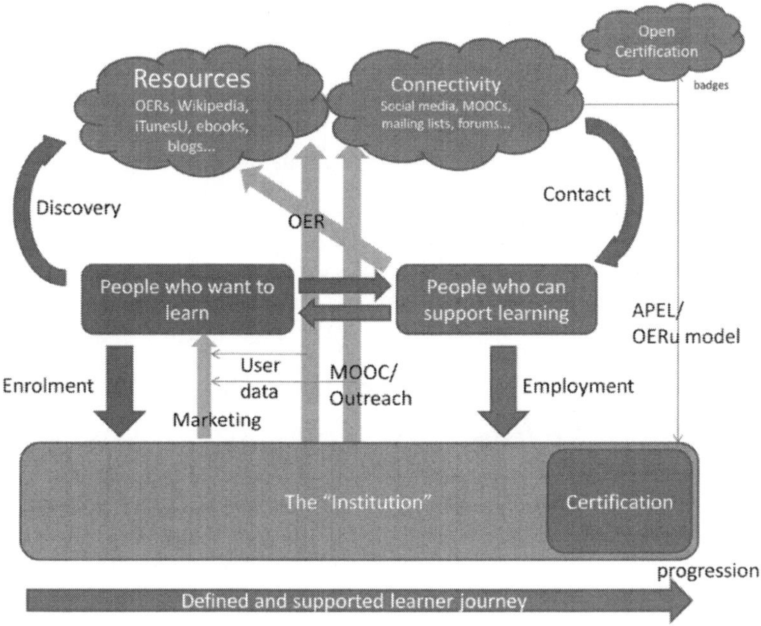

There are three things I really want people to take away from this very simple model.

Students are at the heart of the system

Institutions, certification and the "learner journey" aren't.

Learning is the creation of knowledge.

In trying to capture education in any kind of systems model, I'm unavoidably going to end up modelling a significant chunk of what we might call modern human civilisation. I'd be getting in to fairly fundamental ideas about learning as a thing that we do every day rather than as a discrete activity. In short I'm going to overreach my understanding and end up looking rather silly.

The basis for my own mental model of learning and resource sharing comes from the English Folk Music tradition. It often surprises newcomers to this area of culture that there is no canon - no agreed set of tunes, songs, stories and dances. Instead there are numerous competing regional and cultural traditions, and there are variations even within these traditions

Writing about this in "*English Folk-Song: Some Conclusions*", legendary collector Cecil Sharp suggested that "one man sings a song, and then others sing it after him, changing what they do not like". Rob Young, who recently produced a beautifully written history of interest in the English folk music tradition called " *Electric Eden*", explains the idea further:

> *"For [Cecil] Sharp, folk songs existed in constant transformation, a living example of an art form in a state of perpetual renewal [...] Don't seek the 'original' copy, insisted Sharp; focus on the transformations themselves - for they are the substance of the song"*

As soon as we start to record and fix songs - even if we take great pains to capture every variation we have discovered, we have lost what has made them live. Derrida neatly encapsulates this idea as *differance*. In any written or recorded folk music the subject is indeed "not present".

For me, the idea that one can learn any body of knowledge without knowingly or unknowingly altering it seems fundamentally improbable. And these alterations are not chance mutations, these are memetic improvements that are shared and disseminated - or discarded and lost. A history of knowledge would be a history of these refinements - their discovery, their use and their usurpation. And without this movement - this story - knowledge is simply memorisation.

Our modern cultural preoccupation with measurement and accreditation of learning plays against this narrative flow. Too often, I think, we are more concerned with the mastery of a body of knowledge (as if it were static and could be memorised) rather than the way in which the act of learning moves knowledge onwards.

I've interpreted learning as a refining cycle, drawing on resources and on means of connecting to people. Whether this happens within or without an institution is immaterial, the process is the same. The institution is simply and at best a wonderful box to protect and nourish the mechanism. And if our strange and graceful machines can change the shape and nature of this box: allowing the contents to be more visible whilst retaining the resilience, so much the better.

An institution can also steer and nurture enthusiasm, there are many paths that have already been taken and guidance about this should be welcomed. Because are our thoughts our own, or do they come from others? Clearly, the answer here is both - the limits of my reading do not halt my speculation, and my speculation often drives my reading. Surely, I quietly suspect, somebody else has thought about this stuff too?

At worst, the institution is a codification engine, a printer of certificates showing that an approved course through the sum of human endeavour has been plotted and measured. The ability to convince others that you and your thoughts are worthy of attention is perhaps the greatest of social skills - the examination is a very poor proxy measure for this, and the database query is an even poorer proxy for the examination.

Open learning - as painful as it is that we even need these terms - is natural learning. Or even folk learning. It is our own entry into a tradition that lives longer than us, than our cities and countries, than our economies and values. And accreditation? - accreditation is very useful to us as individuals in the short term. It currently has an enormous economic and social value. It is a worthy investment for the present. But we should not pretend that it has anything much to do with learning.

"I can see by the sadness in your eyes that you never quite learned the song"

I've been thinking more about my #openedspace post, and the can of worms I opened in acknowledging that many of my underlying ideas about the nature of the learning process came from folk music. I've been wondering what folk musicians say about learning, and how widely applicable this is.

Richard Thompson is one of those rare guitar players who is always worth listening to, just because no-one (including him) is quite sure what he is going to do next. He doesn't have a blog as such, but is endlessly quotable and keeps a record of these quotes on his website. I've always been attracted to this one:

> *"For me, the best feeling in music is when you're truly improvising and don't know where you're going, but you know you're going to arrive at an interesting place."*

This is a fine example of what I would call a benefit of higher education, the ability to follow any thread or collections of threads in the pursuit of knowledge. Improvised learning is that which is utterly learner-led and unbound by extrinsic motivation. A wonderful thing to aim for, but there is a lot of skill needed to get there. So does my underlying idea base itself on technical mastery of learning?

Dick Gaugan is a very interesting chap, with twin interests in protest songs and web accessibility. He's maintained a proto-blog since the early days of the web and one of his sporadic posts concern the limits of technical mastery. The closing paragraphs are worth quoting in full:

> *"Mastery of technique is not the job of a musician, it is merely the*

> *basic toolkit for learning to do the job of a musician. The most essential element of the job of a musician is the skill to intelligibly communicate ideas and emotion from the musician to the listener via sound. The absence of that means it is not music, it is a programmed sequence of noises, regardless of however pleasant and harmonious those noises might be.*
>
> *In the words of Mike Heron's Hedgehog Song, "You know all the words and you sing all the notes but you never quite learned the song . . ."*

A very odd song, but one chosen as a Desert Island Disc by none other than the former Archbishop of Canterbury, Rowan Williams. Who has also written and spoken a fair bit about learning, including a lecture to the Centre of Anglican Communion Studies in 2004 where he makes almost the same point as Gaugan does from the opposite direction. *"It is possible, you see, to learn quite a lot about let us say the history of music, about musical theory. It is possible even to recognise patterns of a page of black marks on a white background which tell you how a composition moves. But it would be strange, as I have said, if that were all pursued in the absence of any acquisition of a skill - any capacity to do something in a particular way."*

Both Rowan Williams and Dick Gaugan are arguing that learning requires both the mastery of a set of skills and the ability to set these within a wider pattern that can communicate ideas and emotion to others. However, much of current orthodoxy in educational policy sees the former as an end in itself, which is as unhelpful and uneducational as the occasional focus on the latter as the point of higher education.

But there is one key aspect of folk music missing from this picture, the idea of learning as the reinterpretation rather than the reproduction of knowledge. This is what I touched on in the #openedspace post when I quoted song collector Cecil Sharp. But Richard Thompson, in a song that is at once a folk song and not a folk song, expresses the idea thus:

"We used to say
That come the day
We'd all be making songs
Or finding better words
These ideas never lasted long"

There's been surprisingly little written about this idea of "finding better words", but it seems like it has a lot to say a mainstream education that is still reeling from the implications of the read/write web. An encyclopaedia that is rewritten by any reader to reflect their experience is, at heart, a very similar idea to a ballad or tune that is adapted by all those that experience it. In both instances, a certain level of technical mastery is required and a sense of the overarching pattern of the source material is required. Competence, Experience, Appreciation.

Or, if you'd rather: purity, truth, beauty.

The Future

Imagine universities of 2050

I really don't want to link to this post (from @popenici - and from which I have borrowed the title of this post), but feel I have to so you can have some context to why I'm writing this. I read quite a lot (OK, an awful lot) of HE and technology related blogs in my position as wonk-in-waiting, but I do tend to choose the vaguely politically and socially aware ones.

This is an example of one of the "others". Rather than pull it apart line-by-breathlessly-technodeterminist-line, I thought I'd write my own alternate version.

By 2050 "traditional" on campus attendance is increasingly rare. Not because of any explosion in technology-supported learning, but because the price of fossil-fuel derived energy is such that travel is essentially the preserve of the super-rich. So, largely, is the internet - with increasing attacks on net neutrality leaving the speed of non-commercial traffic unusably slow, even the ubiquitous, cheap low power devices left over from before the plastics rush are primarily used with offline storage.

A little over 2% of young people in the UK attend one of 20 or so traditional institutions. The benefits of doing so are primarily social, these are the sons and daughters of the elite, networking and pairing off. Most regular people experience post-compulsory education via employer training - which is increasingly rare and is very seldom accredited for transferable use. Low wages and long hours have effectively killed the personal learning culture (though the resurgence of trade unions has begun to correct this), and following the growth of corporate-owned schools since the launch of the "Free School" movement in 2010 few people have the skills or intellectual curiosity to learn outside of work.

Globally, the picture is broadly similar to the UK - though only in England does government spending on Higher Education top 5% of GDP. Nearly all of this is used to write off student loans against fees, taken out more than 30 years ago: due to mass unemployment and low wages very few of these were ever paid back. This led to sharp rises in initial fees for students, driving the majority of institutions out of business. Anyone who does study at a University does so in one within their own country - international travel is rare and very expensive.

For a while in the mid-late teens, there was an explosion in online learning, but this tailed off as a tightening of financial margins in traditional institutions meant that the largely voluntary content development and student support processes stopped being supported. Increasing corporatisation of internet connectivity rendered online discussion prohibitively expensive, with both Facebook and Twitter closing accounts belonging to low net-worth individuals in 2019. The demands of advertisers drove this threshold up sharply, until the Second Great DotCom Bubble of 2020 and the collapse of Google rendered the old "free" internet largely unviable. Most connectivity these days is via single use applications able to link to resources on only a small number of severs.

In the corporate training world BlackBoardSharePointPearsonNewsCorp is the dominant provider, delivering an end-to-end managed hardware and software ecosystem for direct delivery of information to staff. It's very much on a just-in-time basis, with content being key and having more in common with the manual than the textbook. BBSPPNC is most people's only contact with online information other than paid-for access to traditional mass media (news, television, music) and email/IM.

In many ways, the world of 2050 has more in common with the world of 1950 than any intervening time. Years of austerity have depleted public services and social mobility, and standards of living are broadly similar. The expected growth in new industries was stifled by continued economic stagnation - most jobs in 2050 would be recognisable to a visitor from 1950, with manufacturing, small-scale farming, mining, heavy industry, and service industries (including security and medical roles) being primary employers in the UK. Welfare is next-to non-existent, and extended family living is now normal, with most people born in 2050 expecting to die within 25 miles of their place of birth, 50-60 years or so later.

It may be already clear that only those who are not in thrall to the dying myths of the age will be able to see the 2050 as anything other than a slightly enhanced version of life a century ago. Institutions (and countries) aware of their supposedly crucial importance to knowledge generation, innovation and their overall contribution to society and economy have no time to waste if they want to be part of the scene in 2050. This is why vision - and knowledge to achieve this vision - may be one of the most valuable commodities in 2012.

9 things to watch out for in 2014

1. **Virtual Reality**

A lot of people in education seem to be playing with Oculus Rift. At first look you'd be forgiven for thinking it was a retro-geek Virtual Boy, but Moore's Law has brought a greater degree of immersion and realism to the structure. The combination of immersion and haptic/gesture technology (the Xbox Kinect system going some way to normalise this) could be useful in simulations for medicine and engineering to name but two.

The overlay of information onto a live video image from a phone camera is another idea that may finally be having its day. Projects like Scarlet are using such technologies successfully with artefacts and images, a more focused implementation than the very early experiments of just overlaying Wikipedia on the view from your office window.

Those of us who have been round for a while will be thinking "second life" at this point - but given the experiences of stuff like fathom.com the xMOOC shouldn't have happened even slightly. I prefer to draw the analogy with the animated GIF - a supposedly antiquated technology that enough interesting people are doing interesting things with that it just might become unexpectedly everywhere.

2. **Algorithmic policy and the knowledge worker shift**

Gone are the days when you could look knowledgeable just by using the words "big data" in conversation. Without going through any of the usual meaning-making or testing processes, it suddenly is an (enormous) fact of life. I think 2014 will be the year when we see policy development staff begin to be replaced by databases. After all, if big data can reduce every problem to a bar chart, you don't need people to choose the option that the machine tells you will make the numbers go up.

Already we have machines that generate internet memes (often with truly terrifying results) as a warning regarding what can happen when you take humans out of decision making. One of your holiday tasks is to watch "All Watched Over By Machines Of Loving Grace" again. And start thinking about telling better stories about how humans add value to decisions.

3. **Data literacy**

Leading on from the above, those of us who wish to continue being knowledge workers need to start making sense of data (and for that matter finance, but that's maybe another story). If every policy position is "justified" by a slew of numbers, we need more people that can make sense of these numbers. Maths - naturally - is hard and we'd all rather be shopping or watching cat videos. But if we want to understand the decisions that affect the world around us, we need to learn to read numbers and to be confident in disputing them. Policy is now quantitative - we need to get better at teaching people how to participate.

4. **Personal data trails**

Our government's loan shark friends Wonga already mine social media data when allocating loans. Moves by Facebook, Microsoft, sonny and especially google (the so called "Nymwars") to use real names in online social interactions makes this process easier.

We've all heard the horror stories of graduates losing jobs because of photographic Facebook evidence of them enjoying themselves in some way. But the implications are greater than this. Slane Girl's youthful indiscretion would once have been something she regretted in the morning and laughed about ten years later - in 2013 she was named and pilloried within hours. One mistake, one unguarded thought expressed online, and your life could be ruined.

My own position has always been is that if someone wants to attack you, they will find and use something online. Without context, without human feeling, every tweet is a weapon that can be used against you. Perhaps 2014 will be the year that we can no longer convince our learners to share.

5. **Corporate courses** (or whatever happen to the MOOC?)

With Udacity and Coursera moving towards to the corporate provision that early competitor Udemy moved to a long time ago, and even newcomer FutureLearn trumpeting employer and industry sign-ups rather than participation rates (I wonder if 90% of employers will drop out in the first 5 weeks?) the "open" O feels like a very bad joke. But these entities aren't leaving higher education entirely in search of profits, they are attempting to destabilise one of the most profitable parts of it.

MBAs and related courses are a huge earner for traditional institutions, not least because fees are generally paid by employers and can be ratcheted up to astronomical levels without your average blue-chip blinking. They are usually bought for rising stars, but given the growing trend of treating generation X and Y appallingly badly it is not inconceivable that rising stars could be fobbed off with a bad video of Andrew Ng in the future.

Coursera have been making some noises about being a publisher, whilst actual publishers are diversifying into accredited awards and learning technology. Convergence, anyone?

Against earlier expectations, institutions are beginning to ask questions about exactly what they are getting from the MOOC platform they work with, given the amount of staff time and reputation (and often hard currency) they are putting in. But the "pivot" could be seen as a victory for traditional education, when it is just a better profit targeting system.

6. **Open classrooms**

The unexpected stars of the Reclaim Open awards have been "open classes" that run alongside traditional class tuition, but in multiple locations. The venerable ds106 (the weird uncle of the MOOC) has led this movement, with simultaneous iterations in institutions across the world and even inside corporate boundaries. Participants each benefit from participation in the global community around the course, with encouragement and peer learning key to retention.

Coventry University's Phonar, incredibly, is now delivered in hundreds of institutions in hundreds of countries around the world via the World Photo Org. And the FemTechNet DOCC (winner 3 of 5) has a similar nodal structure.

These programmes add value to the experience of traditional paying students whilst encouraging the world to join in. I'd hope and expect to see more of these initiatives in 2014, which manage to make pedagogic and financial sense.

7. **Challenges to institutions**

You may not realise it but 2013 has been a huge year for student and staff activism. Just in the last fortnight 7 UK institutions were in occupation, a major multi-union strike action brought many more campuses to a stand-still and students and staff worked together (#3cosas) to deliver living wages and conditions to some of the very lowest paid staff in the University of London. Despite the fears of educational commodification, we have the most politically active student body for a generation.

Combine this with the sad and sorry rise of casual contracts for academic and support staff, and you have both sides of the "student experience" equation reacting with open hostility to the structures that are constructed to confine and control them. Strikes and activism will be a major theme for UK education in 2014, and my limited understanding of the US, Canadian and major European systems suggest that this is a global movement. (Antipodean, South American, African readers - I'd love to learn if this is true for you too.). Will 2014 be the year in which Higher Education leads the way to a better deal for workers, during a near-decade long wage freeze? We can but hope.

8. **Effectiveness metrics**

More big data, I'm afraid. The way in which you do your job will be measured in more and more intrusive ways. From countless student surveys, to meaningless research impact metrics, to email CRM, much academic time is spend either actively measuring oneself or passively being measured. Older readers may suggest 'twas ever thus, but the corporate fashion for big data and (*shudder*) dashboarding has heightened and increased a tendency already manifesting in bureaucracies. (and I write this as someone who likes bureaucracies-)

Gamification is the other end of this story - students are also measuring themselves against themselves and their (real and imagined) peers, maximising the benefit they get from the work they put in. You can imagine both of these trends expanding in 2014, with much that has so far been experimental becoming mandatory. Looked at long term, it is a cyclical peak that last occurred in the 50s with "time-and-motion" studies, but for those living through it, it is scant consolation. This is another one that needs to be answered with some work on the value of human decision-making next year.

9. **More funding chaos**

Just today, a UK government minister announced the largest expansion in higher education funding since the 90s, all paid for by the dubious practice of selling loan books. Most serious wonks have been tending towards seeing this as a superficially pleasant short term political act, shoring up a broken funding system for the year and a half before the election. But we already know about the black hole in the heart of the BIS budget, and it is increasingly apparent that we will see another painful change in the funding system early in the next parliament.

Institutions in the HE system, meanwhile, have been celebrating the current tsunami of cash in the system by spending some of it on shiny stuff to impress prospective students and banking the rest to build up a reserve for when the whole thing goes pear shaped. The design of the funding system makes investment in running costs, like - er - staff a bad move, so many institutions have been laying off departments and using more casual staff to cover fluctuating course sizes.

The big winners, of course, are our friends at Pearson, who have coined it in due to a massive growth in fee loans to students studying lower-level HE awards in private colleges. Edexcel (a Pearson company) award most HNC/Ds in the UK via these private colleges.

The UK economy still struggles in the eyes of most of those living in it because the costs of living have risen whilst wages have stagnated. We are in a very fragile "paper" recovery which is meaningless to everyone but treasury accountants. There is not going to be enough money for the continued expansion of the HE system, and I'm predicting the rumours of the cuts to come and poorly managed loan sales to dominate the HE wonk news cycles in 2014. (Ed M, if you are reading this, how launching an independent study into HE Finance? Next year sometime would be good. I could probably round up some wonks for you if you like?)

(Bonus number 10: **User data bubble**- because targeted advertising is still not effective however many billions of dollars of venture capital is betting that it is. I've been saying this for two years, this is a long term prediction but one that scares me more than most of the above because it would make 2008 look like a mild market correction.)

Overarching theme of the year for 2014- the loss of human agency in decisions that affect the lives of human beings. Cheery stuff.

I hate numbers

So does Audrey Watters. At least that, was one of the strangest accusations made of our double-header keynote on day two of #opened13 (a conference I intend to document more fully in due course). Followers of the followers will no doubt have seen the multimedia that I foisted on the audience instead of a proper keynote with inspirational pictures.

But - yes, numbers = bad. Here's two stories I saw on twitter today.

First up, another one of those millionaire rockstars looking to fix broken education with broken business analytics. Paul Tudor Jones is a hedge-fund manager who never learnt anything from his educational experience at all. But still, he feels that education - when properly business-ified - is a path out of poverty for millions. An early quote on his workspace tells us a lot:

> *His computer projects his fund's market positions onto the wall, blinking when any share changes price, its overall performance channelled into a moving graph (which just so happens, as with most days for the past few decades, to be pointing up). "I sit here and watch*

these all day," says Jones, describing his daily work routine.

So here we are, a man who makes things happen by watching numbers. Guess what he wants to do to the US public schools system? Go on, guess.

Jones says his goal is to get the U.S. educational system in the top [*PISA?*] quartile of developed countries in the next ten years. Twenty years from now he wants the U.S. at number one. (The irony: Jones says he himself got very little out of his own education, with the exception of a journalism class. "My B.A. in economics was zero help in my profession today." Instead, he says that countless hours playing games during his school years-poker, chess, backgammon-were the experiences that "prepared me for what I do today.")

Jones says this will entail a "vertically integrated approach at getting all stakeholders in this-the parents, students and teachers-to acknowledge the problem, then get involved in this transformation," by working with schools, teachers and parent-teacher associations in applying the Robin Hood [*the honest-to-god actual name of his charitable foundation*] method of best practices. That means, among other things, longer school days and years, better teacher and principal training and true evaluation and accountability.

Vertically. Integrated.

Just when I thought the day couldn't get any better, it transpires that Michael Barber and his friends at Pearson have been busy repackaging deliverology into the idea of efficacy. You can play along at home, either with a printout or by sharing your innermost educational secrets with a multinational publishing company.

Barber, writing for the new Pearson "Open For Learning" [no really!]

group on LinkedIn says:

> *As we all know, this is an urgent challenge. Every child needs a high quality education, and we must do everything we can to provide this for all.*

So to provide this everyone's favourite educational publisher wants to standardise the collection of learning (output) metrics so it can use graphs and such to prove that it has successful and useful products. As opposed to, I suppose, asking educational professionals whether they work. There's a video, which features Michael Barber talking over some mournful-sounding piano and strings. (I should have patented that.)

The tool itself draws heavily on the Deliverology approaches of traffic-lights (those special red/red-amber/amber-green/green ones) and trajectories, and is a sterling example of Barber selling the same 20 year-old discredited business process to someone else. I take my hat off to you, sir.

So, in both of these cases we have people who by their own admission would rather deal with numbers and measurements than with people. Trying to make education better.

I believe that metrics-first approaches like these are flawed for the following reasons:

Lazy hypothesising. If you start from a premise that a larger number is better, you are buying in to a whole bunch of implicit and often under-theorised assumptions. It is required that we look at the actual measures themselves: what do they mean, what do they tell us, what do they not tell us?

Poor quality data. Education is not, and will never be standardised. This is why serious educational researchers take a lot of care in choosing samples, and attempt to make them representative. You'd think that "big data" would be better than this, but larger samples tend to be self-selecting (e.g. learners that completed or were entered for a certain test). These, and other, artefacts in large data sets need to be identified and compensated for, because-

Incomplete presentation. A graph on an infographic tells you nothing at all about education, without accompanying contextualisation, methodology, and highlighted anomalies. "But policy-makers are too busy to read all that" comes the response: frankly if people are unwilling to properly engage with data they should not be policy makers. It is very tempting just to look at a line-graph and choose the tallest line, but this is not policy making, this is shape-matching. And so many visualisations tell you nothing more than "we have lots of data".

An end to argument. You can't argue with data. Well, you can, but to do so you need a set of conceptual and critical tools that are outside of the grasp of many (pupils, parents…) who interact with education every day. I can sit here on my smug little blog till the cows comes home and pick apart data, but I've benefited from a lengthy and expensive education and work in a role that gives me time to think about and investigate such things. If you start throwing numbers around as if they were facts, you are disenfranchising a large number of people whose voices need to be heard in these conversations.

Comparison. If you give someone two sets of data the temptation is for them to munge them together in some way, so they can compare them. Serious data scientists know how hard this is, policy makers think you can just plot them on the same axis and make valid comparisons.

Nobody - I repeat: nobody - is saying that quantitative approaches to research are invalid, but I am saying that such research should be done with the appropriate safeguards so the results can be used to make high-quality decisions. All too often we see nothing but context-less graphs and tables of test results, and in the wrong hands these are more dangerous than any weapon you care to name.

I don't hate numbers, but I do love people. The individual experience is the most valuable measure of educational effectiveness we have, but it tells us very little about how effective that same education may be for others. What it does tell us, though, is reliable and worth engaging with. We owe it to the world to end our fascination with big data and start engaging with real and messy reality.

The FOTA EduBeardStroke Parabola 2013

Most predictions are wrong. The small number that turn out to be right are largely luck, but we tend to remember them because they reinforce our naive belief that the future can be predicted.

Apophenia, they call it. The predilection of people to perceive patterns in meaningless noise.

Politics, ideology, is the battle for the narrative. The imposition of a pattern on the noise of life. I've talked about it in the past as a branch of storytelling- on reflection I might have been wrong. In storytelling there is a pattern, in politics only the ghostly perception of a pattern.

With enough events, enough data points, you can back up any narrative concerning the immediate past. The rise of "big data" makes this more, rather than less, of a problem. I have found myself, when confronted by a position ostensibly backed by a mass of data (be it university funding or climate change), to treat it the same as an unreferenced opinion. Given all the possible narratives you could construct with that data, *why have you chosen this one?*

People who play with big datasets (and increasingly, people who don't) like to imagine the emergence of unassailable truth within them. A misunderstanding of the scientific method means that the idea of data as backing up a theory until either more data or a better theory comes along and changes everything has been lost.

So it would be unfair to dismiss something like the Gartner Technology Hype Cycle as being wrong because of an absence of hard data. It is wrong for far more interesting reasons than that.

(1) It presents the graph as an external, "natural", process - separate

from human intervention. The cycle (and accompanying guidance) is sold as an investment aid. You "understand" the hype cycle, you don't "use" it. It's a map of the future. A future which cannot be changed.

(2) It reinforces our greatest secular myth - that "it will all turn out right in the end". Technologies, no matter their idiocy, will eventually sail up onto the plateau of productivity. The difficulties - why, that's just the trough of disillusionment. Soon the world will somehow see the light (without intervention, mind you) and the slope of enlightenment will be scaled. Our own experience tells us this is not true, but so desperate are we for it to be true we believe it anyway.

(3) It's NOT A BLOODY CYCLE. There's no iteration. There's no improvements to old technology. Everything is a technology trigger - not an adaption based on findings out there in the real world.

So the hype cycle is just a model of an idealised closed system. It neatly illustrates the danger of too much data - so many technologies have been hyped, trashed, re-evaluated and used that we assume that they all must do.

Now I'm loath to do this, because I know the graphic will be used out of context and people will ask about the datapoints and complain even though I will tell you how it was prepared, but I present the FOTA EdubBeardStroke Parabola 2013:

[*Methodology: This diagram was prepared by taking one person who thinks too much about learning technology, leaving them on a train for a stupid amount of time and then marinating in beer and nachos*]

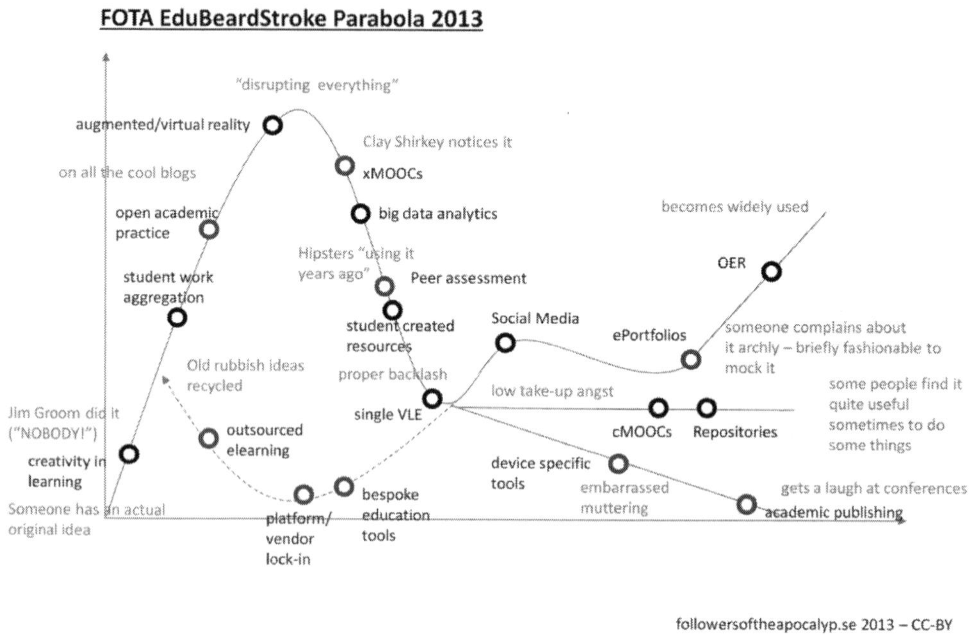

So, in terms of a prediction of what might happen this year it probably works as well as anything else I might do - it's got most of the right things in most of the right places, it's arguable enough to get clicks and comments and it slags off Clay Shirky. Typical cynical blogging really.

If you want something more real - technology (and technology aided learning processes) only work when fun. As soon as they get boring, codified, standardised they stop working. They become a part of the "grind" of education that they initially promised to free us from. They stop being interesting - they stop being chosen and start being imposed.

Most technology is awful, it doesn't work and it causes us endless pain trying to make it work. People will get remunerative careers in helping us to get within touching distance of the initial promise. Eventually they will write books and articles, run conferences and workshops, and the problem will be filed as completed.

It won't be. We will never, never solve education with technology. It won't work. We will solve education with education, and we will solve education with a way of educating that is closer to collaborative play than anything we currently do. Technology might help us start to understand education a bit better. That's it.

(trouble is, I suspect we'll need to solve capitalism before we get there- and I suspect that technology is only going to be a distraction there as well)

The work singularity

> *We are starting to encounter serious bugs with the idea of "work" as what human being should be doing. Humankind is basically engaged in a long price war with machines, and this is a war that it cannot win. It is already unusual (looking globally) to see the work of one human produce enough value to maintain a decent standard of life, and this encroaching trend is not likely to reverse itself any time soon.*
>
> *We are now living in a global state that has been structured for the benefit of non-human entities with non-human goals.*
>
> Charles Stross.

The first industrial revolution begun when it was established that machines were more efficient at manual labour than people. This led to a new area of work, the generation of energy in forms that machines could use, which dominated much of the 20th century.

The second industrial revolution, which began in the middle years of the 20th century, is occurring as machines are becoming more efficient than people at intellectual labour. This too has led to a new area of work, the generation of knowledge (in the form of data) in forms that machines can use.

The third industrial revolution is beginning to occur as machines become more efficient than people at social labour. It can be imagined that this will lead to a new area of work, the generation of people in forms that machines can use.

> *We live in an age in which familiar restraints are being kicked away, and foundations snatched from under us.*

The Dark Mountain Manifesto

Work is humanity's primary means of defining value, so the devaluing of work leads to a devaluing of humanity. Both Marx and Adam Smith, writing at the dawn of the first industrial age, drew a parallel between the "value" of a commodity, and the amount of labour required to produce it.

But as industrial society has moved in to a second phase, the amount of human labour required to produce the same commodities has fallen, and (with design and energy efficiencies) the amount of machine labour - which, after all, is just an abstraction of the human labour required to design and power the machine - has also fallen.

You might, at first, think this would mean stuff has gotten cheaper. But this is to ignore the corollary to efficiency - the less work that has to be done, the less wages are paid to people.

> *"The worker becomes all the poorer the more wealth he produces, the more his production increases in power and range. [...]With the increasing value of the world of things proceeds in direct proportion to the devaluation of the world of men."*
>
> (Marx, on Estranged Labour, 1848)

So the "work singularity" of the title is where **the creation of commodities becomes so efficient that no worker is able to buy them**. I use the term "singularity" because this represents a single, inescapable end-point to our civilisation, and it is not possible to make any meaningful predication as regards what follows. Either civilisation will be radically, unrecognisably, reorganised - or it will collapse.

In education, is it a co-incidence that costs have risen as institutions are under more pressure to deliver efficiency? Perceived student costs have in fact risen as a deliberate political choice in order to drive efficiency in education. The actual cost of educating a student in the US and UK - if you add public investment and student fees - has remained largely static in real terms for the past 10-20 years.

Efficiency - a word I have used variously throughout this post, could usefully be defined in modern terms as the ability to pay less for the same (or similar) results. In education, by far the most expensive outlay is on the wages of educators, so the efficiency agenda has invented various ways to pay them less :rolling temporary contracts, post-graduate students as tutors, casualisation/hourly-paid work/zero-hours, de-professionalisation of support roles, or to get more labour out of them: enlarged class sizes (including the affordances of technology to support this), higher workloads (including the affordances of technology to support this), teaching-only contracts.

(These moves have been paralleled by similar pressures on the workforce more generally - it is important to be clear that this is not a specific attack on academia, rather the academic experience of a more general malaise.)

But what can post-compulsory education offer a workforce entering employment at a time when labour is valued so poorly? And what can be offered as we approach the work singularlity?

First would be an enhanced support for learning literacy - enabling members of a pre- and post-singularity society to re-skill and to adjust to rapidly changing expectations. This also has the advantage of meeting the needs of our current society with its basis on casual labour, but actually refers to a much more profound ability to adapt to whatever comes after the collapse of waged work.

Second would be a documentation and preservation of the knowledge and insight of the existing experts, in academia and elsewhere. Robust and decentralised forms of knowledge-sharing and social media would appear to be a key activity here, as would the archival and replication of resources from these sources.

Thirdly would be an improved understanding around where humans can perform tasks that machines cannot and will not be able to. Mechanised tasks tend to be those that can be standardised, that do not require deep listening skills, and can be logically mapped. There is much that needs to be done that does not "fit" mechanisation, and one of the most important things we can be doing right now is to ensure that the attempt to mechanise these tasks does not destroy our understanding of them.

In certain moods I would add "learning" to this latter category.

The user data bubble?

In many ways the 2000 "dot com" crash was a misnomer - there was nothing fundamentally wrong with the technology. However, what was wrong was the model used to pay for the technology, which was primarily either display advertising revenue or (more commonly) venture capital advanced with the expectations of returns based on display advertising. There were expectations around the revenue generatable from on-line adverts simply because they were online that were just not realisable.

It is difficult to understand, more than 10 years on, quite why people thought that advertising would be more effective online than elsewhere. Advertising Effectiveness is a young science, and much is advanced (and then debunked) based on nothing more concrete than theorising. But many major advertisement placement conglomerates (Google, Microsoft, Apple- sometimes incorrectly referred to as service providers, hardware manufacturers and search engines) are focusing on one particular theory - the idea of personalised advertising based on user data (apologies for linking to a bad Tom Cruise film of a decent Philip K Dick book).

Google is widely reckoned to receive 99% of total income from advertising - around $28 billion in 2011. Facebook partnered with Microsoft in order to gain an estimated $3.8billion via advertising in 2011. And Microsoft itself (in partnership with Yahoo and AOL) are determined to break in to this market despite losing £2.5 billion a year on providing online services, barely breaking even. However, both Google and Facebook have seen recent valuations of substantially more than £100billion dollars, and Apple (a major provider of mobile-targeted adverts) has is valued at $362 billion (more than the UK national debt),very recently holding more cash on deposit than the US government.

Large amounts of these earnings, and much of the assumptions made regarding company values, are based on revenue generated by personally targeted advertising drawing on user data. The data these companies hold on our online (and increasingly, offline) activity represents their most valuable asset. Twitter, a company that doesn't even yet have a revenue model, is valued at more than $12bn (£8bn) simply on the value of the user data it holds.

As we reach the bursting point of the bubble we see increasingly crazy activity. Only today Google launched "search plus your world", using recommendations on social media (initially its own Google+) to serve you search results, and thus advertisements, based on the opinions of your online contacts. The "freezing out" of Facebook and Twitter is not the issue here, it simply breaks search. It relies on your G+ account being well-managed in order to provide you with tailored results. Forgetting that if I want the opinions of my online contacts I will most likely ask them, and most likely disagree with them too.

Tesco, the UKs largest retailer, does not allow you to set up an online account to make purchases without being signed up to their own "Clubcard" user data collection scheme. Simply and startlingly if you don't give them your data, they don't want your money.

Your user data, goes the theory, allows adverts to be specifically targeted to you. Should you buy, for instance, a decent bottle of single malt, you would be likely to receive advertising for other whiskies and spirits. And as a "single malt drinker", your personal data becomes valuable to other companies selling other products and services that other "single malt drinkers" buy. Online, this is easier and quicker, due to data stored by your web browser such as cookies, and search and purchase histories stored by search engines and shopping sites. This makes personal advertisement serving quicker and easier ("looked at data projectors online recently? You'd love to see these ads about data projectors. Never mind that you just bought one, or were researching for a friend..."). Analysts estimate that targeted advertisements drawing on your user data (on and offline) are twice as effective.

To me, all of this seems to be based on a reversal of what I have previously termed "one of the odder beliefs that our culture seems to have developed about markets" - the idea of market efficiency and the rational consumer. Advertisement targeting draws on the idea of our observed behaviour presenting a coherent and realistic picture of our desires and needs. Bluntly speaking, it doesn't. My past spending behaviour likely bears no relation to my spending currently or in the future - circumstances change, tastes change, opportunities change.

All of this sails wonderfully close to Stephen Downes' recent post on learner data. He argues, and I would agree, that data is not "wrong", but it is used in ways which are wrong in that it is used to generate conclusions that it cannot support. As Brian Kelly points out, the NMC Horizon 2012 Preview Report (you can't read it unless you give them your data!!) sees Learner Analytics as a key 3-5 year trend for adoption in HE. And educational technology companies are putting serious money behind the idea.

You can see the effects of this cultural mindset even see this in UK funding policy. Students are expected to make decisions regarding their place of study (or indeed, whether to study at all) based on the Key Information Set [KIS]), an abstracted and highly summarised set subset of user data. This data, it appears, can fix broken markets.

To conclude: estimates of the value of user data are everywhere, and probably overestimate the actual realisable value. True in education and in wider e-commerce. Adjust your investment portfolio or educational predilections as you see fit.

Powder and the mirror: policy, fiction and storytelling

> *"Stories are, in one way or another, mirrors, We use them to explain to ourselves how the world works or how it doesn't work. Like mirrors, stories prepare us for the day to come. They distract us from things in the darkness"* (Neil Gaiman, "Smoke and Mirrors")

A policy-maker is a writer of fiction. And as writers of fiction we use the same narrative techniques and tropes as novelists, poets and film makers. Because what else can we do? The fiction industry - the multi-billion dollar superstructure that exists to entertain and divert us - sets the bar so high.

The mess, the chaos and the arbitrariness of reality will never measure up to the best that the industry can offer. Therefore - we edit; we prune and we cultivate. We collect the shards of experience that suit our purpose, we downplay those that do not.

In the US, we have the American Dream. In the UK, recently, the takes of the "strivers". The "hard-working families". This is a story we can all get behind. Working hard, playing by the rules, going the extra mile (and maybe an enormous amount of spectacularly unlikely luck-). Leads to success.

How much of policy-making cleaves to that story? How much public money props up this clever, counter-factual myth?

Recent variants downplay everything but luck and perseverance. The Olympians. The X-factor. One shining moment of awesome. This is enough to sustain allegiance to the machines of state.

> *"The last page, the final strains of a chord, the curtain falling on an echo of a closing speech, living happily ever after; all that grates on me.*

> *The finality is false, because there you still are, the reader, the observer, the listener, with a gaping chasm in front of you, left out of the resolution of the story that seduced you into thinking yourself inside it. [...] An ending always leaves you standing in the whistling vacancy of a storyless landscape."*(Jenny Diski, "Strangers on a Train")

A writer of fiction can aspire to (or subvert) the closing moment of "happily ever after". A writer of public policy has no such luxury. Or no such requirement. Policy, though it says so much about the future, really concerns nothing but the eternal present of rolling news and social media. The never-ceasing quest for the "announceable".

Most of what you see in the media, reported as announced by the government has either already happened or will never happen. It is a compelling addiction - to present the problem, the diagnosis and the solution in one speech. Your minister does not present policy, he (and it is - still, sadly, in 2012 - nearly always a man) presents a three-act blockbuster.

In UK Higher Education, the problem was the needs of students not being met-Actually, let's do this properly:

"IN A WORLD- where students are unable to take the courses they demand, where business cannot employ the trained staff they need - inflexible and inefficient universities, unchanged for a century, hold all the cards. [sepia shot of Senior Common Room, with glasses of port and evidence of fine dining]. But one man [slow-motion portrait of David Willetts gesticulating] had the vision and the foresight to use government funding and direction to put- STUDENTS AT THE HEART OF THE SYSTEM [chromatic rising choral score, heavy drums, fade to black and then to...] AUGUST 2010."

Problem. Diagnosis. Solution. Compelling, heartwarming and every single iota demonstrably and inarguably a complete lie. And any student of history will tell you that this is a form of lying as old as time - from the Virgin Queen to the Son of Man.

> *"The web is in many ways an internet of attractions more than it is a medium germane to more traditional narrative forms that we have come to expect given our immersion in 20th century film, television and radio."* (Jim Groom, "An internet of attractions")

The rise of social media as a primary policy communications channel is the first chink visible in an increasingly impregnable suit of armour for many years. The opportunity exists because the response comes before analysis. If you read parliamentary reports in newspapers (and you should, as your children will think them as otherworldly as we do public information films) you will note that so much of the skill of the sketch-writer (and just note that job title!) is to turn a series of largely unrelated and frequently absurd events into a narrative. Social media dispenses with that.

As soon as the text of any announcement (generally made available substantially before the announcement is made, to allow journalists a head-start) is public, the ten or fifteen people who really get that micro-policy area will be tearing it to shreds - on a forum, by email, or on twitter. By the time that the details are on the page of an online newspaper, each faction will have agreed and shared a "line" (again, the language is theatrical) which will be hammered to the point of nonsense in the comments below-the-line.

This is new.

We perceive events in isolation. We expect moments of diversion, not narrative super-structures. This is why the mid-90s theories of post-modernism are once again quoted by policymakers as indicative models of an increasingly prismatic reality.

Fox News demonstrated this well on election night, as a carefully constructed worldview was brought crashing down by the continuing liberal bias of US voters. Until this, the success of the right-wing was based on the appeal of the re-affirming narrative - if we could just get back to an imagined past (genuinely, after L.P. Hartley, a foreign country) then all of the uncertainty we face will be over.

But as society becomes more pluralistic and more tolerant, that impulse becomes less and less reliable. The new right insists on the primacy of numbers and the innumerate cousin of the number, the infographic.

There is nothing spectacular or notable about numbers - they are just another way, as open to bias and distortion as any other, of telling a story. They are a tool, not a solution. Relative, not absolute. They are a retreat into another imagined reality, another reflection of whatever truth may be.

> *"Red means run, son, the numbers all add up to nothing"* (Neil Young, Powderfinger)

And why limit ourselves to numbers? The world of fiction; film, music, writing, even rhetoric tell us the power of the other options we have. We know how a graph can reduce something rich and strange into something very easily misunderstood. The fashion is for figures, but if we take policy seriously as an art not a science we owe it to ourselves to stand apart from fashion.

On Singing a Better Song

> *"We do not influence the course of events by persuading people that we are right when we make what they regard as radical proposals. Rather, we exert influence by keeping options available when something has to be done at a time of crisis"* Milton Friedman, "Two Lucky People" (1998) quoted by Dougald Hine in "The End of the University as we know it?" (27 Jan 2011)

I'll admit I was startled when Dougald, whom I know via his work with Dark Mountain (and in an unlikely series of coincidences, briefly played in a band with on Teesside in the early 90s) announced his intention to quote favourably from neo-liberal pin-up Milton Friedman. But when he shared the quote with me, I immediately understood why.

It is a beautiful encapsulation of the nature of resistance to orthodoxy, at the very basic level of ensuring that an alternative to the orthodoxy remains within - as an undertone - the ongoing public discussion. Where an idea seems to prevail, Friedman's counsel suggests that an all-out attack on the idea is not as effective as something more subtle.

I was reminded of this as I read (at the recommendation of Mark Johnson) Roland Bartlett's "Imagining the University" (Routledge 2013). I heard echoes in passages such as:

> *"What is striking about [the] conceptual journey that the idea of the university has undergone - over nearly one thousand years - is that it has gradually shrunk. Whereas the metaphysical university was associated with the largest themes of humanities self-understanding and relationships with the world, the idea of the university has increasingly - and now especially in its entrepreneurial and corporate*

> *incarnations - closed in. The entrepreneurial university is expected to fend for itself, and attend to its potential impact on particular segments of the economy, and become distinctive. This university has abandoned any pretence to be associated with universal themes." (p2)*

The shrinkage of the idea of the university, most notable in the past 30 years, has led to the framing of all possible discourses around the university in terms of "impact" and "viability". Even the alternatives to Bartlett's "entrepreneurial" university are assessed in terms of their impact - in terms of what immediate and tangible benefit that they can offer - even as (again in Bartlett's arresting words) "feasible utopias".

In Christopher Grey's wonderful account of the organisational structure of Bletchley Park (something with I continually refer to with joy) he illustrates wonderfully the idea of an idea enclosing and defining a discourse:

"In a similar way [a] history of the Home Guard notes that it proved impossible to write that history without extensive reference to the popular television comedy 'Dad's Army' because this had so heavily inflected cultural memory and understanding of the topic. This is a very particular and perhaps extreme example, but it is illustrative of the more general significance of the interpretation and re-interpretation of the war in subsequent decades" (pp116-117)

Once you have defined the terms of the debate, it is difficult to avoid dominating it. Culture is riven with such shibboleths, commonplace interpretations and references. And it is these, far more than the facts of any given field, which dominate it.

The stories we tell are far more important that any mere facts, and the stories we contribute to need to be treated as narratives to which richness and delight must be added rather than fictions to be quashed.

In the UK, we've just lived through a concerted and deliberate attempt to define Margaret Thatcher as a universally admired national hero. At first the long-withheld joy (and yes, it feels wrong to define it as joy, so successful has been the narrative engineering) felt by so many who have struggled so long against everything she and her ideology stood for was quashed by an instruction to think of the feelings of her family (respectively a fraud who attempted to destabilise a sovereign state and a quasi-celebrity racist). Then, after an unprecedented 7 hours of Parliamentary eulogies (Churchill, an equally fishy and divisive character - who argued against universal suffrage, lest we forget - was only afforded 40 minutes) we were told it was not a time for party political point-scoring!

The lasting effects of the resistance to this will not be the protests at the cortege or the street party in Glasgow, it will be the open and public commentary of thousands of ordinary people - on social media and to each other. Our Mass Observation project will be soliciting diaries on 12th May 2013- I can only urge people who care to write about Thatcher and what they felt at her passing. The recently released (JISC-funded, no less!) archives from the 80sare equally illuminating as a definition of a serious and politically active 80s light-years away from yuppies and electro-pop.

An owned discursive space is a striated and predefined space, where even resistance is a codified reinforcement of the dominant position. The "riots" against Thatcher became a part of her canonisation by the British establishment - a signifier that those who opposed her opposed all forms of public decency and order. Thinking again about the narratives of the future of the universities, Bartlett suggests:

> *"Is not academic life across the world increasingly striated [after Deleuze and Guattari], with severe limits placed upon it and entreated to run its course in certain directions. [...] "No nomadism here" might be the sign over the university's entrance." (P103)*

A long way from the Abbey at Theleme! Rabelais inscribed the rather more permissive "**Do What Thou Wilt**" as the one abiding rule governing the intellectual and pleasurable pursuits of his novitiates. And Newman, in his "Idea of the University" suggested

> *"An assemblage of learned men, zealous for their own sciences, and rivals of each other, are brought, by familiar intercourse and for the sake of intellectual peace, to adjust together the claims and relations of their respective subjects of investigation. They learn to respect, to consult, to aid each other. Thus is created a pure and clear atmosphere of thought, which the student also breathes, though in his own case he only pursues a few sciences out of the multitude. He profits by an intellectual tradition, which is independent of particular teachers, which guides him in his choice of subjects, and duly interprets for him those which he chooses. He apprehends the great outlines of knowledge, the principles on which it rests, the scale of its parts, its lights and its shades, its great points and its little, as he otherwise cannot apprehend them. Hence it is that his education is called "Liberal." (Discourse 5)*

Newman saw knowledge holistically as a set of narratives that intermeshed - there were none of the constraining striations that Bartlett warns against. Any attempt to limit this "Liberal" education would lessen its impact. And the striations do limit the impact of what universities are doing and are able to conceive doing.

My "feasible utopia" would be an unconstrained, Newman-esque academy. But I'm not quite naive enough to think that going around demanding one is going to get me any way towards it actually existing.

I've not been using all these scholarly references to show off how smart, or how widely read, I am. I've been using them because they are a helpful way of structuring and scaffolding an argument I am building. The argument I am building is that resistance, that critique, that just preserving the idea of another way, is valuable in itself. I'm able to build it because I am lucky enough to have had the chance to exist and grow, briefly, in an unstriated space and to have been astute enough to recognise this at the time.

To even recognise the critical basis of an attack on the university as unsustainable and unviable is to empower the attack. A final point from Bartlett:

> *"[In] an instrumental age, any serious exercise of the imagination has to face the jibe 'But you are not living in the real world'. The proponents of this view fail, of course, to recognise that their reference to the "real world" is question-begging, for what is to count as "the real world"? Is "the real world" the contemporary world, with its gross inequalities, its destruction of the natural environment, its diminishing of the humanities (as it gives the highest marks to the sciences and science and mathematics-based technologies and its valuing of higher education only insofar as higher education yields a return in the knowledge economy? The imagination, in other words, may be working to bring about a different "real world" (p31)*

If you accept the premise that an alternative has to be grounded in the "real world", you've lost. Those arguing for the "entrepreneurial university" and the like are arguing - as Baudrillard put it "neither in a logic of war, nor a logic of peace, but a logic of deterrence." Later, he continues:

> *"We are no longer in the logic of the passage from virtual to actual but in a hyperreal logic of the deterrence of the real by the virtual".*

This idea of the "real world", as I've gone over again and again on these posts, is a pointillist idea that does not bear close inspection. The people arguing that we must take account of the reality do not live in it, because it simply does not exist.

And I may perhaps be excused for not building my arguments on the meagre and constrained dreams of our ruling class. And I may instead work on substituting, artfully and subtly, our dreams for theirs in the collective reinterpretation of our lived history.

> *"I decided I wasn't coming here again. I went to the pub. 'They were all singing, all of 'em.[...] 'oh, some song they'd learned from the jukebox 'And I thought, "Just what the frig am I trying to do? Why don't I just pack it in, stay here and join in with the singin'?" [...] I did join in the singing, but when I turned around, me mother had stopped singin', and she was cryin'.I said, "Why are you crying, Mother?" And she said, "There must be better songs to sing than this." And I thought, "Yeah, that's what I'm trying to do, isn't it?" Sing a better song."*
>
> (Educating Rita)

Hipsters, MOOCs and the KLF: In, Against and Beyond the Accelerationist University

Allow me to start with an infomercial.

This, if you can make it out through the 19th generation VHS hiss and extreme Scottishness, is none other than Bill Drummond, who would go on to release a string of what were possibly the greatest pop recordings of the early 90sas one half of the KLF, and then burn the proceeds in the name of art before disavowing recorded music in favour of the experimental amateur choir The17.

"The Manager" (occasionally, "The Manager's Speech") was the B-side to a very early single entitled "Julian Cope Is Dead" - Drummond had briefly managed Cope's band (The Teardrop Explodes) and worked as a manager/A&R man at WEA records (now Warner). In it, he laments that *"the music- THE MUSIC- is spiritually bankrupt, there is nothing there-"*, and sets out a basic three point plan to reform the industry.

> *1. Musicians are not allowed to spend any more than 10 days recording any one LP*
>
> *2. The Musician's Union have to formulate a standardised contract with all the record companies.*
>
> *3. As for advances, they go, we don't have them anymore.*

Further clarity and rulings can apparently be gained by sending a cheque for £100 to "The Manager" at a PO Box address somewhere in Aylesbury, but I am not sure whether this is still valid. Which is a shame, as further clarity is always welcome.

I mention this here not only because it is a damned interesting bit of UK music history, but because this first act prefigured so much of the rest of Drummond's artistic work. If you like, he has made a career out of appearing to turn away from artforms he used to enjoy back to earlier (and to him, more meaningful) forms of art. From 90s acid house, to 80s hardcore (one of the pivotal moments of my musical history - 1992 Brit Awards no less!), to 60s conceptual art and now to the unrecorded (literally!) depths of musical history.

So far, you may think, so proto-hipster. We know all about the fetishisation of early mass production - a chicken in every pot, jobs for all, forty acres and a mule, and a can of Pabst in the ironic velour saddle-bag of every fixed-wheel bike. We all know that none of these promises were ever fulfilled too - and that a colder, poorer and less equal society now lurches from crisis to economic crisis.

Within this painful reality, we can and should all have our personal searches for reality within the maelstrom of art that it is possible for one to experience, sitting alone at a laptop computer in the UK during the early second decade of the third millennium. But has even this well been poisoned? Certainly Drummond states that:

> *Within days of getting [an] iPod, I was having unforeseen problems - I found myself skipping through tracks. I would hear a few bars of one of my all-time favourites and then decide it was not what I wanted to listen to and skip to something else. Nothing seemed to satisfy, even though in theory I had every recording on it that I had ever wanted to listen to. Was this just part of the ageing process? Was my palette getting jaded? Then I noticed other people doing the same thing, people in their early teens, 20s, 30s, not just blokes like me who were fast approaching 50. The iPod was changing something in all of our relationships with music. I love it when things change.*

There's two responses to this. One is to yearn fervently for the death of the iPod, the internet and similar technologies and a return to the artistic Fordism of the 60s and early 70s - a time when people would form intense personal relationships with mass-produced copies of artworks. The other is Drummond's way, to welcome the change as a necessary one - a required clear-out of the old processes and practices, and the chance for something better. Far from heading into the past, Drummond is excited about the possibility of a more meaningful music in the future.

You could read the #Accelerate Manifesto as a political restatement of this excitement in moving beyond old systems and towards new ones, that may (I emphasise the "may") provide a better deal. Or you could read it as a reclamation of the idea of "progress" by a political left who are often seen as protesting against every change ("We need a National Union of Students that fights for something, not just against something" as current president Toni Pearce notes). Or, as Charles Stross (an interesting article, go read) cites Joshua Johnson as saying:

> *Accelerationism is the notion that rather than halting the onslaught of capital, it is best to exacerbate its processes to bring forth its inner contradictions and thereby hasten its destruction*

In, against and beyond capital, if you will.

I work in the fast-moving field (haha! no really!) of education technology - an area where everyone seems to be "revolutionising learning - for an uncertain future". Some appear to want to use technology to bolster and support educators and the institutions that support them, others to see both done away with. Most are agreed that everything needs to be done faster and more.

I've written before about the need for "slow policy", but even in the supposed ivory towers speed is of the essence. How many times have you heard institutional leaders urged to board the MOOC train before it leaves? Often this is obviously driven by financial interests, sometimes by a genuine desire to try something new, but perhaps also by those who see that existing structures are unsustainable and want to get past them to something less painful.

Tempting, but no. The pressures on institutions, on people, on nations exist not through some natural calamity, or via market forces and the doctrine of disruption. The pressures have been designed. Designed by people - often very smart people who should know better - who are in thrall to the logic of capital. We (and they) can rationalise this by pointing to a bright future beyond, but it is difficult (though sadly not impossible) to imagine a way an education system could put more of those who work and learn in it under intolerable pressure.

Seventy percent of academic staff in the US no longer have even the chance of a dependable full-time job. Do we believe that when it gets to 90% there will be some miracle that catapults us into utopia? With management structures already beholden to speed and capital, do we believe that substituting them with more efficient capitalists (who either run or invest in the big edtech darlings) will improve our lot?

Of course not, which is why the Accelerationists propose that we *"must develop both a cognitive map of the existing system and a speculative image of the future economic system."* Using - and I'm just picturing Audrey Watters' face as I write this - BIIIIIIG DAAAAATAAAAA! Now, there are only two things you can actually do with big data - map existing systems (badly) and make (bad) predictions of the future state of these systems, or use data from existing measures of behaviour to plan new means of controlling this behaviour which totally work.

Maybe - and this is a maybe - there will come a time in the future where teaching is entirely automated, along with a range of similar intellectual roles, resulting in an enormous surplus of knowledge workers. Who is thinking about what these knowledge workers will do? What is the job of academia outside teaching - how many do we need? As of yet, no-one is asking - much less answering these questions.

So you'll excuse me for not wanting to "Immanentize the eschaton" just yet - which brings us to discordianism, a huge influence on the art and music of Bill Drummond. And right now, I need a word with the manager-

Managing the transition - academia in a post-scarcity knowledge economy

Post-scarcity economics is an imaginary concept more usually found in "hard" science fiction than in contemporary public policy. It describes a situation where resources are near unlimited, and able to match the near unlimited range of human needs and desires comfortably. In some formulations of the hypothetical situation, automation has meant that human labour is based on interest and pleasure (creativity) rather than required to be exchanged for resources needed (or wanted) in order to survive. It's not a new idea, by any means - Stallman was all over it in 1985!

Simply put: in a post-scarcity system there are no barriers (financial or pure availability) preventing us from having what we want. You can politicise this from either dominant perspective, as it demonstrates either the final triumph of the free market, or its inevitable destruction. Possibly both.

It is usually imagined across the entire range of an economy - a post-scarcity situation regarding all (food, medicine, technology, information-) human needs - deliberately not using the Mazlow hierarchy as it doesn't mention information (and more generally because it is flawed, which is maybe a post for another time).

However, my suspicion is that we are facing a situation currently where certain elements of human needs are scarce, and others are post-scarce.

Information is now post-scarcity. If knowledge exists, we can easily and near-instantaneously gain access to it. If openness really is the enemy of knowledge, with enemies like these, who needs friends?

Digital media, meaning the digital objects themselves and their distribution, is also post-scarcity. This one gets a lot of people into a lot of trouble.

The problem we face as a culture arises because a lot of the other stuff we need to live is very definitely running on a scarcity model, which leads us to want to make a post-scarity system act as if it was a scarcity system in order to derive value from it that can be exchanged in other places.

This has led, via the growth of Digital Rights Management and restrictive licensing online, to a corporate- and government-backed attempt to import an artificial scarcity into a post-scarcity economy. Unsurprisingly, this has failed and will continue to fail. DRM and licenses are routinely broken and ignored, both knowingly and unknowingly, in day-to-day online life.

People point to the likes of amazon and iTunes (yeah, they don't need the hits…) as examples of successful business models in this area, but really what they are selling is a user experience - specifically friendly and accurate search. If it was as trivial to find, download and listen to an album on a torrent as it is to find one on iTunes, there would be no business model for iTunes (I'm not counting insidious ecosystem lock-in-). It's even possible to suggest that UI is the one thing that people will (indirectly) pay for online. (as an aside, it's worth noting just how steep the technical hurdles are - torrenting, usenet, drm removal - that people routinely negotiate to access digital content. I'd love to hear more about this in the digital literacies space)

The digital economy has it's own currency already - reputation. Yes, like "down and out in the magic kingdom". (or "Accelerando", if you'd rather. And, yes, I would). However, until the (unlikely) emergence of a reputation-$ exchange rate, it will remain as a parallel economy with only second-order impact on participation in the non-scarcity economy via stuff like "professional reputation" and "credibility" impacting on earning potential.

In the education world we are seeing a huge tension between the ideals of academic openness, and the "reality" of the market-driven exploitation of academic labour. Neither of these are going to make anyone any money. And happily, neither describe how academics generate income. Getting paid for having done something once is an exception, getting paid for having the ability to keep doing things - or to keep do things to order - is the rule. We have (or had) a system for the employment of creative people that supported this, which naive links to the monetised exploitation of content artifacts can only undermine.

This, as I've outlined above, is a massive global cultural issue. It's not that we urgently need to find a means of financially sustaining academic online sharing. It's that we can't, because the business models that worked in tangible-object publishing for the 300 years since the enlightenment simply don't work in this universe. The fix for this isn't going to be micro-payments, or usage tracking. It's going to be a wholesale reorganisation of our cultural concepts. And academia should seriously be at the cutting edge of that.

What we do is one of the few things that is - and will likely remain - scarce. The development and training of highly optimised and highly adaptable human mind - capable of drawing links and parallels from a variety of sources in to a coherent whole, that provides an insight into something interesting and important. As above, the insights aren't the point, the point is we are set up to keep doing them. And there's no short-cuts to being able to do this. Just years of training and experimentation. These skills work in a post-scarcity world. We just need to manage the transition.

Always crashing in the same car

The UK Institute of Directors has recently recommended that the UK invest in infrastructure for space travel, supporting a growing private space sector. NASA has recently celebrated the first private-financed delivery of materials to the International Space Station. And a consortium of billionaires (do any three words sound more like the plot for a bad superhero movie?) have announced their intention to mine asteroids for precious minerals.

Meanwhile, mainstream film and science fiction, from Doctor Who to Iron Sky, draws on the retro-futuristic ideas of "steampunk", a conceptualisation of the future as it may have been dreamt in the past. Whilst brass cogs and filigree woodwork art is undeniably beautiful, it would seem to have little in common with the privatisation of space travel.

I'd argue that we now have the first generation of business leaders who were brought up on pulp science fiction, from Star Wars right the way back to Atlas Shrugged. But the individualistic pioneering world of the hero, the future that they dreamed about as children, is not the world they find themselves living in. Our future (and this is, lest we forget, two-thousand-and-twelve) is one where the primary problems to be addressed are not marauding alien armies or governments restricting the glory of private enterprise, but the trivial issues of how to feed, clothe and comfort seven billion people. The fervent mental preparations for space adventures clearly have been of limited use.

But, as Douglas Adams put it in *Mostly Harmless*:

> *"[...]This didn't, of course, deter their crews from wanting to fight the battles anyway. They were trained, they were ready, they'd had a*

> *couple of thousand years' sleep, they'd come a long way to do a tough job and by Zarquon they were going to do it."*

Despite the pressing nature of the social and environmental problems the world does face, and despite the clear need for collective action, we still see the old Randian battles for objective individualism re-erupting. And in steampunk-influenced science fiction, we see an explicit wish to return to the simple problems that can be solved by the unfettered heroism of one man (and it is always a man-), without the stifling need to think to deeply about the real needs of others.

Compare the "nerd triumph" - problems fixed by technology, with little reference to the needs of the end user- indeed, with the expectation that the end user will adapt themselves and their lives to the solution.

As I am contractually obliged to mention higher education at least once in these blog posts, let it be here: who *really* wants an online degree that can be squeezed in between shifts in order to reach the post of supervisor? What I believe people actually want is the ability to be immersed in learning in their own time and at their own pace - but rather than sort out the much harder social and economic problems that would make this possible it is far far easier to invoke "reality" as if it was something we couldn't change and produce some streaming videos and a chatroom.

In our cultural response to the current crisis of capital, it is the ideas of earlier battles - the 30s positions of Keynes and Hayek - that economists have reached back to. But within the new saviour mythology of the entrepreneurial start-up the sacred texts are by the nameless writers of *Astounding Stories*, the expanded-universe industry built around George Lucas and - inevitably - Rand.

Hence, I imagine, the drive for private space programmes. A chance to live those early dreams, to become the people that a generation of - fifteen year-old boys so badly wanted to be. To spend the working day mining asteroids, to take the evening Virgin Galactic flight to the Playboy Space Hotel. And you just know those rockets will be gleaming silver with 50s-style fins. And very, very tall indeed.

Using the billions of pounds our work and lives have earned them, they will return humanity to the correct path of the unified "future histories" postulated by writers in the early-to-middle twentieth centuries. Fighting the easy to win battles, ignoring the work of societal and cultural change. Both in terms of their battle against the state, and their battle for the stars.

Everyone is miserable. We are uninformed. We are lonely and scared

So, the right own the future, the left are trapped in the past. So says John Harris in the Guardian, at least. This is a perplexing argument, as I agree with much of what he says about the problems that he enumerates (changing nature of work, environmental issues, ageing population) but it is clear that all of these require long-term, structured and global collective action (which is pretty old fashioned socialism, frankly) if we are to have any chance of even beginning to address them.

I started thinking a while ago about a Generation X "to-do list", given that the preceding generation has utterly failed to sort any of this stuff out (seriously, come *on* people-). So this is the list of stuff we literally have to do in the next 10-20 years if we have any ambitions of either surviving and/or flourishing as a species.

I'm well aware that everything that follows is hopelessly naive. I don't care.

1) **Everyone is miserable.** Human life in the c21st is so rarely an enjoyable experience for anyone that the entire basis of civilisation is up for question. If we've build this huge machine to live in which is making most of us unhealthy, tired and lonely we should fix it or build something else.

> Q1a) **Waged work is fundamentally flawed.** The dominant model of survival we have is that where we are allocated value based on the work we do for others, and can use this value to purchase goods or other work from other people. But with the

"purchase" side of the system driven by a need to reduce production costs - using technology and/or straight up human exploitation, the odds are stacked against the "realisation of value" end. In other words, if we want to buy cheap stuff we will have to employ less people.

1a1) **we need to buy less stuff.** Buying stuff is a rubbish proxy for happiness. Time, human contact and the pleasure of creation, are much better ways of realising the goal of happiness so-

1a2) **we need to work less.** For the first time in history there is less work that needs to be done than there are people to do it. A lot of people are doing work that doesn't need to be done, either because there are machines to do it or it is just flat-out useless. But we have an economic system where if people don't work they freeze/starve.

1a3) **the way we share stuff is utterly unsustainable.** A few people have everything, most people have nothing. This is not going to end well for either group.

A1a) **Global Basic Citizens Income.** Everyone receives a basic income sufficient to live happily on. Where people do choose to work, some of the value realised could be in additional money, or other opportunities. The remainder of the value realised (and all the value realised by automated labour) should be used to fund the global basic income. This is going to need multilateral state government agreement, and there is no other way of running it that as a (global) state owned project.

Q1b) **the environment we live in is horrible.** It is either disgustingly expensive or unhealthy, often both. Much of this is driven by waged work [1a)]. People "have" to live in horrible places because they have to work nearby. But it is also driven by the myriad stupid things we do to the planet in the name of facilitating our economic model.

> 1b1) **there are few spaces for humans to live.** There are actually loads of places for humans to live, but the majority of us live in places designed for workers. They're all piled up on top of each other near (enough) where we work so we can get there. We spend most of the money we get from work on them, thus perpetuating the waged work cycle. The spaces for workers who don't work, where these exist (and they are becoming fewer and fewer) are in the same places and have the same problems.
>
> 1b2) **there are very few spaces for anything else to live.** Because we all live piled up together, the accumulated filth has to go somewhere else or it would be literally deadly. So we burn some of it, pump some in the sea, and put the rest in the ground. This poisons all of the other wonderful things that we share the earth with. And us, of course.

A1b) **we need to better manage the places that we live.** Living in huge cities is a very unhealthy state of affairs, both for those who live in them and everything that lives outside. We need to think, on a global level about where and how people live, and relocate and re-educate people in how to do so. This - again - is a global managed solution that needs state control. It will not just happen, no matter how many "downsize" articles are written and read by rich people.

Q1c) **we are using too much power.** It's an expensive and dirty business being this miserable. Historically we've solved this in the time-honoured manner of burning stuff. We started with burning other living things, then we graduated to digging stuff out of the ground and burning that. These days we're all about causing huge cracks to appear in the ground with explosions and then burning what comes out. All of these things are running out, so are increasingly expensive and increasingly dirty.

> 1c1) **our way of living uses too much power.** For half the year we burn stuff to make our buildings hotter, for the other half we use poisonous substances and burn stuff to make our buildings cooler. We occasionally want to go to other buildings, and to do this we burn more stuff in engines.
>
> 1c2) **Power is dirty.** Even the newer, "cleaner", ways of generating power we can use are pretty messy. Partly because we need so much of it, and partly because we need it cheaply and quickly, this is not seen as an issue. But it will become one.

A1C) **radically rethink the way we live.** We need to use less machines, and the ones we do use need to be as efficient as possible. We can use machines to replace labour, and in some cases we already do where it is cheaper than employing people. But we should use any surplus to ensure that the machines are cleaner than employing people. This requires tough new laws, and only some kind of government can make them. Or, more likely, it requires government control of industry.

2) **We are uninformed.** I'm not saying that we are stupid, because we are not. But most of us know very little, and what we do know is of very little use. There's a whole range of reasons why this may be the case.

Q2a) **our education system is focused on preparing us for waged work**, and this is increasingly explicit. We are training generations of people to function in a structure that will depress and eventually kill them. And we are designing out the creative, lateral thinking that would allow us to adapt as this model of civilisation breaks down. As a delightful foretaste of work, our education system is also making people ill, and making the places we live horrible.

A2a) **we need to redesign that system** to prepare people for the world that they will (hopefully!) live in, rather than the rather horrible world we do. This takes firstly a global will to dream of a less miserable future - a big job in itself - and secondly the support of the kind of institution and people that could offer the education the people would need. Both these, with the best will in the world, require political will at a global level.

Q2b) **it is almost impossible to get good quality information.** Here, we can grudgingly award a mark to the generation before us, as the internet is unquestionably the best thing to happen in this space for a long time. But then we remove that mark for the internet we now have, which is no longer neutral and is generally becoming another way to buy things we don't need and/or make each other miserable. Away from this, much knowledge is locked away in expensive books and journals, and read by very few. However, we have a great deal of "information" about new things to buy and a lot of gossip.

A2b) **Set knowledge free.** It should be a human right for anyone to access any knowledge that interests them, and to use it in the ways they want or need to, and to share the results. Of all the "answers" in this list, we are closest to this one because of the existence (in some spaces) of excellent library systems and because of the open education movement. But both of these are under pressure from commercial interests, and the big solution is to enshrine this access in some kind of international law. (if we have A1a implemented here the copyright issue becomes much less of an issue and we could safely abolish it.).

Q2c) **we don't know how to make anything we are proud of.** Most of what we use every day, be it food, art, or artefact, is mass-produced. Very few people are able to produce things for themselves, and self-produced things are mostly seen as inferior to mass produced things.

A2c) **Make stuff, dammit.** A population with more time, a better aptitude to learn, and less need to "earn" would be far better placed to begin to enjoy the delights of making things. Be this food, art or anything else. Those lucky enough to have leisure time and disposable wealth are already beginning to re-discover these things- there's been a huge growth around the "maker" movement, gardening, digital arts. But this is not yet widespread, and a much larger global cultural change is needed to give everyone these opportunities.

3) **We are lonely and scared.** We are trained from an early age to see everyone we meet as potential competition. Competition for the chance to work, competition for housing, competition for resources. So it is difficult for any of us to experience the pleasure of trusting and being trusted. Our constant suspicion tends to undermine temporary states of happiness, and to get beyond this we self-medicate with various legal and illegal drugs, and with consumption. Our consumption and ability to consume has become such a marker of status that we fear crime and physical attack.

Q3a) **our status is more important than our friendships.** In general, people develop friendship groups amongst those they work with, and marry (a good "official measure" of friendship) within their own demographic group. We tend to interact with people that are "like us" in terms of education, background and lifestyle - and whereas in some ways this is very human and is bounded by opportunity, in others it can lead to isolation and polarisation.

Q3b) **Interaction has become commercial.** The ways in which people interact, both socially, as peers doing the same things, and romantically are now seen as an opportunity to sell products and experiences. This serves to normalise interaction into scripted events that are opportunities for consumption.

A3) **we need to change the way we think and act** which will also involve shifting the underlying contours of our economy and civilisation - which is a job for us, as the facilitators or those who run it. Of all of the tasks I've set out here, I think this is the hardest one as it is reliant on so many of the others and yet is almost a prerequisite. It is very, very difficult to change a lifetime of taught behaviour concerning the way we interact with others.

In particular this requires acting together as a species and as a planet, something which we have yet to master. Fixing a single state would be hard enough, and would require a governance by and for the people. Fixing an entire global civilisation is, well it is something that the futurologists of my youth predicted would be easy. It won't be. But we should at least try - and we need to use tools and structures we own to do it right.

Further reading:

On the work/employment stuff this recent post by Charlie Stross is a nice overview.

On the culture/creativity and environmental stuff see Dark Mountain

On the education and labour angle see (always) Richard Hall or Brian Lamb.

I believe in faeries

"there is no dream that sings anymore, that ship sailed a long time ago
but true as the rust and the soil and the trees lord i still believe" (asmz)

i believe in faeries

i sincerely and truly believe in faeries in sprites in spirits in pixies and elves
and woodfolk
in life and water and air and stars
because today i want a truth that sings

i wish for the credulous soul of a child open to wonder
and of an old poet unshackl'd from fear

i wish for the moment of dawn where the world is still and the light
untarnish'd
i wish for the aethereal music that pours out like water from my fingers
for people who still delight in things that are pure

washing the suffering from long days
forcing down future narratives of the new crusades
putrid heroic stories of the coming war
the only story is a sacrifice
is our sacrifice

the only sacrifice is a hope of something somewhere anything anywhere that is

MORE TRUE THAN THIS
that here and now could be more than we see

and to lose a single moment that shines is to lose everything
and that is why I believe in faeries

because in the race to define and measure the bleakness that surrounds and will engulf us;
we will lose and we will lose because we care
we should be proud to lose the game of despair

This my invocation. I'm tired of believing in growth and sensation. I'm tired of believing in progress and measurement. And I'm tired of believing in capital and power.

I don't want to measure or quantify, because none of the things I can honestly say I care about are measurable or quantifiable. My liturgy is not written by a business consultant. My truth is not a 140 character condensation of a management textbook. I am not going to "follow my dream" until I have a dream worth following.

I've spent long enough on the traditional collapse of the west. I've got my apocalypse, now is the time for what comes afterwards.

And the ideas that go beyond the mundane have more to say to me than technology, spectacle or property. Give me purity, truth and beauty. Give me what it is to be human, and to connect to others.

Welcome, all followers of the *Followers,* to the future.

Author's Note

Barring a few spelling and grammar tweaks, and the occasional addition or deletion of dates where it helped the article, these are unexpurgated blog postings as written on my platform - http://followersoftheapocalyp.se - during the period 2010-2014. Some of them were quite the social media sensation, others languished largely unread. I don't do blog statistics so I don't know which the most popular posts are, but the collection you have just read represents my favourite writing during the period.

If you are reading the print version of this book you may note that the hyperlinks do not work, please see the eBook version or original posts for references and links.

Purity – Truth – Beauty.

David Kernohan, 14/11/2014

Index